100 MATHS FRAMEWORK LESSONS

TERMS AND CONDITIONS

IMPORTANT – PERMITTED USE AND WARNINGS – READ CAREFULLY BEFORE USING

Licence

YEAR 3

Scottish Primary 4

Minimum specification:
- PC or Mac with a CD-ROM drive and 512 Mb RAM (recommended)
- Windows 98SE or above/Mac OSX.1 or above
- Recommended minimum processor speed: 1 GHz

For all technical support queries, please phone Scholastic Customer Services on 0845 603 9091.

Ann Montague-Smith and
Ann Morgan

CREDITS

Authors
Ann Montague-Smith and
Ann Morgan

Series Consultant
Ann Montague-Smith

Development Editor
Niamh O'Carroll

Editor
Sara Wiegand

Assistant Editors
Ruth Burns, Jennifer Regan
and Margaret Eaton

Series Designers
Micky Pledge and Joy Monkhouse

Designers
Melissa Leeke, Micky Pledge, Geraldine Reidy and Yen Fu

Illustrations
Garry Davies and Mark Ruffle
(Beehive Illustration)

CD-ROM development
CD-ROM developed in association with Vivid Interactive

Published by Scholastic Ltd
Villiers House
Clarendon Avenue
Leamington Spa
Warwickshire CV32 5PR

www.scholastic.co.uk

Designed using Adobe InDesign.

Printed by Bell and Bain Ltd, Glasgow

3456789   7890123456

Text © 2007 Ann Montague-Smith and
Ann Morgan

© 2007 Scholastic Ltd

British Library Cataloguing-in-Publication Data
A catalogue record for this book is
available from the British Library.

ISBN 978-0439-94548-6

ACKNOWLEDGEMENTS

Extracts from the *National Numeracy Strategy* (1999) and the Primary National
Strategy's *Primary Framework for Mathematics* (2006)
www.standards.dfes.gov.uk/primaryframework
and the Interactive Teaching Programs originally developed for the National
Numeracy Strategy © Crown copyright. Reproduced under the terms
of the Click Use Licence.

Every effort has been made to trace copyright holders for the works reproduced in this
book, and the publishers apologise for any inadvertent omissions.

Contents

100 Maths Framework Lessons

About the series

100 Maths Framework Lessons is designed to support you with the implementation of the renewed *Primary Framework for Mathematics*. Each title in the series provides clear teaching and appropriate learning challenges for all children within the structure of the renewed Framework. By using the titles in this series, a teacher or school can be sure that they are following the structure and, crucially, embedding the principles and practice identified by the Framework.

About the renewed Framework

The renewed *Primary Framework for Mathematics* has reduced the number of objectives from the original 1999 Framework. Mathematics is divided into seven strands:
- Using and applying mathematics
- Counting and understanding number
- Knowing and using number facts
- Calculating
- Understanding shape
- Measuring
- Handling data.

The focus for teaching is using and applying mathematics, and these objectives are seen as central to success for the children's learning. While the number of objectives is reduced, the teaching programme retains the range of learning contained in the 1999 Framework. There are, though, significant changes in both the structure and content of the objectives in the new Framework and this series of books is designed to help teachers to manage these changes of emphasis in their teaching.

About this book

This book is set out in the five blocks that form the renewed *Primary Framework for Mathematics*. Each block consists of three units. Each unit within a block contains:
- a guide to the objective focus for each lesson within the unit
- links with the objectives from the 1999 objectives
- the 'speaking and listening' objective for the unit
- a list of key aspects of learning, such as problem solving, communication, etc.
- the vocabulary relevant to a group of lessons.

Within each unit the 'using and applying' objectives are clearly stated. They are incorporated within the individual lessons through the teaching and learning approach taken. Sometimes they may be the only focus for a lesson.

Lessons

Each lesson contains:
- A guide to the type of teaching and learning within the lesson, such as Review, Teach, Practise or Apply.
- A starter activity, with a guide to its type, such as Rehearse, Reason, Recall, Read, Refine, Refine and rehearse, or Revisit.
- A main activity, which concentrates on the teaching of the objective(s) for this lesson.
- Group, paired or individual work, which may include the use of an activity sheet from the CD-ROM.
- Clear differentiation, to help you to decide how to help the less confident learners in your group, or how to extend the learning for the more confident. This may also include reference to the differentiated activity sheets found on the CD-ROM.
- Review of the lesson, with guidance for asking questions to assess the children's understanding.

You can choose individual lessons as part of your planning, or whole units as you require.

What's on the CD-ROM?

Each CD-ROM contains a range of printable sheets as follows:
- **Core activity sheets** with answers, where appropriate, that can be toggled by clicking on the 'show' or 'hide' buttons at the bottom of the screen.
- **Differentiated activity sheets** for more or less confident learners where appropriate.
- Blank core activity sheets or **templates** to allow you to make your own differentiated sheets by printing and annotating.
- **General resource sheets** (such as number grids) designed to support a number of lessons.
- **Editable curriculum grids** (in Word format) to enable you to integrate the lessons into your planning.

In addition, the CD-ROM contains:
- **Interactive whiteboard resources** - a set of supporting resources to be used with the whole class on any interactive whiteboard or on a PC for small group work. These include number grids, money, clocks and so on.
- **Interactive Teaching Programs** - specific ITPs, originally developed for the National Numeracy Strategy, have been included on each CD-ROM.
- **Whiteboard tools** - a set of tools including a 'Pen', 'Highlighter' and 'Eraser', have been included to help you to annotate activity sheets for whole-class lessons. These tools will work on any interactive whiteboard.
- **Diagrams** - copies of all the diagrams included on the lesson pages.

How to use the CD-ROM
System requirements

Minimum specification:
- PC or Mac with a CD-ROM drive and 512 Mb RAM (recommended)
- Windows 98SE or above/Mac OSX.1 or above
- Recommended minimum processor speed: 1 GHz

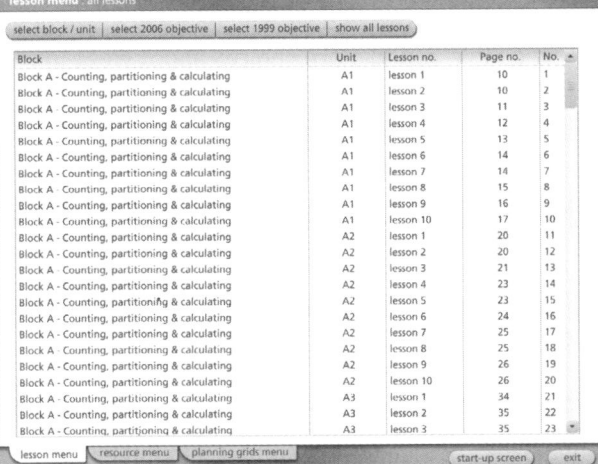

Getting started

The *100 Maths Framework Lessons* CD-ROM should auto run when you insert the CD-ROM into your CD drive. If it does not, use **My Computer** to browse the contents of the CD-ROM and click on the '100 Maths Framework Lessons' icon.

From the start-up screen there are four options: click on **Credits & acknowledgements** to view a list of acknowledgements. You should also view the **Terms and conditions** of use and register the product to receive product updates and special offers. Finally, you can access extensive **How to use this CD-ROM** support notes and (if you agree to the 'Terms and conditions') click on **Start** to move to the main menu.

Each CD-ROM allows you to search for resources by block, unit or lesson. You can also search by Framework objective (both 2006 and 1999 versions) or by resource type (for example, activity sheet, interactive resource or ITP).

Planning

The renewed Framework planning guidance sets out the learning objectives in blocks, and then subdivides these into units. The blocks are entitled:
- **Block A:** Counting, partitioning and calculating
- **Block B:** Securing number facts, understanding shape
- **Block C:** Handling data and measures
- **Block D:** Calculating, measuring and understanding shape
- **Block E:** Securing number facts, relationships and calculating.

Within each block there are three progressive units, which set out the learning objectives for a two- or three-week teaching period. Because of the interrelated nature of learning in mathematics, some of the same learning objectives appear in different blocks so that the children have the opportunity to practise and apply their mathematics.

	Block A: Counting, partitioning and calculating (6 weeks)	Block B: Securing number facts, understanding shape (9 weeks)	Block C: Handling data and measures (6 weeks)	Block D: Calculating, measuring and understanding shape (6 weeks)	Block E: Securing number facts, relationships and calculating (9 weeks)
Autumn	Unit A1	Unit B1	Unit C1	Unit D1	Unit E1
Spring	Unit A2	Unit B2	Unit C2	Unit D2	Unit E2
Summer	Unit A3	Unit B3	Unit C3	Unit D3	Unit E3

It is recommended that planning for the year takes the blocks and units in the following order:
However, the book has been structured in block order (Block A1, A2, A3 and so on), so that teachers can plan progression across units more effectively, and plan other configurations of lessons where required. You can use the different menus on the CD-ROM to find suitable teaching and learning material to match your planning needs.

In each unit in this book, the 1999 Framework objectives are listed, so that it is possible to use materials from previous planning alongside these lessons. The CD-ROM has a facility that allows for filtering by 2006 and 1999 learning objectives in order to find suitable lessons.

The blocks and units, taught in the order above, make a comprehensive teaching package which will effectively cover the teaching and learning for this year group.

Differentiation

Each lesson contains three levels of differentiation in order to meet the wide variety of needs within a group of children. There are differentiated activity sheets for many lessons that can be accessed on the CD-ROM (see 'What's on the CD-ROM', above). The units within a block are placed together in this book. This is in order to enable you to make choices about what to teach, when and to which children, in order to encourage more personalised learning.

Assessment

Within this book the guidelines for 'Assessment for learning' from the Framework are followed:
- Assessment questions are provided within each lesson in order to identify children's learning and to provide the children with effective feedback.
- The questions encourage children to be actively involved in their own learning.
- Many activities are undertaken in groups or pairs so that children have the opportunity to plan together and assess the effectiveness of what they have undertaken.
- The assessment outcomes give the teacher the opportunity to adjust teaching to take account of the results of assessment.
- The crucial importance of assessment is recognised, and the profound influence it has on the motivation and self-esteem of children, both of which are essential for learning.
- The assessment questions offer children the opportunity to understand what they know, use and understand and also to understand how to improve.

Counting, partitioning and calculating

Key aspects of learning
- Social skills
- Problem solving
- Communication
- Reasoning

Expected prior learning
Check that children can already:
- talk about their methods and solutions to one-step problems, identifying and recording the number sentences involved
- read, write, partition and order two-digit numbers, explaining what each digit represents
- recall all addition and subtraction facts for each number to at least 10, all pairs with totals to 20 and all pairs of multiples of 10 with totals up to 100
- add or subtract mentally pairs of one-digit numbers
- recall multiplication and division facts for the 2, 5 and 10 times-tables.

Objectives overview
The text in this diagram identifies the focus of mathematics learning within the block.

Solving one- and two-step word problems involving numbers, money or measures

Reading, writing, ordering, partitioning and rounding two- and three-digit numbers

Explaining methods and reasoning, orally and on paper

BLOCK A: Counting, partitioning and calculating

Addition and subtraction

Mental methods: one- and two-digit numbers

Written methods: one- and two-digit numbers

Multiplication and division

Multiplying one- and two-digit numbers by 10 or 100

Informal written methods: multiplying and dividing TU by U; rounding remainders

Unit 1 ▢ 2 weeks

Counting, partitioning and calculating

Speaking and listening objective
● Explain a process or present information ensuring that items are clearly sequenced and that relevant details are included.

Introduction
In this unit children are encouraged to describe how they solved a problem and to explain the mathematics and methods that they chose to use. They are encouraged to be systematic in how they record their work so that it is clear to both themselves and others how they went about solving the problem. They are encouraged to explain to others the process that they used and to present information in a clearly sequenced way, showing the relevant details.

Using and applying mathematics
● Describe and explain methods, choices and solutions to puzzles and problems, orally and in writing, using pictures and diagrams.

Lesson	Strands	Starter	Main teaching activities
1. Teach and practise	Counting	Count on from and back to zero in single-digit steps or multiples of 10.	Read, write and order whole numbers to at least 1000 and position them on a number line; count on from and back to zero in single-digit steps or multiples of 10.
2. Teach and practise	Counting	Multiply one-digit and two-digit numbers by 10 or 100, and describe the effect.	As for Lesson 1
3. Teach and apply	Counting	Read, write and order whole numbers to at least 1000.	As for Lesson 1
4. Teach and apply	Counting	Count on from and back to zero in single-digit steps or multiples of ten.	**Partition three-digit numbers into multiples of 100, 10 and 1 in different ways.**
5. Teach and apply	Counting	Read, write and order whole numbers to at least 1000 and position them on a number line.	As for Lesson 4
6. Teach and practise	Knowledge	As for Lesson 5	**Derive and recall all addition and subtraction facts for each number to 20.**
7. Teach and apply	Knowledge	As for Lesson 5	**Derive and recall all addition and subtraction facts for each number to 20, sums and differences of multiples of 10.**
8. Teach and practise	Calculate	**Partition three-digit numbers into multiples of 100, 10 and 1 in different ways.**	**Add or subtract mentally combinations of one-digit and two-digit numbers.**
9. Teach and practise	Calculate	As for Lesson 8	As for Lesson 8
10. Teach, apply and evaluate	Calculate	As for Lesson 8	As for Lesson 8

Lessons 1-5

Preparation
The interactive resource 'Number line' can be used as an interactive whiteboard resource, copied onto transparency and used with an OHP, or enlarged to A3 and attached to a flipchart; enlarge CD page 'Paper abacus' to A3.

You will need
Photocopiable pages
'Counting patterns' (page 16) and 'Paper abacus' (page 17) for each child.
CD resources
Support and extension versions of 'Counting patterns' and 'Paper abacus'; 'HTU arrow cards' (see General resources). Interactive resource: 'Number line'.
Equipment
Jars containing different quantities of cubes (from about 50 to 100); Blu-Tack; 13 small counters for each child.

Learning objectives

Starter
● Count on from and back to zero in single-digit steps or multiples of 10.
● Multiply one-digit and two-digit numbers by 10 or 100, and describe the effect.
● Read, write and order whole numbers to at least 1000 and position them on a number line.

Main teaching activities
2006
● Read, write and order whole numbers to at least 1000 and position them on a number line; count on and back to zero in single-digits or multiples of 10.
● Partition three-digit numbers into multiples of 100, 10 and 1 in different ways.
1999
● Read and write whole numbers to at least 1000 in figures and words.
● Order whole numbers to at least 1000, and position them on a number line.
● Know what each digit represents, and partition three-digit numbers into a multiple of 100, a multiple of ten and ones (HTU).

Vocabulary
problem, solution, calculate, calculation, answer, method, explain, reasoning, pattern, predict, place value, partition, digit, ones, tens, hundreds, one-digit number, two-digit number, three-digit number, compare, order, equals (=), count on, count back

Lesson 1 (Teach and practise)

Starter
Rehearse: Ask the children to count in ones from zero to 50, then back until you say *Stop*. Ask: *What was the last number you said? What would the next number be? And the next? How do you know that?* Repeat this for counting in twos from zero to 40 and back again, fives from zero to 50 and tens from zero to 100.

Main teaching activities
Whole class: Continue with the counting activity from the Starter, this time counting in steps of three from zero to 30 and back, then fours from zero to 40 and back. Ask questions such as *What is 40 subtract 4? And 36 subtract 4? How do you know that?* Repeat the counting activity for counting in sixes in the same way.
Group work: Provide each child with activity sheet 'Counting patterns'. They complete counting forward and back patterns.

Differentiation
Less confident learners: Give these children the support version of 'Counting patterns' which has counting patterns in twos, threes, fives and tens.
More confident learners: Provide these children with the extension version of the sheet, which gives no number clues for starting the patterns.

Review
Begin a counting pattern, such as counting up or back in fours. Say: *Stop. What number did you just say? What was the number before that? What will the next number be? How do you know that?* Repeat this for other counting patterns. Now ask the children to work out the counting pattern, starting on 2, and counting in threes. Invite the children to think for a minute, then to say the pattern together. Ask: *What will come next? How do you know?* Repeat this for a counting back pattern, such as starting on 52 and counting back in sixes.

Unit 1 2 weeks

Lesson 2 (Teach and practise)

Starter
Review counting in tens from and back to any two-digit number. Say: *Start on 23. Count on in tens until I say 'Stop!' Then count back to the start number.* Repeat this several times with different start numbers, such as 17, 32, 26. Now choose a larger two-digit start number, such as 87. This time, ask the children to count back to as close to zero as they can go. Say: *Who can predict which number we shall stop on if we count back in tens? Yes, 7. Why do you think that?* Repeat this for other start numbers, such as 76, 99, 84.

Main teaching activities
Whole class: Reveal the 'Number line' interactive resource. Write 123, 156 and 176 onto the board. Now ask, for 123: *How many hundreds... tens... units in this number? How can you tell that?* Repeat for the other two numbers. Invite a child to write these numbers, in order, onto the number line. Repeat for other HTU numbers.
Paired work: The children take turns to choose a HTU number and write this on their whiteboard until they have four numbers. They say which is the hundreds, tens and units digit, then write their numbers onto an empty number line, in ascending order.

Differentiation
Less confident learners: Decide whether to ask these children to work with TU numbers.
More confident learners: Ask these children to order eight HTU numbers each time.

Review
Invite the children to write their sets of numbers onto the empty number line. Ask: *Where would you put ___? Why does it come there? How did you find the smallest/largest number in your set of numbers? What clues did you use?*

Lesson 3 (Teach and apply)

Starter
Reason: Explain that you will give a fact about a three-digit number. Ask the children to write a number that fits that fact on their whiteboard and to hold it up when you say *Show me*. Say, for example: *Write a number that has a seven as a hundreds/tens/units digit. Write a number that is even/odd. Use the same digits as the number on your board; don't rub it out. Now, write the number that has the largest digit in the hundreds/tens/units space.*

Main teaching activities
Whole class: Count in steps of 10, 20, 30, 40, 50, 60 and 100, as in Lesson 1. Discuss the relationship between, for example, counting in twos and counting in 20s. Encourage the children to explain how they can use their knowledge of counting in twos to help them to count in 20s.

Show the children a jar of cubes and ask: *How many cubes do you think there are here?* Invite a child to open the jar and count the cubes. Discuss how these can be counted most efficiently, such as counting in twos or fives. Repeat for another jar.
Group work: Provide each group of four children with a jar of cubes to estimate, then check by counting. Invite the children to say how close their estimate was to their count. Ask: *How did you count the cubes?* Praise those children who grouped the cubes for ease of counting. Ask: *How did you group these?* Discuss how large amounts of items can be grouped in, for example, fives, tens or 20s, then counted.

Differentiation
Less confident learners: Provide fewer objects for counting.
More confident learners: Challenge the children to try different groupings, and to be ready to report back during the Review on which ways they found more effective, and why.

Review
Invite the more confident learners to report back on their findings. Encourage them to explain which ways were easier for them and why they think this. Now practise counting in steps of 20, 30, 40, 50, 60 and 100, as in the main teaching activity. Ask: *What number comes next? How do you know? How does knowing how to count in twos... help you to count in 20s...?*

Lesson 4 (Teach and apply)

Starter

Reason: Repeat the Starter for Lesson 1, but this time invite the children to count across the hundreds 'bridge'. For example, count on from 94 to 194 and back again; count down from 187 to 87 and back again, and so on.

Main teaching activities

Whole class: Write the headings 'Hundreds', 'Tens' and 'Units' on the board. With Blu-Tack, stick the 100-card from CD page 'HTU arrow cards' onto the board under the Hundreds heading. Now put the 10-card under the Tens heading and the 1-card under the Units heading. Ask the children to read each card. Combine the cards to make 111 and ask the children to read this. Write 100 + 10 + 1 = 111. Repeat for randomly chosen arrow cards, each time making the complete number.

Erase what is written on the board. Now write up 415 and ask: *What does the four/one/five represent? What is this number? Who can write it in words for me?* Invite the children to jot down another number which uses all three of the digits 1, 4, 5. Ask: *What number did you write?* Invite a child to write this on the board for you, and ask what each digit represents.

Group work: Provide each child with a copy of activity sheet 'Paper abacus' and several small counters. Ask them to use the three digits on their sheet to make as many HTU numbers as they can, modelling each number using the counters on the abacus. They write the numbers as: hundreds add tens add units; as an HTU number; in words.

Differentiation

Less confident learners: Give these children the support version of 'Paper abacus' which asks them to make TU numbers.
More confident learners: The extension version of the sheet asks children to order their sets of numbers from largest to smallest.

Review

Review the core version of 'Paper abacus', using the A3 version pinned to the board. Ask: *How did you decide where to put your counters?* Invite a child to write the first set of numbers in order, from smallest to largest. Ask: *Which number is the smallest? How can you tell? So which is the largest?* Write another set of three digits on the board, and challenge the children to say which numbers can be made from these. Encourage them to think about which would be the smallest, and which would be the largest numbers that they can make.

Lesson 5 (Teach and apply)

Starter

For the Starter, reveal the interactive resource 'Number line'. Explain that you will say a two-digit number and would like the children to say where it should fit on the number line. Ask: *What is the largest/smallest number that I could say?* Continue to fit up to 20 different numbers onto the line.

Main teaching activities

Whole class: Review the work from Lesson 3. Write 256 on the board and ask: *How many hundreds... tens... units?* Repeat for other three-digit numbers.

Now write up the digits 2, 4, 6, 8. Ask the children to write down as many three-digit numbers as they can make, using three of the digits each time. Give the children five minutes to do this. Then ask them to draw their own empty number line and to place their numbers onto the line, in order. Decide whether to limit the less confident learners to choosing two digits each time to make a TU number. Challenge the more confident learners to write two sentences: to explain how they found the smallest number; to explain how they found the largest number.

Review

Work as a class to build the empty number line using the HTU numbers the children found. Choose two numbers, such as 648 and 684. Ask: *What other numbers will fit between these two? How do you know that?*

Lessons 6-10

Preparation
Prepare two sets of 0 to 9 numeral cards for each pair.

You will need
Photocopiable pages
'Adding and subtracting multiples of ten' (page 18) and 'Working mentally' (page 19).
CD resources
Support and extension versions of 'Adding and subtracting multiples of ten' and 'Working mentally'; core, support and extension versions of 'Money problems (1)'; 'Numeral cards 0-20' (see General resources).
Equipment
Two sets of 0-9 numeral cards for each pair.

Learning objectives

Starter
● Read, write and order whole numbers to at least 1000 and position them on a number line.

Main teaching activities
2006
● Derive and recall all addition and subtraction facts for each number to 20, sums and differences of multiples of 10.
● Add or subtract mentally combinations of one-digit and two-digit numbers.
1999
● Know by heart: all addition and subtraction facts for each number to 20; all pairs of multiples of 100 with a total of 1000 (eg 300 + 700); all pairs of multiples of 5 with a total of 100 (eg 35 + 65).
● Derive quickly all number pairs that total 100 (eg 62 + 38, 75 + 25, 40 + 60).
● Use mental calculation strategies - several objectives, including: use known number facts and place value to add/subtract mentally; add and subtract mentally a 'near multiple of 10'; add mentally three or four small numbers; find a difference by counting up.

Vocabulary
problem, solution, calculate, calculation, answer, method, explain, reasoning, pattern, predict, count on, count back, add, subtract, multiply, times, divide, share, group, sum, total, difference, plus, minus, pound (£), pence (p), note, coin

Lesson 6 (Teach and practise)

Starter
Recall: Provide individual whiteboards and pens. Ask the children to draw an empty number line and to label one end of the line 550 and the other end 600. Explain that you will say a number and that you would like them to decide where it fits onto the number line. Say, for example: 575; 590; 565. Ask the children to show you their whiteboards when you say *Show me.* This will enable you to identify those who understand and those who need more practice in ordering numbers.

Main teaching activities
Whole class: Explain that in this lesson the children will learn how to use what they know about addition and subtraction to 10 to derive additions and subtractions to 20. Begin by writing on the board 1 + 9 = and ask for the answer. Write it in. Now write 11 + 9 and ask: *What is the answer? How did you work that out?* Discuss how one way is to remember that 1 + 9 = 10 and that 11 is the same as 10 + 1. Write on the board 10 + 1 + 9 = 19 + 1 = 20. Repeat for other additions, such as 15 + 4, 12 + 6 and so on. Now ask the children to find the answer to 8 - 5, then 18 - 5 and to explain their methods. Write on the board 18 - 5 = 10 + 8 - 5 = 10 + 3 = 13. Ask: *Do we need to write all of this out each time? Who can see a quicker way of finding the answer?* Agree that if 8 - 5 = 3 then 18 - 5 must be 13 because the 'ten' is left unchanged. Repeat with other examples, such as 19 - 6, 14 - 3. Now remind the children that they can bridge through 10 to find additions such as 8 + 6 (8 + 2 + 4 = 10 + 4 = 14), and subtractions such as 14 - 8 (14 - 8 = 10 - 8 + 4 = 6).
Group work: Ask the children to work in pairs. They write all the addition sentences they can find for □ + □ = 18 and 18 - □ = □. Ask them to think

about how they will record their work, reminding them that if they find a way to order their number sentences, then they will be able to see what is missing.

Review

Review the work together that the children have done. Ask questions such as: *How did you order your work? Beginning with 1 + 17 = 18, then 2 + 16 = 18: how did this help you to spot what was missing?*

Now ask questions, writing responses on the board for all to see, such as: *Tell me all the pairs of numbers that total 16. How did you find these? Tell me all the numbers, in the range to 20, that give a difference of 6. How did you work that out?*

Differentiation

Less confident learners: Suggest to these children that they count up/down in their heads, or use a number line to help them in order to find totals and subtractions.

More confident learners: Challenge these children to repeat this for another start number, such as 19.

Lesson 7 (Teach and apply)

Starter

Recall: Repeat the Starter from Lesson 6. Now ask the children to suggest numbers that will fit between, for example, 550 and 565. Repeat for other pairs of numbers.

Main teaching activities

Whole class: Write on the board: 50 + 80 and ask: *How can we work this out?* Agree that this can be found because the children know that 5 + 8 = 13, so therefore 50 + 80 = 130. Repeat for other examples. Now write on the board 156 + 10 and ask: *What is 156 add 10? Add 20? Add 30? What pattern do you see?* Repeat for other examples where the children add or subtract a multiple of 10 to or from a two-digit or three-digit number. Each time write the number sentence on the board.

Paired work: Provide copies of activity sheet 'Adding and subtracting multiples of ten'. Ask the children to work in pairs and to take turns to choose two numbers from the top grid to make the total or difference in the second grid. Their partner decides if they think the answer is correct. They keep score by writing their number sentences on their sheet.

Differentiation

Less confident learners: Give these children the support version of the activity sheet which involves adding multiples of 10 to single-digit numbers.

More confident learners: The extension version of the sheet involves larger three-digit numbers.

Review

Ask: *What is 40 + 70? How did you work that out? And 110 subtract 40?* Repeat for other examples of adding/subtracting multiples of 10. Now extend to multiples of 100, such as 300 + 600, 900 – 400, and so on.

Lesson 8 (Teach and practise)

Starter

Recall: On the board draw this table:

Number	+ 1	– 1	+ 10	– 10	+ 100	– 100

Write a three-digit number into the first column, such as 236, and ask the children to say the answer for each column as you point along the table. Repeat this for other three-digit numbers. Keep the pace sharp so that the children have to think quickly in order to respond. You may wish to ask individual children to respond to particular parts of the table, to check that they can add/subtract 1, 10 or 100.

Main teaching activities

Whole class: Explain that today the children will use the mental strategy of putting the larger number first in order to count on. On the board, write 5 + 26 and ask: *How should we begin to do this mentally?* Accept the suggestion of rewriting the sentence as 26 + 5. You may find it helpful to use an empty number line:

Unit 1 ▭ 2 weeks

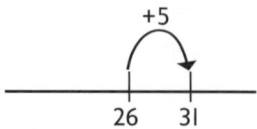

When the children have understood the modelling using an empty number line, provide further examples of adding a single-digit to an TU number, such as 7 + 38.

Now write up 30 + 53 and explain that the same method can be used to calculate this. Draw an empty number line:

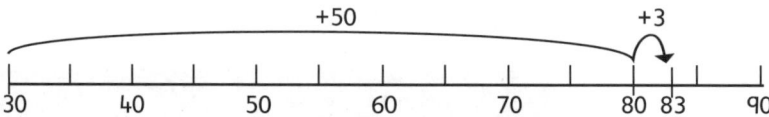

Explain that this can also be calculated by starting at 53 and counting on three tens. Show this on the number line by marking in the three tens.

Now ask children to try this counting along a mental number line. Say: *What is 40 + 57?* Invite children to explain how they calculated: 57 + 10 is 67; add 10 is 77; add 10 is 87; add 10 is 97. So 40 + 57 is the same as 57 + 40 which is 97.

Group work: Ask the children to work in pairs. Give each pair two sets of 0-9 numeral cards and ask them to shuffle the cards together. One of them takes two cards and generates a TU number; the other takes a single card. They write an addition sentence, putting the larger number first and counting on mentally to find the answer. Ask them to generate ten such questions, shuffling the cards after each one. Then they take turns to take two cards to make a TU number and take one more card, to which they add a zero to make a decade number. Again, they write the addition sentence and calculate mentally. Again, ask them to generate ten such questions.

Review
Invite children from each ability group to write up one of their number sentences, without the answer, on the board. Ask the class: *How can we solve this?* Invite the children to explain how they calculated the answer.

Differentiation
Less confident learners: Suggest to the children that they make TU add U sentences, and draw a blank number line if they need help.
More confident learners: Challenge these children to calculate HTU add decade numbers.

Lesson 9 (Teach and practise)

Starter
Recall: Shuffle together three sets of 0-9 cards. Explain that you will hold up three cards at a time to make an HTU number. Ask the children to say the number. Repeat this several times, keeping the pace sharp. Now invite individual children to write the number in words on the board (for example for the less confident you might choose 57; for the more confident you might choose 307 or 370) and ask questions such as: *What does the zero represent?*

Main teaching activities
Whole class: Explain to the class that today they will be adding and subtracting to/from a two-digit number, crossing the tens boundary. Begin with subtracting a single-digit number from a teens number, such as 16 - 7. Explain that this can be done in two steps: 16 - 6 - 1, so that the calculation could be written as 16 - 6 - 1 = 10 - 1 = 9. Repeat this for other examples, such as 13 - 7, 15 - 8, 14 - 9. Now ask the children to respond to questions that you write on the board such as: 14 - 8 = ☐; 14 - ☐ = 6; ☐ - 8 = 6. Discuss how if you know one fact, others can be found.

Now write on the board: 57 + 6 = and explain that this can be calculated by crossing the tens boundary like this: 57 + 6 = 57 + 3 + 3 = 60 + 3 = 63. Repeat for further examples, such as 45 + 8, asking the children to work mentally and to explain what they did. Write the mental calculation on the board for everyone to see. Repeat this for subtraction, such as 53 - 8. Then ask the children to work mentally to complete questions that you write on the board: 47 + 6 = ☐; 47 + ☐ = 53; ☐ + 6 = 53; and 74 - 7 = ☐; 74 - ☐ = 67; ☐ - 7 = 67.

Individual work: Provide each child with a copy of the activity sheet 'Working mentally' to complete.

Differentiation
Less confident learners: Provide the support version of the activity sheet, which contains addition and subtraction for crossing 10 and 20.
More confident learners: You may like to use the extension version of the activity sheet which includes some examples of crossing hundreds.

Review

Divide the class into two teams and choose captains. Ask the captains to come to the front. Explain that each team will, in turn, be given a number question to solve, and that the captain will decide who answers. However, the captain must ask a different person each time! Keep a score on the board for correct answers, and the first team to score ten points wins. Ask questions such as: *What is 15 subtract 7? What is 67 + 8? 92 - 5? 54 - 8?* When one team has gained ten points, ask: *What strategies did you find helpful to work out the answers?*

Lesson 10 (Teach, apply and evaluate)

Starter

Repeat the Starter for Lesson 9, then extend by asking the children to think of a three-digit number that has a zero in its tens or units; a three-digit number that has a two in its hundreds, tens or units, and so on.

Main teaching activities

Whole class: Give money examples for crossing the tens boundary, such as: *I have to pay 42p to post a letter. I have 36p in my hand. How much more money do I need? If I add two 20 pence coins to £1.45, how much is that?*
Individual work: Ask the children to work individually to answer the one- and two-step problems on the activity sheet 'Money problems (1)'. Remind them that they should show their jottings and these can include number lines, notes and diagrams.

Differentiation
Less confident learners: Provide the support version of 'Money problems (1)' for these children.
More confident learners: The extension version of the activity sheet contains more difficult problems to solve.

Review

Work through the core activity sheet that the children have completed. Ask them to explain the steps that they took to solve the problems. Say: *Tell your partner with which steps in solving problems you feel confident.*

BLOCK A
Counting, partitioning and calculating

BLOCK A

Counting, partitioning and calculating

Name _____ Date _____

Counting patterns

Write the missing numbers to complete these counting patterns.

1. [ ] [ ] 6 9 12 [ ] [ ] [ ] 24 27 [ ]

2. 0 4 [ ] [ ] [ ] 20 24 [ ] [ ] [ ] 40

3. 0 6 12 [ ] [ ] [ ] 36 42 [ ] [ ] [ ]

4. [ ] 36 32 [ ] [ ] [ ] [ ] [ ] [ ] [ ] 0

5. 30 [ ] [ ] 21 18 [ ] [ ] [ ] [ ] [ ] 0

6. 60 54 [ ] [ ] [ ] [ ] [ ] [ ] [ ] [ ] [ ]

Write these number patterns.

7. Keep subtracting 5, starting from 31.

[ ] [ ] [ ] [ ] [ ] [ ] [ ]

8. Keep subtracting 4, starting from 29.

[ ] [ ] [ ] [ ] [ ] [ ] [ ] [ ]

9. Keep subtracting 6, starting from 47.

[ ] [ ] [ ] [ ] [ ] [ ] [ ] [ ]

10. Now write your own subtraction pattern.

[ ] [ ] [ ] [ ] [ ] [ ] [ ] [ ]

What number did you subtract each time? [ ]

Name _____   Date _____

Paper abacus

You will need 13 counters.

Use the counters to make three-digit numbers on the abacus.

Each number must have the digits 2, 5 and 6.

How many different numbers can you make?

Write the value of the numbers that you make in the table below.

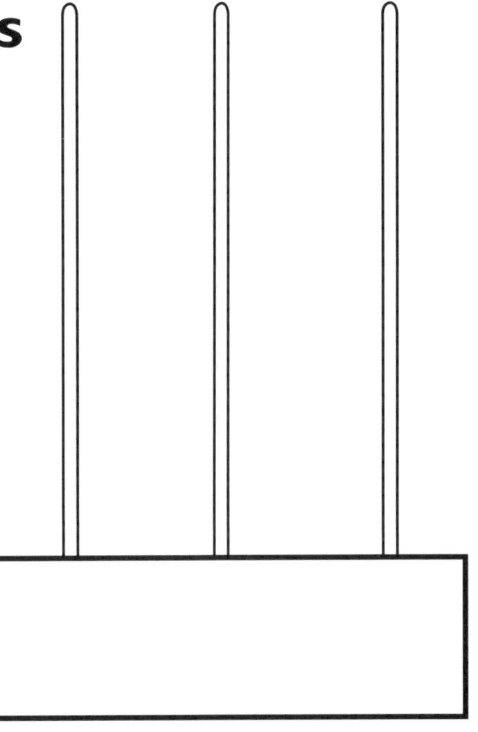

Hundreds	Tens	Units	The number

Now write your numbers again, in words here.

_____

_____

_____

_____

Name _____ Date _____

Adding and subtracting multiples of ten

Work with a partner.

Take turns to choose two numbers from Box A.

Add them in your head to find their **total**. Find the **difference** between them in your head.

Look in Box B. Can you find one of your answers (**total** or **difference**)?

Cross through the numbers in Box A as you use them, and write the number sentences onto the sheet.

Box A

80	90	70	170	120	150
160	240	10	700	50	90
60	70	20	30	90	80
500	480	60	10	20	40

Box B

120	490	130	200	80	170
330	150	110	790	410	60

Take turns to write your number sentences here.

Name	Name

PHOTOCOPIABLE **SCHOLASTIC**

Name _____   Date _____

Working mentally

Complete these number sentences.

1. 16 – 8 = ☐   **2.** 15 – 6 = ☐

3. 17 – 9 = ☐   **4.** 16 – 9 = ☐

5. 35 + 7 = ☐   **6.** 47 + 8 = ☐

7. 64 + 7 = ☐   **8.** 73 + 9 = ☐

9. 65 – 8 = ☐   **10.** 72 – 9 = ☐

11. 56 – 8 = ☐   **12.** 87 – 8 = ☐

Complete this number sentence.

Then write three more number sentences using the same numbers.

64 + 6 = ☐

☐ + ☐ = ☐

☐ – ☐ = ☐

☐ – ☐ = ☐

Now choose your own two-digit number and a single-digit number.

Write four number sentences like the ones you have just done.

☐ + ☐ = ☐

☐ + ☐ = ☐

☐ – ☐ = ☐

☐ – ☐ = ☐

Decide how to work this out.

Write the answer and a number sentence to show how you worked out the answer.

45 + 46 = ☐

BLOCK A

Counting, partitioning and calculating

Unit 2 ▯ 2 weeks

Counting, partitioning and calculating

Speaking and listening objective

● Follow up others' points and show whether they agree or disagree in a whole-class discussion.

Introduction

In this ten-lesson unit, the children listen carefully to other children's points of view and find helpful ways to respond in whole-class discussions especially when they have an alternative point of view. They explain how they solved problems, and use number lines, hundred squares and mental methods to solve problems. They partition three-digit numbers; round two- or three-digit numbers to the nearest 10 or 100, learning the rules for such roundings. They extend the range of mental calculation or recall for addition and subtraction, and for multiplication and division. They continue to learn multiplication and division table facts.

Using and applying mathematics

● Describe and explain methods, choices and solutions to puzzles and problems, orally and in writing, using pictures and diagrams.

Lesson	Strands	Starter	Main teaching activities
1. Teach and practise	Counting	Derive and recall multiplication facts for the 2, 3, 4, 5, 6 and 10 times-tables and the corresponding division facts; recognise multiples of 2, 5 or 10 up to 1000.	**Partition three-digit numbers into multiples of 100, 10 and 1 in different ways.**
2. Teach and practise	Counting	As for Lesson 1	Round two-digit or three-digit numbers to the nearest 10 or 100 and give estimates for their sums and differences.
3. Teach and practise	Knowledge	As for Lesson 1	**Derive and recall all addition and subtraction facts for each number to 20, sums and differences of multiples of 10 and number pairs that total 100.**
4. Teach and practise	Calculate	**Partition three-digit numbers into multiples of 100, 10 and 1 in different ways**	Multiply one-digit and two-digit numbers by 10 or 100, and describe the effect.
5. Teach and apply	Knowledge	As for Lesson 1	Derive and recall multiplication facts for the 2, 3, 4, 5, 6 and 10 times-tables and the corresponding division facts; recognise multiples of 2, 5 or 10 up to 1000.
6. Teach and practise	Calculate	**Derive and recall all addition and subtraction facts for each number to 20, sums and differences of multiples of 10 and number pairs that total 100.**	**Add or subtract mentally combinations of one-digit and two-digit numbers.**
7. Teach and practise	Calculate	As for Lesson 6	As for Lesson 6
8. Teach and apply	Calculate	As for Lesson 6	As for Lesson 6
9. Teach and apply	Calculate	**Add or subtract mentally combinations of one-digit and two-digit numbers.**	As for Lesson 6
10. Teach, apply and evaluate	Calculate	As for Lesson 9	As for Lesson 6

Lessons 1-5

Preparation
Make two sets of 0-9 digit cards using CD page 'Numeral cards 0-20'; copy CD page 'Hundred square' onto an OHT.

You will need
Photocopiable pages
'Missing numbers' (page 29) and 'Multiplying by 2 and 4' (page 30) for each child.
CD resources
Support and extension versions of 'Missing numbers'; 'Numeral cards 0-20', 'Number lines' and 'Hundred square' (see General resources). Interactive resources: 'Number cards' and 'Number line'.
Equipment
Counting stick.

Learning objectives

Starter
● Partition three-digit numbers into multiples of 100, 10 and 1 in different ways.
● Derive and recall multiplication facts for the 2, 3, 4, 5, 6 and 10 times-tables and the corresponding division facts; recognise multiples of 2, 5 or 10 up to 1000.

Main teaching activities
2006
● Partition three-digit numbers into multiples of 100, 10 and 1 in different ways.
● Round two-digit or three-digit numbers to the nearest 10 or 100 and give estimates for their sums and differences.
● Derive and recall all addition and subtraction facts for each number to 20, sums and differences of multiples of 10 and number pairs that total 100.
● Multiply one-digit and two-digit numbers by 10 or 100, and describe the effect.
1999
● Know what each digit represents, and partition three-digit numbers into a multiple of 100, a multiple of ten and ones (HTU).
● Round any two-digit number to the nearest 10 and any three-digit number to the nearest 100.
● Round any positive integer less than 1000 to the nearest 10 or 100.
● Know by heart: all addition and subtraction facts for each number to 20; all pairs of multiples of 100 with a total of 1000 (eg 300 + 700); all pairs of multiples of 5 with a total of 100 (eg 35 + 65).
● Derive quickly all number pairs that total 100 (eg 62 + 38, 75 + 25, 40 + 60).
● Multiply mentally by 10/100 by shifting the digits one/two places to the left.

Vocabulary
problem, solution, calculate, calculation, answer, method, explain, reasoning, pattern, predict, place value, partition, digit, ones, tens, hundreds, one-digit number, two-digit number, three-digit number, compare, order, equals (=), count on, count back, add, subtract, multiply, times, divide, share, group, sum, total, difference, plus, minus

Lesson 1 (Teach and practise)

Starter
Recall: Explain that you will ask for multiplication and division facts from the 2-times table. Keep the pace sharp so that children are encouraged to recall or derive quickly. Ask, for example: *What is 4 multiplied by 2? What is 20 divided by 2? What is 7 times 2? I share 18 sweets between Peter and Paul. How many do they each receive?*

Main teaching activities
Whole class: Use the interactive resource 'Number cards' to drag/drop cards to build the number 156. Ask: *What does the digit 1 represent? And the 5? And the 6? What if I change around the 1 and the 6? What number would it read then?* Agree that this would be 615. Repeat this for other configurations, such as 516, 561, and so on. Now use the drag/drop cards to make 132. Ask the children to count back in tens until they reach the smallest number they can say. Ask them to predict what that number will be.

Unit 2 ▶ 2 weeks

Count together from 132 down in tens and agree that the smallest number they reach is 2. Repeat this for counting back in tens from 194. Now repeat this for counting on from a given number, such as 547. They count in tens to get as close to 700 as they can without crossing the 700 barrier. Again, ask for predictions, then count. Repeat for other three-digit starting numbers.

Paired work: Provide each pair with two sets of 0–9 digit cards. Ask the children to take turns to choose three digit cards from the shuffled pack and to predict the smallest number they would reach when they count back in tens from their number. They count back in tens to check. Ask them to record their prediction and the number they reach. They decide how to record. Ask them to do this ten times. They then make another three-digit number from the cards, and choose a higher stop number which is a hundreds number. They predict, then count on to as close as they can get, without crossing the hundreds barrier. Again, ask them to do this ten times.

Review

Ask the children to give one of their start numbers for counting back in tens. Challenge the others to work out the smallest number that can be reached, and to explain why they think that is the smallest number. Repeat this for several different start numbers. Then repeat for the counting up numbers. Ask questions such as: *Imagine counting back from 164 in tens. Is 56 one of the numbers you say? Why not? Now imagine counting forward in tens from 99. Is 139 one of the numbers you say? Why is that?*

Differentiation

Less confident learners: Decide whether to concentrate on counting on and back within 100.

More confident learners: Challenge this group to choose a stop number where they cross their chosen hundreds barrier.

Lesson 2 (Teach and practise)

Starter

Recall: Repeat the Starter from Lesson 1, this time for the 2-, 5- and 10-times tables.

Main teaching activities

Whole class: Explain that when rounding numbers up or down, there is a simple rule to learn. Write on the board the number 26. Explain that this rounds up to the nearest 10. Ask: *What number will 26 become when rounded to the nearest 10?* (30) Say: *Where the units digit is 5, 6, 7, 8 or 9, the number will round up to the nearest 10.* Write 32 on the board. Explain that this rounds down to the nearest 10 and ask what the rounded number will be. (30) Say: *Where the digit is 1, 2, 3 or 4 the number rounds down to the nearest 10.*

Set the 'Number line' interactive resource to 0–100. Write 48 on the board. Ask: *Where should this number go?* Invite a child to come to the front to point to the appropriate place. Write the number on the line. Say: *Round 48 to the nearest 10.* Agree that this is 50. Repeat for other two-digit numbers.

Now set the 'Number line' interactive resource to 0–1000. Explain that rounding to the nearest 100 also has rules. Say: *Tens digits 50, 60, 70, 80 and 90 round up to the next hundred. Tens digits 10, 20, 30 and 40 round down to the nearest hundred.* Write 360 on the board and ask: *Where does this number fit on the number line? How will it round?* Repeat for other three-digit numbers.

Paired work: Provide copies of general resource sheet 'Number lines'. This shows a 0–100 number line and a 0–1000 number line. Ask the children to work in pairs with two sets of shuffled 0–9 digit cards. They take turns to: take two cards and make a TU number; write it on the 0–100 number line; round it up or down; mark with an arrow where the number rounds to. They repeat this nine more times and record what they have done in the space below. They repeat this for rounding three-digit numbers on the 0–1000 number line.

Review

Invite children to give examples of their roundings. Record these, as before, on an appropriate number line. Ask questions such as: *Why does 64 become*

Differentiation

Less confident learners: Let these children concentrate on rounding TU numbers on the 0–100 number line.

More confident learners: Challenge the children to try rounding larger numbers to the nearest hundred, such as 1562.

60 when rounded to the nearest 10? Why does 78 round up to 80? Why does 345 round down to 300 when rounded to the nearest 100? Round 659 to the nearest 100. Explain why the answer is 700.

Lesson 3 (Teach and practise)

Starter
Recall: Repeat the Starter from Lesson 2, this time including some 3-times table questions. Again, keep the pace sharp to encourage rapid recall.

Main teaching activities
Whole class: Write on the board 4 + 5 = and write the answer. Now write underneath 40 + 50 and ask: *How can we use the fact that 4 + 5 = 9 to help us to find 40 + 50?* Agree that when adding multiples of 10 it is the tens digits that can be added, so that 40 + 50 = 90. Now write 400 + 500 and ask: *How does 4 + 5 = 9 help us here?* Repeat this for subtraction, such as: 7 - 4, 70 - 40, 700 - 400, and so on.

Now ask the children to say pairs of numbers that total 20. Write these on the board, ordering them so that the pairing begins with 0 + 20 = 20, to 20 + 0 = 20. Discuss the patterns that the children can see in the ordered pairs. Repeat this for pairs of multiples of 10 which total 100, such as 40 + 60, again ordering these. Ask: *How does knowing all the pairs of unit numbers that total 10, such as 3 + 7, help you to find multiples of 10 which total 100?*

Invite the children to respond to finding complements to 100. Say, for example: *What must I add to 37 to make 100? How did you work that out?* Repeat for other examples.

Paired work: Provide each pair with a copy of the general resource sheet 'Hundred square' and two coloured pencils. They take turns to point to a number. Their partner finds the number which, when added to the first number makes 100. Their partner can challenge if they disagree, and show the correct answer. The winner of each round colours in both numbers. The child with more squares coloured in wins the game.

Review
Play the game together as a class. Put the class into two teams each with a captain. One captain chooses a number; the other captain chooses someone from their team to find the complement to 100. The first team captain can challenge if they disagree. Emphasise that the captains must choose a different person each time to answer. Now ask questions such as: *What must I add to 57p to make £1? How did you work that out? Did everyone use the same method? Which method do you think is best? Why do you think that?*

Differentiation
Less confident learners: Decide whether to work together to play the game. The children can use their copy of 'Hundred square' to count up to 100 to find the missing number; ask them to shut their eyes and to visualise the hundred square and to count up mentally.
More confident learners: Decide whether to provide each pair with a timer. Set a limit such as ten seconds for each of the children to find an answer.

Lesson 4 (Teach and practise)

Starter
Recall: Play the Buzz game. The children stand in a circle and each child says a number in sequence ascending from any three-digit number. Each time a child says an odd number they should also say 'Buzz'. Encourage the children to do this at speed. Repeat the game counting backwards from any three-digit number.

Main teaching activities
Whole class: On the board write 5 × 10. Ask: *What is 5 multiplied by 10?* Write 50. Repeat this for other ×10 of single-digit numbers. Ask: *What happens when you multiply by 10?* Write TU headings above 5, then 50, 6 and 60 and so on. Elicit understanding that when multiplying by 10 the digits shift one place to the left. Now ask: *What is the value of 5 in 5? 50?* Then introduce the concept of dividing by 10 by writing on the board 40 ☐ 10 = 4. Ask:
● *What is 30 divided by 10?*

Differentiation

Less confident learners: This group multiples and divides by 10 only using the support version of 'Missing numbers'.
More confident learners: Distribute the extension version of the sheet. This group has to follow two functions being used, eg ☐ × 10, then ☐ ÷ 10. This emphasises the inverse nature of multiplication and division. The group should also have access to a calculator to check and to assist with the investigation of ☐ × ☐ × ☐ = 300. (Two possible likely solutions are 3 × 10 × 10 or 5 × 6 × 10.) Tell the children that you would like them to suggest answers to this question in the Review and be prepared to explain their thinking. Ask them whether the order they input their calculation in the calculator makes any difference to the product.

- *What is 500 divided by 10?*
- *What is 1000 divided by 10?*

Discuss how the digits move when multiplying and dividing by 10, then when multiplying and dividing by 100.

Invite the children to come up with three questions they can ask the rest of the class to solve, such as: *What is 6 multiplied by 10?* Use some of the children's questions with the whole class. Encourage the more confident children to ask and answer multiples of 100 questions.

Group work: The children complete activity page 'Missing numbers', which contains calculations such as 2 × 10 ☐ 10 = 2.

Review

Ask the more confident children to give answers to ☐ × ☐ × ☐ = 300. They can write their responses on the board. For each response, using the OHP calculator, demonstrate the multiplication for others to see. Now ask questions such as:

- *What is 5 multiplied by 10? By 100?*
- *What happens to the digits when you multiply by 10? By 100?*
- *What is 500 divided by 10? By 100?*
- *What happens to the digits when you divide by 10? By 100?*
- *Multiply 5 by 10. And by 10 again. What has happened to the value of the digit 5?*

For each question write the number sentence and answer on the board, so that the answer and the reasoning are clear.

Lesson 5 (Teach and apply)

Starter

Recall: Explain that you will ask the children multiplication and division questions from the 2-, 5- and 10-times tables. Say, for example: *What is 3 multiplied by 5? 7 multiplied by 2? 20 divided by 10? 20 divided by 5?* Keep the pace sharp to encourage quick recall.

Main teaching activities

Whole class: The children should be able to apply doubling and halving strategies to help them calculate quickly by the end of this lesson. Begin by using a counting stick. Label one end of the stick 0 and the other end 20, and ask the children to count along the stick in twos with you. Now point to any position on the stick, such as 8, and ask: *What number goes here? Two multiplied by what makes 8?* Repeat this for other positions on the stick. Now wipe the numbers from the stick and re-label it 0 to 40, so you can count in fours as the children count along with you. Now point to any position on the stick and ask the class to say what number is at that position. Challenge the children to say the 4-times table fact for, for example, 12 (3 × 4 = 12).

On the board write up the 2-times table facts. Now write up the beginning of the 4-times table facts, 0 × 4 and 1 × 4, then 2 × 4, so that the 'doubles' appear next to each other in a list. Ask the children to supply the answers. Ask the children to explain what they see; that is, that if the 2-times table facts are doubled, then the result is the 4-times table facts.

Cover the table facts on the board so that the children can no longer see them, and ask questions such as: *What is double 4? 5? 8? 10? How did you work that out? What is the product of 6 and 4?* Repeat, this time asking for halves, such as: *What is half of 20? 40? 36? How did you work that out?* Write up the halves as a division sentence, such as 20 ÷ 2 = 10. Invite the children to give examples of doubling and halving that they have noticed in real life, such as 'buy one get one free', 'two for the price of one', 'half-price sale', '50% off'.

Now ask: *What is double 16?* Write on the board 16 × 2 = 32. Ask: *What is half of 32?* and write up 32 ÷ 2 = 16. Discuss how multiplication and division facts are linked, and that if you can recall a multiplication fact then you can

Unit 2 ⬜ 2 weeks

find the linked division facts. Repeat for other examples, such as: 18 × 2 and 36 ÷ 2.

Draw this grid on the board:

×	2	4	1
1			
2			
4			

Point to a square and ask for suggestions as to what should be written in it. Check that the children understand that they multiply the row and column numbers together for the chosen square. For each answer ask: *How did you work that out?* Children may have remembered facts, and used doubles.

Individual work: Provide each child with a copy of activity sheet 'Multiplying by 2 and 4'. Ask them to complete the tables chart, then challenge them to work out the doubles for the numbers entering the function machine.

Review

Ask the children to say together the 4-times table facts as a chant. To begin with, the children can read the answers from their sheet. Now ask them to cover their sheet and to say these number facts again, this time without a prompt. Remind them that they can use doubling to help them. Ask questions such as: *What is 8 × 4? So what is half of 32? How do you know this?* Repeat for other facts from the 4-times table.

Differentiation

Less confident learners: If necessary, provide number lines or 100 squares as an aid for this group to calculate their 4-times tables facts. You may prefer them to work as a group to find the answers for the function machine challenge.

More confident learners: Challenge these children to work quickly to complete the table facts. Decide whether to provide more numbers for doubling, such as 26, 27, 29 and 30.

Lessons 6-10

You will need

Photocopiable pages
'Counting on' (page 31).

CD resources
Support and extension versions of 'Counting on'; core, support and extension versions of 'Inspector Add-it'; 'Hundred square' and 'Number lines' (see General resources).

Equipment
Calculators; OHP calculator; large sticky notes.

Learning objectives

Starter

● Derive and recall all addition and subtraction facts for each number to 20, sums and differences of multiples of 10 and number pairs that total 100.
● Add or subtract mentally combinations of one-digit and two-digit numbers.

Main teaching activities

2006
● Add or subtract mentally combinations of one-digit and two-digit numbers.
1999
● Use mental calculation strategies – several objectives, including: use known number facts and place value to add/subtract mentally; add and subtract mentally a 'near multiple of 10'; add mentally three or four small numbers; find a difference by counting up.

Vocabulary

problem, solution, calculate, calculation, answer, method, explain, reasoning, pattern, predict, place value, partition, digit, ones, tens, hundreds, one-digit number, two-digit, number, three-digit number, compare, order, equals (=), count on, count back, add, subtract, sum, total, difference, plus, minus

Lesson 6 (Teach and practise)

Starter

Recall: Explain that you will say a number between 0 and 20, and challenge the children to say the number that adds to your number to make 20. So, if you say 5, the children say 15, and so on. Begin slowly, giving the children about ten seconds thinking time. As they become more confident, increase the pace.

Main teaching activities

Whole class: Explain that in today's lesson, the children will be asked to put the larger number first and count on. Write on the board 7 + 56. Invite the children to count on from the larger number. Say together: *56 and 57, 58, 59, 60, 61, 62, 63.* Agree that 7 + 56 is 63. Some children may point out that they can add 4 to 56 to take them to 60, then another 3 because 4 + 3 = 7. If children are unsure, model this using an empty number line. Provide further examples such as: 7 + 136, 8 + 237, each time counting on in ones from the larger number. Now write up 30 + 44. Invite suggestions for how this can be calculated. Suggest that counting on in tens from 44 would be useful and say together: *44 and 54, 64, 74. So 30 + 44 = 74.* Repeat the counting in tens procedure for other examples.

Individual work: Provide each child with a copy of the activity sheet 'Counting on' and invite them to complete the addition sentences using the counting on in ones or tens strategy.

Review

Write on the board 40 + 57 and ask: *How would you work this out?* Invite a child to demonstrate adding by counting on in tens. Repeat for 9 + 133 for counting on in ones. Provide further examples.

Differentiation

Less confident learners: The support version of 'Counting on' contains simpler numbers.
More confident learners: Provide the extension version of the sheet which involves adding three numbers.

Lesson 7 (Teach and practise)

Starter

Recall: Explain that you will keep a steady beat by clapping quietly. Ask the children to say the number that adds to make 100 to the number that you say. Begin with 10, then 20, and so on up to 100. Repeat this, this time clapping a little faster but still keeping a steady beat.

Main teaching activities

Whole class: Explain that today the children will be adding by finding pairs that total 9, 10 or 11. Write on the board 15 + 6 + 2 + 8 and ask: *Which numbers shall we pair? Why did you choose those?* A solution would be: (15 + 5 + 1) + (2 + 8) = 20 + 1 + 10 = 31. Repeat this for other examples, such as 16 + 7 + 5 + 3, where one way of calculating would be: (16 + 5) + (7 + 3) = 10 + 6 + 5 + 10 = 31. In this example children can make 11 by adding 6 and 5. Now provide an example where the children can add to make a 9, such as 13 + 8 + 6 + 5 = (10 + 3 + 6) + (8 + 5) = 19 + 13 = 10 + 10 + 9 + 3 = 32.

Individual work: Write up some addition sentences, such as: 14 + 7 + 8 + 1; 19 + 2 + 7 + 3... Also include some with missing numbers such as 15 + ? + 5 = 33 for the children to complete.

Review

Review the number sentences on the board. Invite children from each ability group to explain how they calculated. There is likely to be more than one way of doing this for some questions, so ask, for example: *Who tried a different way? Tell us what you did. Was this easier/harder to do than Marc's way?*

Ask the more confident children to write up their own sentences and invite all the children to suggest how these could be calculated.

Differentiation

Less confident learners: If necessary, provide adult support to work with this group.
More confident learners: Challenge the children to write three addition sentences of their own and swap these with a partner. Ask them to explain their calculation strategies during the Review session.

Lesson 8 (Teach and apply)

Starter

Recall: Repeat the Starter from Lesson 7, but this time use a faster, steady pace. Repeat, increasing the pace so that the children will need to answer almost immediately. This will give you the opportunity to identify who has rapid recall of these facts.

Main teaching activities

Whole class: Explain that in today's lesson the children will be partitioning into '5 and a bit' when adding. On the board write 19 + 8 and ask: *How can* *we work this out?* The children may reply: (10 + 5 + 4) add (5 + 3). Write up, for example: 10 + 5 + 4 + 5 + 3 = 10 + 5 + 5 + 4 + 3 = 20 + 7 = 27. Explain that breaking down the numbers 6, 7, 8 and 9 into '5 and a bit' is a very useful strategy. Provide more examples, such as 27 + 36 and 28 + 29, and invite individual children to demonstrate the method of partitioning and recombining, writing this on the board.

Paired work: Write these numbers on the board: 26, 37, 48, 29. Ask the children to work in their pairs and to take turns to choose two of the numbers. They both write addition sentences, partition into '5 and a bit' and recombine. They compare what they have done, then combine two more of these numbers until they have completed all six possible addition combinations.

Review

Invite pairs to explain how they worked out their answers. Ask: *How would you partition 48/57/69/96 into '5 and a bit'?* Remind the children that this week they have considered putting the larger number first; looking for pairs that make 9, 10 or 11, and today partitioning into '5 and a bit'.

Lesson 9 (Teach and apply)

Starter

Recall: Provide the less confident children with a 100 square or 0–100 number line. Explain that you will say a two-digit number. Ask the children to work mentally to find the number that when added to your number totals 100. Say, for example, 3, 9, 17, 32, 64... Give some thinking time so that the majority of the children have had time to calculate the answer mentally.

Main teaching activities

Whole class: Explain to the class that they will be adding small numbers, using the strategies that they have learned so far in this unit. Ask them to add the following numbers, making jottings as they choose (some children will need to be reminded to use an empty number line if they need to): 10 + 15 + 10 + 11 = ☐. Take suggestions from the children how they could do this, such as 10 + 10 + 5 + 10 + 10 + 1 = 20 + 20 + 6 = 46. Using an OHP and OHP calculator, show the children that they still obtain the same answer if they input the numbers in a different order.

Now ask the children to try another example, this time adding mentally: 15 + 7 + 15 + 3. Invite a child to explain how they worked this out. They may have doubled 15, then added 7 and 3, to make 40. Invite other suggestions. Discuss whether any ways of adding were more efficient and why this is so. Provide calculators and invite the children to use the calculators to check their answer, by inputting the numbers in a different order. Repeat this for other examples, still working mentally.

Individual work: Ask the children to complete the activity sheet 'Inspector Add-it'. Core group and more confident children can check their answers using a calculator.

Review

Ask a child to show how they would calculate 10 + 17 + 13 = ☐. Acknowledge that personal preference is allowed so spotting that 17 + 13 = 30 and then adding the 10 is fine. Write the numbers in the sum on large sticky notes and change their order. Invite the children to work out the answer each time you move the notes. Now write up 10 + ☐ + 10 = 35. Ask: *What do you think the missing number is? What number must be in the units position of this number? Why do you think that?* Ask for examples of what the number *couldn't* be if the children are struggling to explain.

Now ask the children to work in pairs. Prompt them to find three numbers which, when totalled, make 40. Challenge the more confident children by asking them to find four numbers which total 60; decide whether to limit the range for the less confident children to three numbers to total 20.

Differentiation

Less confident learners: Decide whether to simplify the TU numbers, using, for example, 16, 17, 18 and 19.
More confident learners: Decide whether to challenge the children to total three of these numbers each time.

Differentiation

Less confident learners: The support version of the activity page focuses on smaller totals.
More confident learners: The extension version of the activity page focuses on crossing the tens boundary when adding.

Lesson 10 (Teach, apply and evaluate)

Starter
Repeat the Starter for Lesson 9, this time reducing slightly the thinking time in order to encourage quicker mental recall or calculation.

Main teaching activities
Whole class: Review the work done in Lesson 9. Use more examples, including checking with a calculator, such as $15 + 14 + 9$, $8 + 9 + 6$...
Paired work: Prompt the children to find three numbers which, when totalled, make 40. Challenge the more confident children to find four numbers which total 80; if necessary, limit the range for the less confident children to three numbers that total 20.

Review
Discuss what the children have done during their paired work and ask: *Which strategies did you use to find the totals?* Invite the children to discuss with their partner the strategies with which they feel confident.

Name _____   Date _____

Missing numbers

Work out the missing numbers and then check your answers with a calculator.

1. 2 × 10 = 20

   2 × 10 × 10 = ⬚

2. 4 × 10 = 40

   4 × 10 × 10 = ⬚

3. 6 × 10 = ⬚

   6 × 10 × 10 = ⬚

4. 200 ÷ 10 = ⬚

   20 ÷ 10 = ⬚

5. 400 ÷ 10 = 40

   40 ÷ 10 = ⬚

6. 600 ÷ 10= ⬚

   60 ÷ 10 = ⬚

Name _____   Date _____

Multiplying by 2 and 4

Write in the missing numbers.

Use halving and doubling to help.

	1 times-table	2 times-table	4 times-table
1	1		
2			
3		6	
4			
5			
6			24
7			
8	8	16	
9	9		
10	10		

Challenge

Double these numbers.

19

21

22

23

25

Name _____   Date _____

Counting on

Add the numbers.

Count on in ones from the larger number.

Write your answer.

1. $9 + 45 =$ ☐   **2.** $8 + 165 =$ ☐

3. $7 + 85 =$ ☐   **4.** $6 + 137 =$ ☐

5. $9 + 124 =$ ☐   **6.** $5 + 178 =$ ☐

Count on in tens from the larger number.

Write your answer.

7. $30 + 46 =$ ☐   **8.** $40 + 56 =$ ☐

9. $20 + 48 =$ ☐   **10.** $30 + 67 =$ ☐

Now try these.

Decide whether to count on in ones or in tens.

Write your answer under the heading of the method that you used.

Add	Count on in ones	Count on in tens
7 + 168		
30 + 49		
40 + 58		
9 + 154		

Unit 3 ▢ 2 weeks

Counting, partitioning and calculating

Speaking and listening objective
● Actively include and respond to all members of the group.

Introduction
In this ten-lesson unit children solve problems for addition, subtraction, multiplication and division. They work in groups, pairs and individually. Where they work in groups or pairs, encourage the children to listen to the others and to give positive comments about their work. This will help the children to develop ways of responding without hurting others' feelings, even when they disagree. They round numbers to the nearest 10 or 100, add and subtract mentally and develop written methods for addition and subtraction. They begin to recognise and use vertical methods for computation. They continue to develop their rapid recall of multiplication table facts and to derive division ones. They find remainders after division and decide whether to round up or down. They continue to develop their written methods for multiplication and division.

Using and applying mathematics
● Solve one-step and two-step problems involving numbers, money or measures, including time, choosing and carrying out appropriate calculations.

Lesson	Strands	Starter	Main teaching activities
1. Teach and practise	Counting	**Add or subtract mentally combinations of one-digit and two-digit numbers.**	Round two-digit or three-digit numbers to the nearest 10 or 100 and give estimates for their sums and differences.
2. Teach and practise	Calculate	As for Lesson 1	**Add or subtract mentally combinations of one-digit and two-digit numbers.**
3. Teach and practise	Calculate	As for Lesson 1	As for Lesson 2
4. Teach and practise	Calculate	Derive and recall multiplication facts for the 2, 3, 4, 5, 6 and 10 times-tables and the corresponding division facts; recognise multiples of 2, 5 or 10 up to 1000.	Develop and use written methods to record, support or explain addition and subtraction of two-digit and three-digit numbers.
5. Teach and practise	Calculate	As for Lesson 4	As for Lesson 4
6. Teach and practise	Calculate	As for Lesson 4	As for Lesson 4
7. Teach and apply	Knowledge	As for Lesson 4	Derive and recall multiplication facts for the 2, 3, 4, 5, 6 and 10 times-tables and the corresponding division facts; recognise multiples of 2, 5 or 10 up to 1000.
8. Teach and practise	Calculate	As for Lesson 4	Use practical and informal written methods to multiply and divide two-digit numbers (eg 13 × 3, 50 ÷ 4); round remainders up or down, depending on the context.
9. Teach and apply	Calculate	As for Lesson 4	As for Lesson 8
10. Teach, apply and evaluate	Use/apply	As for Lesson 4	Solve one-step and two-step problems involving numbers, money or measures, including time, choosing and carrying out appropriate calculations.

Lessons 1–6

Preparation
Make sets of 0 -9 digit cards, using CD page 'Numeral cards for 0 to 20'; copy onto card and cut up CD page 'Multiples of 5 cards'.

You will need
Photocopiable pages
'Addition empty number line' (page 41) for each child.
CD resources
Support and extension versions of 'Addition empty number line'; 'Numeral cards 0–20', 'Hundred square' and 'Multiples of 5 cards' (see General resources).
Equipment
Beanbag; Blu-Tack; large 200-300 number line.

Learning objectives

Starter
● Add or subtract mentally combinations of one-digit and two-digit numbers.
● Derive and recall multiplication facts for the 2, 3, 4, 5, 6 and 10 times-tables and the corresponding division facts; recognise multiples of 2, 5 or 10 up to 1000.

Main teaching activities
2006
● Round two-digit or three-digit numbers to the nearest 10 or 100 and give estimates for their sums and differences.
● Add or subtract mentally combinations of one-digit and two-digit numbers.
● Develop and use written methods to record, support or explain addition and subtraction of two-digit and three-digit numbers.
1999
● Round any two-digit number to the nearest 10 and any three-digit number to the nearest 100.
● Use mental calculation strategies – several objectives, including: use known number facts and place value to add/subtract mentally; add and subtract mentally a 'near multiple of 10'; add mentally three or four small numbers; find a difference by counting up.
● Use informal pencil and paper methods to support, record or explain HTU ± TU, HTU ± HTU.
● Begin to use column addition and subtraction for HTU ± TU where the calculation cannot easily be done mentally.

Vocabulary
problem, solution, calculate, calculation, answer, method, explain, reasoning, pattern, predict, place value, partition, digit, ones, tens, hundreds, one-digit number, two-digit number, three-digit number, compare, order, equals (=), count on, count back, add, subtract, sum, total, difference, plus, minus

Lesson 1 (Teach and practise)

Starter
Recall: Ask the class to stand in a circle to play a game, as follows: Give a beanbag to a child to hold and ask him/her to say a two-digit number. He/she then passes the beanbag to his/her left. The next person has to add 10 to the number, pass on the beanbag, and so on, until someone says 'Inverse reverse'. This means the rule changes to subtract 10 and the direction of the beanbag also changes. Tell the children that they may each say 'Inverse reverse' only once during the game.

It may take a few tries before the children can pick up speed! If you have a large class, you could double up children by asking one child to stand behind a partner and to whisper the answer for the person in front to call out.

Main teaching activities
Whole class: Explain to the class the conventions of rounding numbers to the nearest 10: numbers ending in 1 to 4 round down; numbers ending in 5 to 9 round up. Then ask the children to round these distances to the nearest 10km: 24km (20km), 36km (40km), 12km (10km) and 55km (60km). Now explain that numbers can be rounded to the nearest hundred, and that this time it is the tens digit which is important for rounding: tens digits which are 1 to 4 round down; tens digits which are 5 to 9 round up. Write on the board 160 and ask: *What number will this be if it is rounded to the nearest hundred? 200, because there are six tens so that it rounds up.* Repeat this

for other numbers, such as 340, 890, 450 and so on, each time checking that the children can explain the rounding. Now include numbers with a digit other than zero in the units place and explain that when rounding to the nearest 100 the units digit is ignored. Give examples such as 456, 137, 222, 361 and so on.

Group work: Ask the children to work in groups of four. They take turns to draw three single-digit cards from a pack of 0–9 cards. They make a three-digit number, then say what that number is rounded to the nearest 100. This can be recorded on paper if you wish. Challenge the children to work quickly.

Differentiation

Less confident learners: Decide whether to limit this group to making two-digit numbers, and rounding to the nearest 10.

More confident learners: Challenge these children to make six different three-digit numbers with their three cards, such as for the cards 5, 6, 3: 563, 536, 653, 635, 356 and 365. The children then round each of these numbers to the nearest 100.

Review

Ask the children to think of a question that might give the answer 60, such as: *A tailor needed 55cm of cloth, so he rounded the measurement up to 60cm so there would be plenty of material.* Share some of the responses from the children.

Ask each child to write a three-digit number on their whiteboard. They then pass their whiteboard along to another child who writes the number to the nearest hundred (rounded up or down as appropriate). The children then pass their whiteboards back to each other to check the answers. Remind the class that you are interested to know when they next use the rounding up/down strategy.

Lesson 2 (Teach and practise)

Starter

Recall: Repeat the Starter from Lesson 1, but extend the game so that the children now say 'Inverse reverse 100', and count forwards and backwards in hundreds.

Main teaching activities

Whole class: Explain that today the children will be totalling several small numbers. On the board write 17 + 4 + 3 + 6 and ask: *How can we work this out?* Discuss how the 17 and 3 can be combined to make 20, and the 4 and 6 to make 10. Now ask the children to consider this example: 19 + 8 + 4 + 7. For example: (19 + 8) + (4 + 7) = (20 + 7) + (10 + 1) = 27 + 11 = 38. Repeat this for a further example, such as 15 + 6 + 8, where 15 + 6 makes 21 or 20 + 1. This relates to adding 11 by adding 10 and adjusting by 1. Now write on the board 14 + 8 + 5, where 14 + 5 = 19 or 20 – 1. This relates to adding 9 by adding 10 and adjusting by 1.

Individual work: Write these numbers on the board: 11, 12, 13, 14, 15, 16, 1, 2, 3, 4, 5, 6, 7, 8, 9 and 10. Ask the children to choose one of the two-digit numbers and three single-digit numbers, and then use them to write an addition sentence and calculate the answer. Ask them to write six addition sentences, making each one different.

Differentiation

Less confident learners: If necessary, let these children choose just two or three of the numbers for each addition sentence.

More confident learners: Challenge the children to include one of these numbers each time: 21, 32, 43, 54 and 65.

Review

Choose some of the number sentences that the children have written and ask them to explain their calculation strategies. Ask questions such as: *How else could we work this out? Can you make a 10, 11, 9? How does that help you? How could you check your answer?*

Ask the more confident children to write up some of their number sentences on the board and to explain how they calculated their answers. Discuss how making a 10 can also be used to make 20, 30, 40 and so on.

Lesson 3 (Teach and practise)

Starter

Reason: Explain that you will write up a number sentence such as 45 + 36 = 81. Ask the children to write on their whiteboards another addition and two subtraction sentences which use the same numbers, such as 36 + 45 = 81; 81 – 36 = 45; 81 – 45 = 36. Repeat for other examples, such as 97 – 43 = 54.

Main teaching activities

Whole class: Write on the board: 36 + 30 = and ask for an answer. Invite children to explain how they worked this out, such as counting on three tens. Now write 36 + 29 and explain that we can use adding 9, 10, and 11 strategies for adding. Write up 36 + 29 = 36 + 30 - 1. Ask the children to calculate the answer. Repeat for another example, such as 45 + 39, or 45 + 40 - 1.

Now write up 64 + 21 and ask for suggestions for calculating this. Write up 64 + 20 + 1 and discuss how this is a development from adding 11 by adding 10 and adjusting by 1. Now write up: 15 + 9 = ; 15 + 19 = ; 15 + 29 = . Ask the children to work out the answer to 15 + 9 (24) and then to deduce the answers to the other two addition sentences. Ask them to continue the pattern of number sentences and to write the answers. Discuss how patterns like this help us to find answers to questions quickly.

Individual work: On the board write: 17 + 11; 17 + 21; 17 + 31. Ask the children to write the answers to these, then to continue the pattern until the total is about 100. Then ask them to begin with 18 + 9 and to continue the pattern to find the answers for themselves. Finally, ask them to continue the subtraction pattern for 78 - 1, 78 - 11, 78 - 21 and so on to 78 - 71.

Review

Challenge the children to say the number sentence pattern as you write these on the board. Begin with 17 + 11... and continue to 17 + 81 = 98. Now ask the more confident children to continue the pattern, prompting the other children to join in as they see this continue: 17 + 91 = 108; 17 + 101 = 118... Ask: *What do you notice?* Discuss how, as the tens number increases in 11, 21, 31... so does the total increase by 10 each time. Repeat this for the 18 + 9 pattern, again, using the more confident children to help to take the answers beyond 18 + 79 = 97.

Differentiation

Less confident learners:
Provide a 100 square for the children to use to count on in tens, if necessary, to help them to find the answers.
More confident learners:
Challenge these children to continue each pattern until the totals are about 200.

Lesson 4 (Teach and practise)

Starter

Recall: Play a class game of Pelmanism. Stick up on the board the 'Multiples of 5 cards' (face down). Divide the class into two teams, nominating a spokesperson for each team. Each team is allowed to come and reveal two cards. If the cards have the relationship of a double, then the team keeps the cards. If they have no doubles relationship, the cards are stuck back (face down) and the other team has a go. The team that finds the most pairs wins.

Main teaching activities

Whole class: Explain to the children that they will be using an empty number line in order to help them to count on in multiples of 1, 10 or 100 as a strategy for addition. On the board write 65 + 34 and draw an empty number line.

Discuss how 65 + 34 can be broken down into 65 + 30 + 4, counting on in tens for the 30 then in ones for the 4. Repeat for 54 + 37.

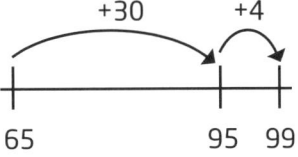

Now repeat this for examples which cross the hundreds boundary. Write on the board 75 + 38 and draw an empty number line. Explain that this example can be broken down like this: 75 + 38 = 75 + 30 + 5 + 3. Encourage the children to count in tens from 75 to 105, then add 5, then add 3. Now try 84 + 37 and some HTU + TU sums, such as 257 + 68 which breaks down into 257 + 60 + 3 + 5, and then for HTU + HTU, such as 348 + 279 (348 + 279 = 348 + 200 + 70 + 2 + 7).

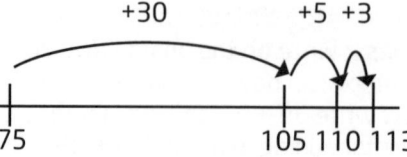

Differentiation

Less confident learners: Decide whether to use the support sheet which only includes examples of TU + TU.
More confident learners: The extension version of the sheet includes more HTU + HTU examples.

Individual work: Provide the activity sheet 'Addition empty number line' for the children to complete.

Review

Work through some examples from the core activity sheet. Invite individual children to draw number lines on the board to demonstrate their addition strategy. Discuss whether different strategies were used by other children, and which they think was more efficient.

Lesson 5 (Teach and practice)

Starter

Recall: Repeat the Starter for Lesson 4, but this time use only the decade cards from general resource sheet 'Multiples of 5 cards'. Explain that one card has to be half the amount of the other. The children will quickly realise this is the same as the game they played in Lesson 4, but with halves, not doubles. For this version, introduce the rule that the second card they turn must be half the first card - so having the correct order is crucial!

Main teaching activities

Whole class: Explain that today the children will use the empty number line in order to subtract by counting up from the smaller to the larger number. Write on the board 76 - 48 and draw an empty number line. Write an addition to show what is added to 48:

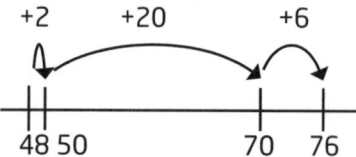

$$48 + \ \ 2 \longrightarrow 50$$
$$+ 20 \longrightarrow 70$$
$$+ \ \ 6 \longrightarrow 76$$

So 20 + 2 + 6 = 22 + 6 = 28. Explain that 76 - 48 = 28. Repeat with another example, such as 94 - 57.
Paired work: Ask the children to work quickly in pairs to try 64 - 36 and 81 - 54.
Whole class: Review the two examples that the children have tried for themselves. Check that the majority understand the method and, if necessary, do some more examples with the whole class. Now demonstrate the same method for HTU - HTU. Write on the board 654 - 367 and draw an empty number line to demonstrate that the answer is 3 + 30 + 200 + 54 = 287. Repeat for another example.
Paired work: Ask the children to work in pairs to complete examples of subtraction by complementary addition. Write on the board: 95 - 47, 61 - 38, 56 - 29, 123 - 45, 246 - 178 and 401 - 238.

Differentiation

Less confident learners: If necessary, limit the examples to just TU - TU.
More confident learners: Include more HTU - HTU examples for this group.

Review

Review some of the examples from the board. Invite individual children to draw an empty number line on the board and to demonstrate how they worked out the answer.

Lesson 6 (Teach and practise)

Starter
Repeat the Starter from Lesson 4, then the Starter for Lesson 5 so that children practise deriving doubles and halves of multiples of 5.

Main teaching activities
On the board write 83 – 57 and draw an empty number line, as shown below:

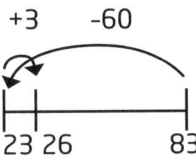

Write: 83 – 57 = 83 – 60 + 3 = 23 + 3 = 26. Repeat for 72 – 36 before deciding whether to demonstrate with an HTU – HTU example (such as 782 – 357). Show the children that this can also be written as:

$$782 - 357 = 782 - 400 + 43$$
$$= 382 + 43$$
$$= 425$$

```
  782
- 357
  382    take 400
+  43    add 43
  300
  120
    5
  425
```

Provide some examples of TU – TU by compensation for the children to try in pairs, such as 76 – 37, 81 – 35 and 62 – 34. (More confident children may like to try some HTU – HTU examples, lining up the hundreds, tens and units on squared paper.)

Review
Review the examples on the board, drawing the empty number line each time and asking a child to write in the appropriate numbers and a horizontal number sentence. Then ask: *How shall we round up? So how much shall we add back on?*

Lessons 7–10

Preparation
Enlarge 'Rounding up and down' to A3; copy CD page 'Two-step problems' onto an OHT.

You will need
Photocopiable pages
'Remainders' (page 42).
CD resources
'Two-step problems'; support and extension versions of 'Remainders'; core, support and extension versions of 'Rounding up and down'.
Equipment
Interlocking cubes or counters.

Learning objectives

Starter
● Derive and recall multiplication facts for the 2, 3, 4, 5, 6 and 10 times-tables and the corresponding division facts; recognise multiples of 2, 5 or 10 up to 1000.

Main teaching activities
2006
● Solve one-step and two-step problems involving numbers, money or measures, including time, choosing and carrying out appropriate calculations.
● Derive and recall multiplication facts for the 2, 3, 4, 5, 6 and 10 times-tables and the corresponding division facts; recognise multiples of 2, 5 or 10 up to 1000.
● Use practical and informal written methods to multiply and divide two-

digit numbers (eg 13 × 3, 50 ÷ 4); round remainders up or down, depending on the context.

1999

● Solve word problems involving numbers in 'real life', money and measures, using one or more steps, including finding totals and giving change, and working out which coins to pay. Explain how the problem was solved.

● Know by heart multiplication facts for the 2, 5 and 10 times-tables; begin to know the 3 and 4 times-tables. Derive quickly corresponding division facts.

● Begin to know multiplication facts for the 6 times-tables.

● Recognise two-digit and three-digit multiples of 2, 5 or 10, and three-digit multiples of 50 and 100.

● Use known number facts and place value to carry out mentally simple multiplications and divisions.

● Begin to find remainders after simple division; round up or down after division, depending on the context.

Vocabulary

problem, solution, calculate, calculation, answer, method, explain, reasoning, pattern, predict, multiply, times, divide, share, group

Lesson 7 (Teach and apply)

Starter

Recall: Explain that you will ask multiplication or division facts from the 2, 3, 5 or 10 times-tables. Ask the children to say the answer together. Keep the pace sharp. Say, for example: *What is 6 multiplied by 3? What is 24 shared between 3? How many times will 2 divide into 20?*

Main teaching activities

Whole class: Explain that in this lesson, the children will use multiples of 2, 5 and 10. Write on the board: 16, 30, 75, 160, 485, 532, 800. Ask: *Which of these numbers is a multiple of 2…5…10? How do you know?* Discuss ways of recognising multiples: multiples of 2 end in an even units digit; multiples of 5 have a 5 or 0 units digit; multiples of 10 have a 0 units digit. Ask the children to say some multiples of 2 which have three digits between 600 and 800. Repeat this for multiples of 5 and 10.

Now say: *Tell me some numbers that will divide exactly by 2… 5… 10. Tell me some numbers that will have a remainder when divided by 2… 5… 10. How did you work that out?*

Say: *I have 36 cakes. These go into boxes which each hold five cakes. How many boxes do I need? How did you work that out? Suppose I fill all the boxes by getting extra cakes. How many cakes will there be then?*

Paired work: Write some three-digit numbers on the board such as: 348, 955, 624, 320, 800. Ask the children to decide which of these numbers can be divided exactly by 2, 5 or 10. Ask them to decide if any of the numbers could be divided exactly by more than one divisor.

Differentiation

Less confident learners: Decide whether to work with these children as a group and to concentrate on two-digit multiples.

More confident learners: Challenge these children to suggest some more three-digit numbers which can be divided exactly by 2, 5 or 10.

Review

Discuss the work that the children have just completed. Ask: *How did you work out which numbers could be divided exactly by 2, 5 or 10? Which numbers will divide exactly by 2 and by 5 and by 10? How do you know that?*

Invite the more confident children to suggest some of their numbers to the rest of the class. Ask: *Which will divide exactly by 2, 5 or 10? How can you tell?*

Lesson 8 (Teach and practise)

Starter
Recall: Explain that you will say a multiple of 5 and that you would like the children to calculate its double. Say smaller multiples of 5, such as 5, 10, 15... up to about 50. Ask: *How did you work that out? If it is a double of a multiple of 5, what will its units digit be?* (0) *How did you work that out?*

Main teaching activities
Whole class: Now write on the board: 43 = 10 × 4 + ☐. Ask: *How can we work out the missing number?* Discuss how 10 × 4 is 40, so 3 more will be needed to make 43. Write up further examples, such as: 54 = 10 × 5 + ☐. Ask the children to suggest an answer, and to explain how they worked this out.
Individual work: Ask the children to complete the activity sheet 'Remainders', which summarises the work from Lessons 7 and 8.

Review
Put the children into two teams, each with a captain. The captain's job is to choose a team member to answer each question (each child can go only once, so all have a turn) and to keep the score on the board. Explain that you will say a division sentence, and that you want the children to give the answer and, where there is one, the remainder. Ask them to say a complete sentence such as '36 divided by 5 is 7 remainder 1'. Use table facts that they know well, such as those from the 2, 3, 4, 5 and 10 times-tables. This will give you an opportunity to check who has understood the concept of division and remainders, and who needs further help.

Differentiation
Less confident learners: The support version of the activity sheet 'Remainders' concentrates on facts from the 2, 5 and 10 times-tables.
More confident learners: The extensiion version of the activity sheet includes some facts from the 6 and 8 times-tables.

Lesson 9 (Teach and apply)

Starter
Recall: Ask the children to derive the half fact for doubles of multiples of 5 to 100. Ask: *What is half of 200? What is 150 divided by 2?* Allow some thinking time so that the majority of the children have calculated the answer.

Main teaching activities
Whole class: Explain that in today's lesson the children will solve division problems and decide whether to round up or down. Say: *I have 23 cakes. The cake boxes hold four cakes each. How many boxes do I need for my cakes?* Discuss how 23 divided by 4 is 5 remainder 3, but that all the cakes must go into boxes, so the three cakes left over also need a box. So, in this case, the answer rounds up to six boxes.
Repeat with: *I have 37 cakes. The cake boxes each hold four cakes. How many boxes can I fill?* Discuss how 37 ÷ 4 = 9 r1. Explain that nine boxes can be filled, and that this is an example of rounding down.
Individual work: Provide copies of the activity sheet 'Rounding up and down'. Ask the children to read each problem, write a division sentence and then decide whether to round up or down. They write the new answer.

Review
Using the enlarged core version of 'Rounding up and down', work through the problems with the children. Invite them to explain how they solved each question, whether they needed to round up or down, and why they made that decision.

Differentiation
Less confident learners: The support version of 'Rounding up and down' uses only the 2, 5 and 10 times-table facts.
More confident learners: The extension version of 'Rounding up and down' also includes the 6 and 8 times-tables.

Lesson 10 (Teach, apply and evaluate)

Starter

Revisit: Explain that you would like the children to find the doubles of multiples of 50 to 500. Remind them that they have just practised doubling and halving for multiples of 5. Ask questions such as: *What is double 50? What will its last two digits be? How do you know that?* Repeat for other doubles such as: double 100, 350 and 400.

Main teaching activities

Whole class: Explain that today's lesson will be about solving problems. Say to the children: *I think of a number, double it and add 6. The answer is 66. What was my number?* (30) Invite the children to explain how they worked this out. Discuss how this problem is a two-step problem. Write on the board: 66 – 6 = 60. Half of 60 is 30.

Now ask the children to solve this problem: *I think of a number, halve it and subtract 3. The answer is 17. What was my number?* (40) Encourage the children to work with a partner to solve this, and to make jottings of what they did. Invite a pair of children to write up their jottings and solution on the board. Ask the rest of the class whether they solved the problem in the same way. Suggest to the children that it is helpful to be systematic in writing down their jottings, and that tables or lists can be helpful.

Individual work: Ask the children to solve similar problems from the activity sheet 'Two-step problems'. Show these using the OHT. Ask the children to decide how to record their work with jottings, and to write the answer as a sentence. This will encourage the children to work independently of a pre-formatted activity sheet.

Review

Using the OHT 'Two-step problems', discuss each problem in turn, and how the children responded to it. Discuss the types of jottings that the children made, and how useful these have been. Encourage them to read out their answer sentences. Discuss the vocabulary used in these, and check that the children are using the vocabulary of multiplication, division, remainders and rounding appropriately. If the more confident children have invented some problems of their own, ask them to share these with the whole class. Invite children, in pairs, to identify any table facts that they need to learn. Suggest that they make a list of these and learn them for homework.

Differentiation

Less confident learners: If necessary, provide adult support for this group. Encourage the children to make jottings, which they should read back to the adult helper to check that they are suitable.

More confident learners: Challenge this group to make up some similar problems for themselves and to swap these with a partner's problems. They solve each other's problems.

Name _____   Date _____

Addition empty number line

Write the answers to these addition sentences.

Show your working out on the empty number lines.

54 + 73 =	339 + 57 =
76 + 45 =	463 + 78 =
87 + 68 =	246 + 321 =
134 + 54 =	354 + 265 =
257 + 62 =	338 + 276 =

Name _____   Date _____

Remainders

Write the answers to these questions.

1. $16 \div 5 =$ ⬚

2. $25 \div 4 =$ ⬚

3. $36 \div 10 =$ ⬚

4. $48 \div 5 =$ ⬚

5. $31 \div 2 =$ ⬚

6. $64 \div 10 =$ ⬚

7. $28 \div 3 =$ ⬚

8. $17 \div 3 =$ ⬚

9. $84 \div 10 =$ ⬚

10. $34 \div 4 =$ ⬚

Now write in the missing numbers.

1. $45 = 10 \times 4 +$ ⬚

2. $63 = 6 \times 10 +$ ⬚

3. $18 = 4 \times 4 +$ ⬚

4. $26 = 5 \times 5 +$ ⬚

5. $31 = 10 \times 3 +$ ⬚

Securing number facts, understanding shape

Key aspects of learning
- Problem solving
- Reasoning
- Social skills
- Communication
- Enquiry
- Managing feeling

Expected prior learning
Check that children can already:
- Solve one-step problems in the context of numbers, measures or money
- check solutions make sense in the context of the problem
- recognise patterns in numbers or shapes and predict and test with examples
- recall addition and subtraction facts for each number to at least 10, all pairs with totals to 20 and all pairs of multiples of 10 with totals up to 100
- recall multiplication facts for the 2, 5 and 10 times-tables and the related division facts
- recognise multiples of 2, 5 and 10 up to 100
- describe the properties of and sort common 2D and 3D shapes and recognise them in pictures
- identify and draw lines of symmetry
- identify right angles in shapes and as quarter turns.

Objectives overview
The text in this diagram identifies the focus of mathematics learning within the block.

Solving one- and two-step problems involving numbers, money or measures.

Dividing and recalling number facts for all operations

Estimating and checking

Identifying and using patterns and relationships to solve problems

Block B: Securing number facts, understanding shape

Recognising, using and drawing right angles

Drawing and comparing angles

Interpreting drawings of shapes and using reflective symmetry to draw and complete shapes

Securing number facts, understanding shape

Speaking and listening objective
- Sustain conversation, explaining or giving reasons for their views or choices.

Introduction
In this 15-lesson unit, two lessons are specifically devoted to solving problems in the context of money (Lessons 1 and 2). Children use empty number lines to help them to solve problems. They are encouraged throughout the unit to explain their thinking, the mathematics they chose, and to give reasons for their views or choices. During lessons encourage the children, when working in pairs or groups, to hold sustained conversations so that they develop discussion skills.

Using and applying mathematics
- Represent the information in a puzzle or problem using numbers, images or diagrams; use these to find a solution and present it in context, where appropriate using £.p notation or units of measure.
- Identify patterns and relationships involving numbers or shapes, and use these to solve problems.

Lesson	Strands	Starter	Main teaching activities
1. Teach and practise	Use/apply	Derive and recall multiplication facts for the 2-, 5- and 10-times tables and the corresponding division facts.	Represent the information in a puzzle or problem using numbers, images or diagrams; use these to find a solution and present it in context, where appropriate using £.p notation or units of measure.
2. Teach and practise	Use/apply	**Derive and recall all addition and subtraction facts for each number to 20.**	As for Lesson 2
3. Teach and reason	Knowledge	As for Lesson 2	**Derive and recall all addition and subtraction facts for each number to 20.**
4. Teach and apply	Knowledge	As for Lesson 2	**Derive and recall all addition and subtraction facts for each number to 20, sums and differences of multiples of 10 and number pairs that total 100.**
5. Teach and reason	Use/apply	Derive and recall multiplication facts for the 2-, 5- and 10-times tables and the corresponding division facts.	Identify patterns and relationships involving numbers or shapes, and use these to solve problems.
6. Teach and apply	Shape	**Derive and recall sums and differences of multiples of 10 that total 100.**	Relate 2D shapes and 3D solids to drawings of them; describe, visualise, classify, draw and make the shapes.
7. Teach and apply	Shape	As for Lesson 6	As for Lesson 6
8. Teach and practise	Shape	Use knowledge of number operations and corresponding inverses, including doubling and halving.	As for Lesson 6
9. Teach and reason	Use/apply	**Partition three-digit numbers into multiples of one hundred, ten and one in different ways.**	Identify patterns and relationships involving numbers or shapes, and use these to solve problems.
10. Teach and reason	Use/apply	As for Lesson 9	As for Lesson 9
11. Teach and practise	Knowledge	Derive and recall multiplication facts for the 2-, 3-, 4-, 5-, 6- and 10-times tables.	Derive and recall multiplication facts for the 2-, 3-, 4-, 5-, 6- and 10-times tables and the corresponding division facts; recognise multiples of 2, 5 or 10 up to 1000.
12. Teach and practise	Knowledge	As for Lesson 11	As for Lesson 11
13. Teach and practise	Knowledge	**Derive and recall all addition and subtraction facts for each number to 20.**	Use knowledge of number operations and corresponding inverses, including doubling and halving, to estimate and check calculations.
14. Teach and practise	Knowledge	Read, write and order numbers to at least 1000 and position them on a number line.	As for Lesson 13
15. Teach, practise and evaluate	Knowledge	**Derive and recall all addition and subtraction facts for each number to 20.**	As for Lesson 13

Lessons 1-5

Preparation

Enlarge CD pages 'Multiplication facts for 2-, 5- and 10-times tables' and 'Price tags' to A3 onto card to make teaching sets. Make individual number fans for each child using CD page 'Number fans'.

You will need

CD resources

Core, support and extension versions of 'Money problems 2' for each child; 'Multiplication facts for 2-, 5- and 10-times tables', 'Number fans' and 'Price tags' for each child, 'Blank price tags' for each less confident child (see General resources).

Equipment

Large sheets of sugar paper and pens; pots of coins containing 5p, 10p, 20p, 50p, £1 and £2 coins; £5 and £10 notes.

Learning objectives

Starter

● Derive and recall multiplication facts for the 2-, 5- and 10-times tables and the corresponding division facts.
● Derive and recall all addition and subtraction facts for each number to 20.

Main teaching activities

2006

● Represent the information in a puzzle or problem using numbers, images or diagrams; use these to find a solution and present it in context, where appropriate using £.p notation or units of measure.
● Derive and recall all addition and subtraction facts for each number to 20, sums and differences of multiples of 10 and number pairs that total 100.
● Identify patterns and relationships involving numbers and use these to solve problems.

1999

● Choose and use appropriate operations (including multiplication and division) to solve word problems, and appropriate ways of calculating: mental, mental with jottings, pencil and paper.
● Recognise all coins and notes. Understand and use £.p notation (for example, know that £3.06 is £3 and 6p).
● Know by heart: all addition and subtraction facts for each number to 20; all pairs of multiples of 100 with a total of 1000 (eg 300 + 700); all pairs of multiples of 5 with a total of 100 (eg 35 + 65).
● Derive quickly all number pairs that total 100 (eg 62 + 38, 75 + 25, 40 + 60).
● Solve mathematical problems or puzzles, recognise simple patterns and relationships, generalise and predict. Suggest extensions by asking 'What if...?'
● Describe and extend number sequences.
● Investigate a general statement about familiar numbers or shapes by finding examples that satisfy it.

Vocabulary

problem, solution, calculate, calculation, operation, answer, method, explain, reasoning, pattern, predict, add, subtract, sum, total, difference, plus, minus, pound (£), pence (p), note, coin

Lesson 1 (Teach and practise)

Starter

Recall: Explain to the children that you will hold up a card which has a 2-, 5- or 10-times table fact on it. Ask the children to use their number fans to show the answer when you say *Show me*. Keep the pace sharp as this is an opportunity for children to recall these facts rapidly.

Main teaching activities

Whole class: Explain that today the children will be finding totals and giving change. Provide them with pots of coins and notes so that they can model the questions. Show the children the £5 note and explain that it is worth £5, before asking them to work quickly in their groups to find different ways of making £5. Repeat this for the £10 note. Now ask all the children, apart from the less confident ones, to put the coins and notes away so that they work mentally. Say: *You have £5 to spend. Here is a price tag for £3.50. How much change would you receive? How can you work this out?* Invite suggestions, such as counting up to £4 then adding £1. Model this with the children. Draw an empty number line on the board and write on £3.50, £4 and £5. Count up to find the change: *£3.50 and 50p makes £4 and £1 makes £5. 50p and £1 is £1.50, so the change from £5 is £1.50.* Repeat this for other examples, such as £4.60 and £6.85.

Paired work: Provide each pair with a set of price tags from the general resource sheet 'Price tags'. Ask them to take turns to take a tag and work out the change from £10. Remind them that they can use an empty number line to help them to count up if they find this difficult to do mentally.

Review

Invite pairs to model one of their responses. Ask them to explain how they worked out the change. Ask: *Who did it this way? Did anyone use a different method? Which do you think is better? Why do you think that?* Now set a challenge for all the children to try, writing it on the board as you explain: *You have £5 to spend. There are three CDs that you would like but you can only afford to buy two. The prices are £3.15, £2.60 and £1.75. Which two would you choose? How much would they cost in total? How much change would you have?* Give the children about five minutes to solve this. Then ask: *Which did you choose? How did you work out your answers?*

Lesson 2 (Teach and practise)

Starter

Recall: Ask the children to call out the complement of 20 to random numbers you give from one to 20. For example, if you say 18, the children reply: *Two.* Keep the pace sharp.

Main teaching activities

Whole class: Explain that today the children will be solving word money problems. Say: *Cal buys three packets of crisps that cost 35p per packet. How much did he pay altogether? How much change did he get from a £2 coin?* Ask the children to suggest how much they estimate the three packets of crisps will cost and write their estimates on the board. Now ask: *How can you work out the cost of three packets of crisps?* Children may suggest doubling 35p to 70p and adding on 35p. Invite suggestions for finding the change. If children are unsure about counting up mentally, draw an empty number line on the board and demonstrate the counting-up method again (see Lesson 1).

Paired work: Ask the children to work in pairs to solve the following problem: *Paul sends six letters. Each letter costs 30p to send. How much do the letters cost to send in total? How much change does Paul get from £2?* Provide coins for the less confident children to model the problem.

Individual work: Provide each child with a copy of activity sheet 'Money problems 2'. Ask them to record how they worked out the problems as well as their answers.

Review

Review together the problems on the core 'Money problems 2' sheet. Invite children to explain the methods that they chose.

Lesson 3 (Teach and reason)

Starter

Recall: Repeat the Starter from Lesson 2. This time, ask the children to say the appropriate addition sentences. For example, if you say 14, they say: *14 + 6 = 20 and 6 + 14 = 20.* Keep the pace sharp.

Main teaching activities

Whole class: Explain that the children will have the opportunity to recall more addition and subtraction facts to 20. Write the number 15 on the board. Ask the children to think of two numbers that total 15. Write up

Differentiation

Less confident learners: There are blank tags available. These can be used to give this group smaller prices with a starting sum of money such as £2.
More confident learners: Decide whether to use the blank tags and write in more challenging amounts, such as £6.87.

Differentiation

Less confident learners: There is a support version of 'Money problems 2' with totals up to £12.
More confident learners: You may prefer this group to use the extension version of the activity sheet with change from larger amounts of money.

their suggestions as addition facts: 8 + 7; 10 + 5, and so on. Remind the children that if they are unsure, they can use an empty number line. Model the following using an empty number line: 8 + 7 = 8 + 2 + 5 = 10 + 5 = 15. Now ask the children to look at the facts and ask them to think of how these could be ordered and write the list again in order. For example: 0 + 15; 1 + 14, and so on. Ask the children to say the two subtraction facts that complement each addition fact. For 8 + 7 they would say: *15 - 7 = 8 and 15 - 8 = 7.* Now ask them to think of two numbers each less than 20, whose difference is 15. Write their responses on the board and ask for each fact: *What addition fact can you find from this?* For example, for 18 - 3 they would find 15 + 3 = 18 and 3 + 15 = 18.

Paired work: Ask each pair to use only numbers that are equal to 20 or less and to make all the addition statements they can with the total of 17, then to find all the corresponding subtraction facts. Ask them to write these as an ordered list. Remind them that if they need help they can use an empty number line.

Review

Invite the children to respond to probing questions, and invite them to give reasons for their responses. Ask, for example: *What two numbers that are 20 or less give a difference of 12? Think of more pairs that give this difference. How did you work out the answer?* Discuss how knowing one fact can give another such as 18 - 5 = 13 as do 17 - 4 and 16 –3. Ask the children to explain the pattern. Now ask: *What would you add to 8 to make a total of 15? Tell me three pairs of numbers that total 18. Which subtraction facts use these numbers?* Discuss how knowing one fact for addition or subtraction helps you to find three further facts that use the same numbers.

Differentiation

Less confident learners: Decide whether to provide number lines for the children to use as an aid for counting on and back.
More confident learners: Challenge the children to use what they find out to write out the ordered addition facts for 27, then the corresponding subtraction facts.

Lesson 4 (Teach and apply)

Starter

Recall: Repeat the Starter from Lesson 3, this time for subtraction facts. If you say 13, they say: *20 - 13 = 7 and 20 - 7 = 13.* Keep the pace sharp.

Main teaching activities

Whole class: Review complements to 10, then extend this to the complements to 100, such as if 6 + 4 = 10 then 60 + 40 = 100. Repeat for the other complements to 100, linking back to the complements to 10 each time. Extend this to addition and subtraction of multiples of ten, such as 50 + 40 = 90 and 90 - 40 = 50, and so on. Discuss how if the children know one fact, they can find three further facts for addition and subtraction of multiples of ten.

Paired work: The children take turns to say a multiple of 10, up to 100. Their partner gives four facts using this number and 100. For example, for 80 they would give: 80 + 20 = 100; 20 + 80 = 100; 100 - 80 = 20; 100 - 20 = 80. Ask the children to record their facts using lists.

Review

Discuss the facts that the children have found. Challenge everybody by asking the more confident learners to give a pair of their multiples of ten for the others to find the resulting addition and subtraction facts. Remind the children to use an empty number line if they need help with counting on and back in tens to find the solutions.

Differentiation

Less confident learners: Encourage the children to use an empty number line to count on or back.
More confident learners: Challenge the more confident learners to choose two multiples of 10 (such as 80 and 70) and to give two addition facts and the two related subtraction facts for these numbers.

Lesson 5 (Teach and reason)

Starter

Recall: Repeat the Starter from Lesson 1, this time reading out the facts you choose as division rather than multiplication. For example, for a card that reads 3 × 2, you might say: *What is 6 divided by 2?* Keep the pace sharp, asking the children to show their answers using number fans.

BLOCK B

Securing number facts, understanding shape

Main teaching activities

Whole class: Introduce the vocabulary for the lesson, and use with a function machine example on the large whiteboard. Ensure that all the class appreciate that ⟶ represents 'maps onto' and is a mathematical convention.

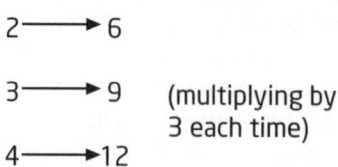

2 ⟶ 6

3 ⟶ 9   (multiplying by
              3 each time)
4 ⟶ 12

Try the same idea but using other items. Ask: *What if we applied a doubling rule to a quarter piece of pizza? What would the pattern be?* (One quarter followed by one half followed by one whole, and so on.) Then ask: *What if a halving rule was applied to 100cm of string? How long would it be before there was nothing much to see?*

Group work: Working in pairs, children choose a rule to investigate from a list you give them. Write these numbers on the board: 2, 8, 3, 6, 5, 9, 4, 7; and all or some of the following rules:

● Add 4 to each number.
● Double each number.
● Multiply each number by 10 and then halve each answer.
● Add 8 to each number.
● Subtract 2 from each number.

Differentiation

Less confident learners:
Suggest that this group selects the rule 'Add 4 to each number'.

More confident learners:
Encourage this group to reason about their answers. For example: *All my answers will be less than 20 if I add 8 because my largest starting number is 9.* Use these reasonings for the Review.

Review

Take each rule in turn, and check the children's responses by asking volunteers to give the answers. The children can 'mark' their own answers. Can the class make reasoned statements relating to each rule? Look for:

● *If I add four to each number, this would have the same effect as adding six and subtracting two.*
● *If I double each number, then odd numbers will map onto even answers and even numbers will still become even numbers.*

Lessons 6-10

Preparation

Enlarge CD page 'Carroll diagram' to A3.

You will need

Photocopiable pages
'Shape descriptions' (page 56), 'Rectangles' (page 57) and 'Equilateral triangles' (page 58) for each child.

CD resources
'Carroll diagram' (see General resources).

Equipment
A tray for each group with 3D shapes; trays of 2D shape tiles; 2D large rectangular shape cut from cardboard; plastic equilateral triangles.

Learning objectives

Starter

● Derive and recall sums and differences of multiples of 10 that total 100.
● Use knowledge of number operations and corresponding inverses, including doubling and halving.
● Partition three-digit numbers into multiples of one hundred, ten and one in different ways.

Main teaching activities

2006
● Relate 2D shapes and 3D solids to drawings of them; describe, visualise, classify, draw and make the shapes.
● Identify patterns and relationships involving numbers or shapes, and use these to solve problems.

1999
● Relate solid shapes to pictures of them.
● Classify and describe 3D and 2D shapes, including the hemisphere, prism, semi-circle, quadrilateral... referring to properties such as reflective symmetry, the number or shapes of faces, the number of sides/edges and vertices, whether sides/edges are the same length, whether or not angles are right angles...
● Make and describe shapes and patterns, eg explore the different shapes that can be made from four cubes.

Unit 1 ▸ 3 weeks

- Solve mathematical problems or puzzles, recognise simple patterns and relationships, generalise and predict. Suggest extensions by asking 'What if...?'
- Describe and extend number sequences.
- Investigate a general statement about familiar numbers or shapes by finding examples that satisfy it.

Vocabulary

triangle, square, rectangle, quadrilateral, pentagon, hexagon, octagon, cube, cuboid, pyramid, sphere, hemisphere, cone, cylinder, prism, face, edge, vertex, surface, solid, side, flat, straight, curved, two-dimensional (2D), three-dimensional (3D), right-angled

Lesson 6 (Teach and apply)

Starter

Recall: Explain that you will give the children two multiples of 10. Ask them to write down on their whiteboards two addition facts for these numbers. For example, if you say *30 and 50,* they write 30 + 50 = 80. Now ask them to write the two related subtraction facts (80 – 3 = 50 and 80 – 50 = 30). When you say *Show me,* they hold up their whiteboard for you to check. Repeat for other pairs of multiples of 10, keeping the total to 100 or less.

Main teaching activities

Whole class: Provide each group with a tray of 3D shapes and have a collection of these shapes for yourself. Ask the children to check that they can name each shape; hold up each shape in turn and ask the children to find it on their tray, and then to volunteer its name. Write the name of each shape on the board. Some may not know the name of the hemisphere, but give this name and write it on the board. Ask: *How would you describe a hemisphere? What is special about it?* Encourage the children to use the vocabulary of 3D and 2D shapes to do this. For example: *It is round; its base is a circle.* Repeat this for the triangular prism. Discuss right angles, and where children can see these (for example, on a triangular prism).

Now explain that some of the shapes can be classified as prisms. Write 'prism' on the board. Say: *If you cut a prism along its length it always has the same face. The end faces of a prism are identical.* Ask the children to sort the shapes into two groups: 'prisms' (cubes, cuboids, triangular prisms) and 'not prisms' (spheres, hemispheres, cones, pyramids, cylinders). Note that prisms have end faces which are polygons, and circles are not classified as polygons, so the cylinder is not a prism.

Point to one of the vertices of the cube and say: *This is one of the cube's vertices.* Write 'vertex' and 'vertices' on the board and say: *A vertex is the point where two lines or edges meet. Two or more are called vertices.* Invite the children to identify the vertices on the shapes in front of them. Explain that both 2D and 3D shapes have vertices, and write 'two-dimensional (2D)' and 'three-dimensional (3D)' on the board.

Paired work: In pairs, using sheets of A2 sugar paper and felt-tipped pens, ask the children to write three clear statements that describe a 3D shape. It should read like a large description tag: 'Our shape is three-dimensional. It has four faces. Each face forms an equilateral triangle'. Remind the children that they can refer to 2D shapes when describing 3D ones, such as: *The shape has a circle as its base.* Ask the children to write statements for three different 3D shapes.

Review

Invite pairs from each ability group to read out statements for one of their shapes. Ask all the children: *Do you agree with this statement? What other statements could be made about this shape?*

Differentiation

Less confident learners: Decide whether to complete the task as a group. This will give the children more opportunity to hear and use the vocabulary of shape.
More confident learners: Challenge the children to write an extra statement for each shape that they choose.

Lesson 7 (Teach and apply)

Starter
Recall: Repeat the Starter from Lesson 6, this time asking the children to respond by putting up their hands. Keep the pace sharp.

Main teaching activities
Whole class: One at a time, hold up the shapes from the tray for Lesson 6 and ask the children to describe the shape. Encourage them to refer to the 2D faces, such as: *It has square faces.*
Individual work: Provide each child with a copy of the activity sheet 'Shape descriptions'. Ask them to read the description and to sketch how they think the shape would look.

Review
Discuss what the children have done. Invite children to show the shapes that they drew, and discuss the range of different shapes that fit each description. For example, the 2D shape with four sides and a right angle does not have to be a square or rectangle!

Differentiation
Less confident learners: You may find that this group will find it helpful to have a selection of 2D and 3D shapes in front of them.
More confident learners: Challenge the more confident children to draw another shape for each description, where possible.

Lesson 8 (Teach and practise)

Starter
Recall: Ask doubling and halving questions such as: *What is double 5... 8... 10... 13... 23? What is half of 40... 36... 28... 14... 8?* Keep the pace sharp.

Main teaching activities
Whole class: Explain that a quadrilateral is any flat shape with four straight sides. Write 'quadrilateral' on the board. Now ask the children to use their whiteboard to sketch a quadrilateral for you that has a mathematical name. They will probably sketch a square or rectangle, but perhaps some more confident children might sketch a parallelogram or trapezium. Provide each group with a tray of 2D shapes and explain that you will describe a shape and you want them to hold up any shape that fits the description. For example:
- *Hold up a quadrilateral. What shape are you holding?*
- *Hold up any shape that has a right angle.*
- *Hold up the shape that is half of a circle. What is this shape called?* (Write 'semicircle' on the board.)
- *Hold up any shape that has five equal sides and five vertices.*
- *Hold up any shape with a line of symmetry.*

Discuss symmetry in 2D shapes, and which shapes have a line of symmetry. Challenge the more confident children to identify shapes with more than one line of symmetry.
Paired work: Ask the children to sort their set of flat shapes. Using the general resource sheet 'Carroll diagram', enlarged to A3, they should write the following headings on the diagram: 'Has straight sides'; 'Does not have straight sides'; 'Has at least one right angle'; 'Does not have at least one right angle'. They then write the names of their shapes into the Carroll diagram, in the correct sections. Then ask the children to sort their shapes into those with a line of symmetry and those without. They can record these as drawings.

Differentiation
Less confident learners: Decide whether to limit the children to sorting by one property into a simplified Carroll diagram, such as 'Has straight sides'; 'Does not have straight sides'; or 'Has at least one right angle'; 'Does not have at least one right angle'.
More confident learners: Challenge the children to suggest their own properties for sorting and to make another four-region Carroll diagram for sorting the shapes.

Review
Invite the more confident children to set their challenge for the other children. Ask them to give one of their sorting properties, and invite the others to find the shapes that fit. Ask questions such as: *Which shapes fit this property? Which shapes do not fit that property? What other sorting properties can you think of? Which shapes would fit that property?*

Lesson 9 (Teach and reason)

Starter

Recall: Explain that you will say a number and how many more than that number you would like the children to write on their whiteboards. When you say *Show me*, the children hold up their boards for you to check. Say:

- *Write the number that is one more/less than 3, 15, 73, 99, 200, 501.*
- *Write the number that is ten more/less than 14, 25, 76, 98, 400, 721.*
- *Write the number that is 100 more/less than 100, 258, 803.*
  Discuss the place value of each digit in the original and new numbers.

Main teaching activities

Whole class: Explain that you are going to investigate some true/false statements using some simple shapes. On the OHP, place a rectangle at an angle so none of the sides are parallel to the edge of the illuminated screen.

Ask the children what they can already tell you about this shape and gather as many facts as possible. What do they think would happen if you cut the shape in half? Ask:

- *Will both shapes have anything in common?*
- *Will the space the two shapes occupy (the area) remain the same or not?*
- *What sorts of angles will both shapes have?*
- *What do your answers depend upon?* (Whether the cuts are horizontal, vertical or diagonal.)

Cut the shape in half to form two rectangles and replace the cut pieces onto the OHP. What can the children say now about both shapes? Emphasise their identical size and the symmetrical nature after cutting.

Paired work: Ask the children to work in pairs to investigate the statement: 'When you cut any rectangle exactly in half, you will always get two rectangles'. They should sketch their findings. Hopefully someone will use a diagonal cut so you can say 'No' to the statement posed initially. (If necessary, prompt this solution with direction.)

Now eliminate the use of diagonal cuts and ask the children to try cutting lots of rectangles from the activity sheet 'Rectangles' before asking: *When you cut any rectangle in half without diagonal cuts, will you always get two rectangles?* Be prepared for the question: *Is a square a rectangle?* (Yes.) Ask the children to measure their rectangles with a ruler. Encourage them to record their work systematically.

Review

Ask the children to make true or false statements to you, for example: 'All my cut shapes had four sides.' 'All my cut shapes had four lines of symmetry.' 'All my shapes had sides longer than 6cm.' Let all the children help show whether the statements are true or false.

Discuss with the children:

- *What have you learned today?* (One child might feel more confident in recognising that a square is a special rectangle.)
- *Can you see the relevance of doing this work?* (Knowing how to cut or fold a rectangle to make two smaller rectangles, and knowing the properties of both shapes are identical, can help predict what might happen when cutting up other regular shapes.)
- *When might an adult use this knowledge?* (When cutting up carpet tiles for laying, for example.)

Emphasise that making a general statement about shapes helps us to understand the properties of shapes.

Differentiation

Less confident learners: Work with this group once they have some findings. Help them to say a sentence each about what they have found out, so that they can contribute to the Review.
More confident learners: Set the challenge: *When you make a horizontal and a vertical cut through a rectangle to make quarters, will all the quarters be rectangles?*

Lesson 10 (Teach and reason)

Starter
Recall: Repeat the Starter for Lesson 9, choosing new numbers and increasing the pace.

Main teaching activities
Whole class: Ask the children to close their eyes and visualise a triangle. Invite them to sketch what they picture on their whiteboards. (Most children will draw an equilateral triangle.)

Discuss the properties of a triangle, drawing examples of scalene, isosceles and right-angled triangles on the board. Check that the children recognise all of these as forms of triangles.

Now ask the children to visualise two equilateral triangles sliding together so two of the sides touch fully. They should sketch what they visualise on their whiteboards before you show this happening on the OHP. Ask: *What shapes can be made? Will the shapes always have four sides if we insist on two sides touching?* (Yes.)

Group work: The children use the activity sheet 'Equilateral triangles'. Explain that equilateral triangles are special and that their sides are all the same length. Ask the children to investigate the statement: 'If two equilateral triangles join so that one side of one triangle always touches a side of the other triangle, the new shape will always have four sides.'

Review
Invite children from each ability group to show their sketches and to say a sentence to explain their results.

Differentiation
Less confident learners: Provide this group with plastic equilateral triangles, as colour can help the children keep track of what they have tried.
More confident learners: What if there were three triangles? Can the children write down their ideas without the cut-out shapes? Distribute the activity sheet 'Equilateral triangles' to the group. Explore with them the idea of using correct mathematical vocabulary to describe what they see. Write all their statements on A2 paper. Cut out the statements into strips and reassemble them in order of clarity.

Lessons 11-15

Preparation
Copy CD page 'Reading and writing numbers' onto an OHT, or enlarge to A3.

You will need
Photocopiable pages
'Aladdin's adding' (page 59) for each child.
CD resources
Support and extension versions of 'Aladdin's adding'; core, support and extension versions of 'Checking answers'; 'Reading and writing numbers' for each child (see General resources).

Learning objectives

Starter
● Derive and recall multiplication facts for the 2-, 3-, 4-, 5-, 6- and 10-times tables.
● Derive and recall all addition and subtraction facts for each number to 20.
● Read, write and order numbers to at least 1000 and position them on a number line.

Main teaching activities
2006
● Derive and recall multiplication facts for the 2- ,3-, 4-, 5-, 6- and 10-times tables and the corresponding division facts; recognise multiples of 2, 5 or 10 up to 1000.
● Use knowledge of number operations and corresponding inverses, including doubling and halving, to estimate and check calculations.
1999
● Know by heart multiplication facts for the 2-, 5- and 10-times tables; begin to know the 3- and 4-times tables. Derive quickly corresponding division facts.
● Recognise two-digit and three-digit multiples of 2, 5 or 10, and three-digit multiples of 50 and 100.
● Begin to know multiplication facts for the 6 times-tables.
● Check subtraction with addition, halving with doubling and division with multiplication.
● Repeat addition or multiplication in a different order.
● Check with an equivalent calculation.

Vocabulary
problem, solution, calculate, calculation, operation, answer, method, explain, reasoning, pattern, predict, multiply, divide, group, sum, double, halve, multiple

Lesson 11 (Teach and practise)

Starter
Rehearse: Ask the children to give multiplication facts table for 3-, 4- and 6-times tables. Keep the pace sharp.

Main teaching activities
Whole class: Explain that you will be asking for more multiplication facts from the 3-, 4- and 6-times tables. Ask the children to find the answers to the multiplication table facts that you ask, such as: *What is 3 × 2? 6 × 4? 8 × 6? How did you find the answer?* Discuss how, if children are unsure, they can work through the table facts until they reach the answer.
Paired work: Each pair take turns to choose a fact from the 3-times table for their partner to give the answer. Ask the children to write down the facts that they say, and to mark those that they are unsure of for them to learn. They repeat this for the 4- and 6-times tables.

Review
Continue to ask questions about the multiplication facts. Say, for example: *What is 8 × 4? How did you find the answer? Did you 'know' or did you say the 4-times table to yourself? This is a good strategy if you do not know the answer.* Say the 4-times table together. Ask: *Which two multiplication facts are either side of 8 × 4? Tell me the answer to 6 × 4 and the two facts either side of this.*

Differentiation
Less confident learners: Ask the children to work as a group with an adult, who asks for the multiple facts and checks the answers.
More confident learners: Decide whether to ask the children to derive the facts for the 8-times table from the 4-times table.

Lesson 12 (Teach and practise)

Starter
Recall: Repeat the Starter for Lesson 11, this time for multiplication tables 2, 5 and 10, keeping the pace sharp.

Main teaching activities
Whole class: Ask the children to say how they know if a number is: a multiple of 2 (it is even); a multiple of 5 (it has a 5 or 0 as its unit digit); a multiple of 10 (it has a 0 as its unit digit). Now say some numbers between 50 and 100 that are multiples of 2, 5 or 10, and ask the children to say which they are, and how they know. Repeat this for numbers greater than 100. Write the following on the board:
- Multiples of 2 between 200 and 250
- Multiples of 5 between 355 and 455
- Multiples of 10 between 260 and 360
- Multiples of 2, 5 and 10 between 150 and 200.

Paired work: Ask the children to work in pairs to find these numbers.

Review
Ask questions such as: *Can I use the digits 1, 2, 4 to make a multiple of 5? Why not? Which numbers between 230 and 240 are multiples of 2... 5... 10? How do you know?*

Differentiation
Less confident learners: Decide whether to work with these children as a group. Ask them to state for each number, why it is a multiple of 2, 5 or 10.
More confident learners: Challenge the children to find all the multiples of 8 between 160 and 240.

Lesson 13 (Teach and practise)

Starter
Recall: Provide the children with individual whiteboards and pens and ask them to work in pairs. Explain that you will write a number trio on the board, which, when placed into an addition or subtraction sentence, will make a true statement. For example: 6, 4, 2 makes 2 + 4 = 6, 6 - 2 = 4, and so on. Ask the children to write two addition and two subtraction sentences for each number trio. When you say *Show me*, they hold up their boards to show what they have written. Ask the pairs to swap over each time, so that they take turns writing addition or subtraction sentences.

Main teaching activities

Whole class: Explain to the children that by the end of this lesson they should be able to re-order the numbers in their calculations so that they can check they have the correct answer. Point out that this is more helpful than just redoing a calculation in the same order as it is easy to repeat a mistake.

Write the following calculation on the board: 2 + 5 + 16 + 4 = □. Ask the children how many different ways they could do this mentally. Choose one child's suggestion, for example: 16 + 4 = 20; 5 + 2 = 7; 20 + 7 = 27.

Discuss how helpful it is to search for pairs of numbers to make a ten (16 + 4 = 20). Explain that when checking addition it is helpful to add again, this time adding the numbers in a different order, and consider another child's method. Repeat this for another addition such as 7 + 19 + 3 + 8 (7 + 3 = 10 and 19 + 8 = 20 + 8 − 1). Discuss how, when checking, children can use an equivalent subtraction sentence to check their addition, and vice versa.

Group work: The children work on marking Aladdin's homework, using activity sheet 'Aladdin's adding', as if they were teachers. Give the children 20 minutes to see how many questions they can check properly, using re-ordering mental methods.

Differentiation

Less confident learners: Ask the children to work on the support version of the activity sheet in pairs. Suggest that they may find using an empty number line helpful when calculating mentally.

More confident learners: Decide whether to use the extension version of the sheet for these children.

Review

Write on the board: 9 + 13 + 11 + 7 and ask: *How could you work this out mentally?* Responses may include: 9 + 11 + 13 + 7, so that children look for two 'tens'. Now ask: *How could you check this?* Encourage the children to suggest other ways of ordering, such as adding the tens, then totalling the units: 10 + 10 + 9 + 3 + 1 + 7. Repeat this for other examples.

Lesson 14 (Teach and practise)

Starter

Using an OHT of activity sheet 'Reading and writing numbers', ask children to mark the three-digit numbers/two-digit numbers/numbers greater than ___ .

Main teaching activities

Whole class: Write up a problem: *Kit Ling gave £1.20 of her pocket money to her brother. She had £2.30 left. How much pocket money did Kit Ling have left?* Invite the class to explain how they might solve this before asking a child to write it as a money number sentence, such as £1.20 + £2.30 = £3.50. Ask: *How can we check this using subtraction?* Write up £3.50 − £2.30 = □ and invite an answer.

Individual work: Provide the differentiated activity sheet 'Checking answers' for the children to complete.

Review

Write 56p + 8p on the board and ask: *How can we work out the answer?* The children may suggest: 56p + 4p + 4p = 60p + 4p = 64p. Now ask: *How could we check our answer?* They may suggest: 64p − 8p = 64p − 4p − 4p = 60p − 4p = 56p.

Lesson 15 (Teach, practise and evaluate)

Starter

Recall: Repeat the Starter for Lesson 13, choosing different number trios and extending to totals up to 20.

Main teaching activities

Whole class: Explain that multiplication can be checked with division, and doubling with halving. Say: *What is 20 divided by 4? Can we check this with multiplication? Yes, 20 divided by 4 is 5, and 4 multiplied by 5 is 20.* Repeat for other examples from the 2-, 3-, 4-, 5-, 6- and 10-times table facts.

Unit 1 ⬛ 3 weeks

Ask the children to estimate division using the 4-times table: 17 divided by 4; 21 divided by 4, and so on.

Now ask: *If half of 50 is 25, what is double 25?* Repeat for other doubling and halving facts.

Paired work: Ask the children to work in pairs. They take turns to choose a division fact from the 3- or 4-times table and say this to their partner. They both write down the division fact and the corresponding multiplication fact. Then ask the children to take turns to say and write halving facts, followed by the corresponding doubling fact.

Review

Ask questions such as: *What is 40 + 30? How can this help us to estimate 43 + 37? What is 28 divided by 4? So how can we check this with multiplication? Use the 4-times table to estimate 23 divided by 4. If half of 28 is 14 what is double 14?* Invite the children that you are targetting for assessment to give examples of how multiplication can be checked by division, halving by doubling, and vice versa.

Differentiation

Less confident learners: Decide whether to work as a group. Begin by reciting the 3-times table facts and choose division facts from this table, before repeating this for 4-times table facts.

More confident learners: Challenge the children to try the paired work for the 6-times table facts as well.

Name _____   Date _____

Shape descriptions

Read each description of a mathematical shape.
Sketch the shape in the space and write its name.

1. This shape is two-dimensional (2D). It has four
   straight sides and at least one right angle.
   What could it look like?

   _____

2. This shape is two-dimensional (2D). It has three straight sides.
   No side is the same length. What could it look like?

   _____

3. This shape is three-dimensional (3D). It has six faces.
   Each face is a rectangle. What could it look like?

   _____

4. This shape rolls easily along the floor. It is the same shape as a football.
   It is 3D. What could it look like?

   _____

Name _____   Date _____

Rectangles

Work with a partner.

Cut out the rectangles.

> **Investigate the statement:** 'When you cut any rectangle in half without diagonal cuts, you always get two rectangles.'

Make some sketches and write some sentences to explain what you find out.

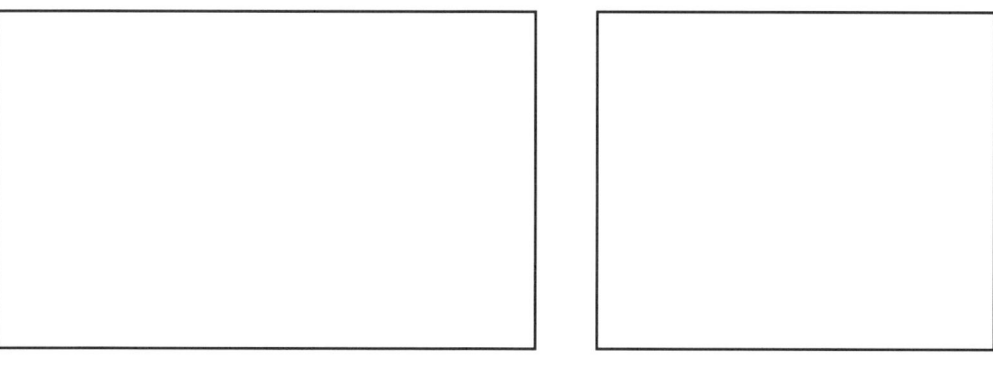

BLOCK B

Securing number facts, understanding shape

Name _____   Date _____

Equilateral triangles

Cut out the triangles at the bottom of this sheet.

Join them together as your teacher described.

Continue to join them together.

Sketch your results here.

Write a sentence to explain your results.

_____

_____

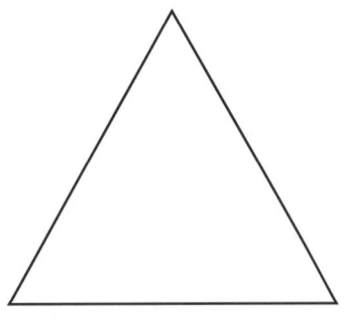 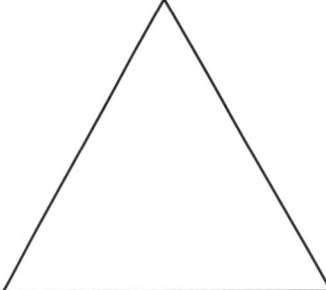 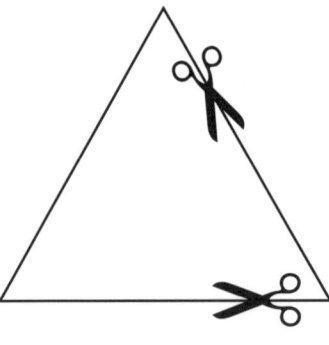

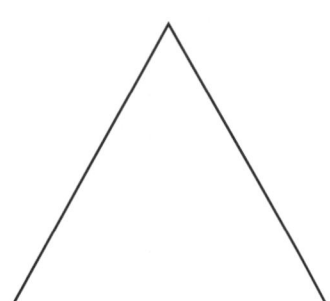 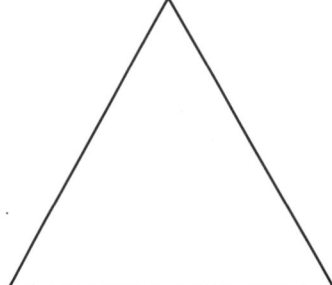 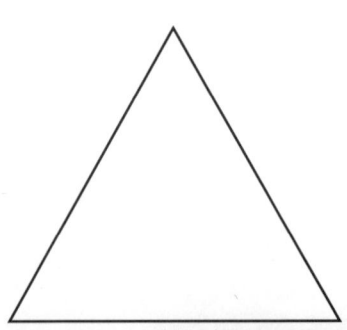

BLOCK B

Securing number facts, understanding shape

Name _____   Date _____

Aladdin's adding

Put X or ✔ next to the answer then write what you did mentally to check.
The first one has been done for you.

Aladdin's calculation and answer	Is he right? Use a tick or cross	How you checked it
2 + 3 + 15 + 2 = 11	X	15 + 2 + 3 + 2 = 22
3 + 4 + 15 + 1 = 23		
6 + 3 + 12 + 4 = 26		
7 + 13 + 5 + 1 = 29		
8 + 4 + 6 + 1 = 19		
2 + 1 + 15 + 2 = 11		
3 + 3 + 15 + 1 = 22		
6 + 14 + 2 + 1 = 26		
7 + 13 + 5 + 3 = 29		
8 + 14 + 2 + 1 = 26		

Securing number facts, understanding shape

Lesson	Strands	Starter	Main teaching activities
1. Teach and practise	Use/apply	Identify patterns and relationships involving numbers or shapes, and use these to solve problems.	Solve one-step and two-step problems involving numbers, money or measures, including time, choosing and carrying out appropriate calculations.
2. Teach and apply	Use/apply	As for Lesson 1	As for Lesson 1
3. Teach and practise	Knowledge	Derive and recall multiplication facts for the 2-, 3-, 4-, 5-, 6- and 10-times tables and the corresponding division facts; recognise multiples of 2, 5 or 10 up to 1000.	Derive and recall multiplication facts for the 2-, 3-, 4-, 5-, 6- and 10-times tables and the corresponding division facts; recognise multiples of 2, 5 or 10 up to 1000.
4. Teach and apply	Use/apply	As for Lesson 3	Represent the information in a puzzle or problem using numbers, images or diagrams; use these to find a solution and present it in context, where appropriate using £.p notation or units of measure.
5. Teach and reason	Use/apply	As for Lesson 3	As for Lesson 4
6. Teach and reason	Use/apply	As for Lesson 3	Identify patterns and relationships involving numbers or shapes, and use these to solve problems.
7. Teach and apply	Shape	Read, write and order whole numbers to at least 1000 and position them on a number line; count on from and back to zero in single-digit steps or multiples of 10.	Relate 2D shapes and 3D solids to drawings of them; describe, visualise, classify, draw and make the shapes.
8. Teach and apply	Shape	Derive and recall multiplication facts for the 2-, 3-, 4-, 5-, 6- and 10-times tables and the corresponding division facts; recognise multiples of 2, 5 or 10 up to 1000.	As for Lesson 7
9. Teach and apply	Shape	Derive and recall all addition and subtraction facts for each number to 20, sums and differences of multiples of 10 and number pairs that total 100.	Draw and complete shapes with reflective symmetry; draw the reflection of a shape in a mirror line along one side.
10. Teach and apply	Shape	As for Lesson 9	As for Lesson 9
11. Teach and practise	Counting	As for Lesson 9	Read and write proper fractions (eg $3/7$, $9/10$) interpreting the denominator as the parts of a whole and the numerator as the number of parts; identify and estimate fractions of shapes; use diagrams to compare fractions and establish equivalents.
12. Teach and apply	Counting	As for Lesson 9	As for Lesson 11
13. Teach and practise	Counting	Read and write proper fractions (eg $3/7$, $9/10$) interpreting the denominator as the parts of a whole and the numerator as the number of parts; identify and estimate fractions of shapes; use diagrams to compare fractions and establish equivalents.	As for Lesson 11
14. Teach and reason	Counting	Read, write and order whole numbers to at least 1000 and position them on a number line; count on from and back to zero in single-digit steps or multiples of 10.	As for Lesson 11
15. Teach, apply and evaluate	Counting	As for Lesson 14	As for Lesson 11

Unit 2 ▢ 3 weeks

Speaking and listening objective
- Sustain conversation, explaining or giving reasons for their views or choices.

Introduction
In this 15-lesson unit, using and applying mathematics and speaking and listening apply to every lesson. Children are encouraged to discuss with each other, give their reasons and listen to others' points of view. They solve problems, discussing the methods that they chose and identifying patterns and relationships. They make 2D shapes and investigate lines of symmetry. They sketch shapes, and compare their sketches, discussing differences and similarities. They identify simple fractions, make these fractions from shapes and find equivalent fractions.

Using and applying mathematics
- Solve one- and two-step problems involving numbers, money or measures, including time, choosing and carrying out appropriate calculations.
- Represent the information in a puzzle or problem using numbers, images or diagrams; use these to find a solution and present it in context, where appropriate using £.p notation or units of measure.
- Identify patterns and relationships involving numbers or shapes, and use these to solve problems.

Lessons 1-5

Preparation
Copy CD pages 'Word problem frame' and 'Word problems' onto OHTs; Copy CD page 'Multiplication facts for the 2-, 5- and 10-times tables' onto card to make a teaching set.

You will need
Photocopiable pages
'Spot the pattern' (page 73) and 'Sparky – Queen of the chickens (part 2)' (page 74) for each child.
CD resources
Support and extension versions of 'Spot the pattern' and 'Sparky – Queen of the chickens (part 2)'; 'Word problem frame' for each child and 'Word problems' for the teacher's/LSA's reference; 'Hundred square' for each child, 'Multiplication facts for 2-, 5- and 10-times tables', 'Sparky – Queen of the chickens (part 1)' (see General resources). Interactive resource: 'Number grid'.
Equipment
Coloured counters; Blu-Tack.

Learning objectives

Starter
- Identify patterns and relationships involving numbers or shapes, and use these to solve problems.
- Derive and recall multiplication facts for the 2-, 3-, 4-, 5-, 6- and 10-times tables and the corresponding division facts; recognise multiples of 2, 5 or 10 up to 1000.

Main teaching activities
2006
- Solve one- and two-step problems involving numbers, money or measures, including time, choosing and carrying out appropriate calculations.
- Derive and recall multiplication facts for the 2-, 3-, 4-, 5-, 6- and 10-times tables and the corresponding division facts; recognise multiples of 2, 5 or 10 up to 1000.
- Represent the information in a puzzle or problem using numbers, images or diagrams; use these to find a solution and present it in context, where appropriate using £.p notation or units of measure.

1999
- Solve word problems involving numbers in 'real life', money and measures, using one or more steps, including finding totals and giving change, and working out which coins to pay. Explain how the problem was solved.
- Know by heart multiplication facts for the 2-, 5- and 10-times tables; begin to know the 3- and 4-times tables. Derive quickly corresponding division facts.
- Recognise two-digit and three-digit multiples of 2, 5 or 10, and three-digit multiples of 50 and 100.
- Begin to know multiplication facts for the 6-times tables.
- Choose and use appropriate operations (including multiplication and division) to solve word problems, and appropriate ways of calculating: mental, mental with jottings, pencil and paper.
- Recognise all coins and notes; understand and use £.p notation (for example, know that £3.06 is £3 and 6p).

Vocabulary
problem, solution, calculate, calculation, operation, inverse, answer, method, explain, reasoning, pattern, predict, estimate, approximate, multiply, divide, group, multiple

Lesson 1 (Teach and practise)

Starter
Recall: Firstly, practise with the children walking forwards and then backwards four steps. You could do this to music. The children count one on the first step then count two and clap on the second step, count three on the third step then clap and count four on the fourth step. Moving backwards, they say five, clap on six, say seven, clap on eight. Ask whether they are clapping on odd or even numbers. Continue the pattern up to 40. Change the starting number to 15. What happens? Invite the children to suggest two-digit numbers to start on, discussing the odd and even patterns each time.

Main teaching activities
Whole class: Explain to the class that they will be using mental calculation strategies to solve problems. Solve the following problem with the class using an OHT of general resource sheet 'Word problem frame'. Say: *There are 17 books on the top shelf, 8 books on the middle shelf and 13 books on the bottom shelf. How many books are there altogether?* Invite the children to say what sort of calculation they will need to do and write their suggestions on the board, such as 17 + 8 + 13. Ask: *How shall we work this out?* Children may suggest adding 17 and 13 because they can 'make a ten'. Write on the OHT: 17 + 13 + 8 in the first column; 10 + 10 + 10 + 8 in the second column; and the answer 38 in the third column.

Repeat for another example, which this time is a two-step problem: *There are 15 apples, 22 pears and 28 bananas. If I eat three of each of the fruit, how many pieces of fruit are left?* (56)

Paired work: Put an OHT of the activity sheet 'Word problems' on the OHP and ask the children to work in pairs to complete these, using a copy of 'Word problem frame'. Ask them to read each question carefully, discuss with their partner how to solve it, and fill in the table for each problem.

Review
Review each question, and how the children solved it. Discuss the strategies that they used. Where different strategies were used, invite the children to compare them and discuss which is more efficient and why that is.

Differentiation
Less confident learners: Decide whether to work with these children as a group. Discuss for each question how it can be calculated and say the calculation through together, counting on in ones as appropriate.
More confident learners: Decide whether to limit the children to working mentally, rather than mentally with jottings.

Lesson 2 (Teach and apply)

Starter
Recall: Use the Starter from Lesson 1, but this time concentrate on counting backwards.

Main teaching activities
Whole class: Write on the board: 12 + 6 + 8 + 9 and ask: *What could the word problem be?* Give the children a few minutes to decide on their word problem, then take suggestions and together solve the addition sentence. Discuss the strategies that the children used, and their efficiency.
Paired work: Ask the children to work in pairs and to write some addition sentences choosing three numbers from a given list each time: 13, 14, 15, 17, 18, 19, 4, 5, 6, 7, 8, 9, 10 and 11. Write the list on the board. Now ask the children to write, using general resource sheet 'Word problem frame', a word problem in the first column as well as the calculation, and complete the rest of the row. Challenge them to write five problems in all.

Review
Invite children from each ability group to give examples of their number sentences and, using the OHT of 'Word problem frame', write up their calculations, strategies and answers. Ask the more confident children to demonstrate some of their two-step problems.

At the end of the lesson, ask: *Which strategies do you feel confident in*

Unit 2 ⬜ 3 weeks

using now? You may like to ask the children to write this down, and to write down which strategies they feel they need to practise more. Set a problem. Say: *Eggs come in boxes of six. How many boxes do I need to buy if I need 24 eggs?* Ask: *How did you work out this problem?*

Lesson 3 (Teach and practise)

Starter

Recall: Explain to the children that you will show them a multiplication card for the 2-, 5- or 10- times tables from general resource sheet 'Multiplication facts for 2-, 5- and 10-times tables'. Ask them to say quietly the answer to the question on the card when you hold up your hand. Give them a few seconds of thinking time, so that most have time to recall the table fact. Give very little time as the children should all know these well by now. You may prefer to sort the cards and to deal with, for example, the 2-times table first.

Main teaching activities

Whole class: Show the children the general resource sheet 'Hundred square', enlarged to A3. Using one colour of counters, ask the children to say the pattern of two starting on 2, and cover each number said with a counter, sticking it with Blu-Tack. You could also use the interactive resource 'Number grid', set to a hundred square for this activity, using the electronic pen to cover the relevant numbers. Repeat this for counting in fives, starting at 5, using a different colour counter, then in tens, starting at 10. Now ask:
- *Does the pattern of twos cover odd or even numbers? Can you explain why this is?*
- *What do you notice about the pattern of fives? What are the digit numbers?*
- *Which numbers are in both the pattern of fives and tens? What about in the pattern of twos and tens? And twos, fives and tens?*

Now use paper to mask parts of the hundred square so that only the squares 1 to 25 are visible. Ask the children to count in threes, starting from 2, and again cover the numbers said with a counter. Ask: *What do you notice about this pattern?* (It forms diagonal lines.) *What would the next number in the sequence be?* (26.) *And the next?* (29.) *Would 41 be in the sequence?* (Yes.) *How do you know?*

Remove the counters and ask the children to think out the pattern of counting in threes, this time starting on 1. Ask: *What would the pattern be?* Repeat this, moving the masking sheets so that the number squares 1 to 36 are visible. Ask the children to count in steps of four from 1, then from 2, then in steps of five, and so on.

Paired work: Provide copies of activity sheet 'Spot the pattern' for each child. Ask the children to work in pairs to complete the sequences. Encourage them to discuss the sequences. They may find it helpful to say each one aloud so that they hear the numbers making the pattern. Some children may find a copy of the 'Hundred square' helpful.

Review

Use an A3 version of 'Spot the pattern' and have the 'Hundred square' handy. Invite individual children to give missing numbers. Ask a child to point to each number in the sequence on the hundred square for the others to check the pattern. You may wish to use the Blu-Tacked counters again to cover the numbers to help the less confident children to keep the pattern in their heads. Ask questions such as: *Does this sequence make a pattern on the hundred square?* (For example, straight line, diagonal, every other number...) *What would the next number in the sequence be? And the number before the first in the sequence?* (Where the pattern begins, for example, with a teen number.)

Lesson 4 (Teach and apply)

Starter
Recall: Use the cards from general resource sheet 'Multiplication facts for 2-, 5- and 10-times tables'. Ask the children to respond quickly to the multiplication facts. They write the answer each time on their whiteboards and when you say *Show me,* they hold this up for you to see. Keep the pace sharp. This activity will give you the opportunity to check which children have rapid recall and which need further practice.

Main teaching activities
Whole class: Explain that today's lesson is all about using the appropriate calculation to solve problems. Invite the children to respond by writing a symbol (+, -, × or ÷) on their whiteboards during the following story. Pause each time you want them to do this, as there is a calculation to do. Now read the story below, from the general resource sheet 'Sparky – Queen of the chickens (part 1)'.

Poultry Productions Presents... the story of Sparky Queen of the chickens! Sparky had been playing lead guitar with the 'Screaming Bantams' for two decades.

Ask: *How many years is this?* (20.) Pause for × or + sign and the calculation.

She had played to many chickens in many coops. Looking back it must have been at least three concerts a week. Ask: *How many concerts is that every month?* (12.) Pause for × or + and the calculation.

There were only four of them left in the band. That's half what we started with, she remembered. Ask: *How many were in the band when they started?* (8.) Pause for ÷ sign and the calculation.

Read the story again. This time ask, for each pause: *How can you tell which calculation is needed? What clues are there in the story?* Discuss the vocabulary that is used and what it tells about the calculation needed.

Group work: Ask the children to use their version of 'Sparky – Queen of the chickens (part 2)' and to solve the problems, deciding which calculation to use each time.

Review
Read through the core activity sheet 'Sparky – Queen of the chickens (part 2)' together and ask for answers. Invite children to explain which strategies they used for working out their answers. Repeat this for the support and extension versions of the sheet. For each question ask: *Which calculation do you think you should use? What tells you that in the sentence?* Extend the work by suggesting a new scenario. For example: *Imagine four plates that each have four cakes. Make up a word problem for this. What is the answer? How did you work it out?*

Differentiation
Less confident learners: This group has smaller numbers to work with, using the support version of the sheet 'Sparky – Queen of the chickens (part 2)'.
More confident learners: More complex numbers are used on the extension activity sheet.

Lesson 5 (Teach and reason)

Starter
Recall: Repeat the Starter from Lesson 4. This time, ask for a division fact for the multiplication on the card that you choose.

Main teaching activities
Whole class: Invite the children to think about coins. On the board, list all the different coins that there are. Then say to the class: *Sammy gave two silver coins to pay for a 16p toy. Which coins do you think he chose? How much change did he get?*

Encourage the children to suggest different solutions for this and write their calculation strategies on the board.

Paired work: Set a similar problem for the children to tackle in pairs. Say to the class: *You have a 50p piece. You buy a toy and receive two silver coins as change. Which coins could these be? How much did the toy cost?* Remind

▷ the children that there are several answers to this, and challenge them to find as many as they can.

Review

Review the children's answers and ask questions such as: *Which calculation/strategy did you use to work that out?*

Lessons 6-10

Preparation

Photocopy three sets of 0 to 9 digit cards onto A3 from CD page 'Numeral cards 0-20'; copy CD page 'Pictures of 3D shapes' onto an OHT; prepare eight 3D 4-cube models (all different) from interlocking cubes and seal each one inside an opaque carrier bag (keep aside two of the models to use in during the lesson; make a shape with five interlocking cubes, ensuring that at least one cube will be hidden from view when the shape is placed onto the OHP.

You will need

CD resources

'Lines of symmetry'; 'Numeral cards 0-20', 'Pictures of 3D shapes' and 'Symmetry' for the teacher's/LSA's reference (see General resources).

Equipment

Interlocking cubes; gym mats; small safety mirrors; pegs and pegboards.

Learning objectives

Starter

● Derive and recall multiplication facts for the 2-, 3-, 4-, 5-, 6- and 10-times tables and the corresponding division facts; recognise multiples of 2, 5 or 10 up to 1000.

● Read, write and order whole numbers to at least 1000 and position them on a number line; count on from and back to zero in single-digit steps or multiples of 10.

● Derive and recall all addition and subtraction facts for each number to 20, sums and differences of multiples of 10 and number pairs that total 100.

Main teaching activities

2006

● Identify patterns and relationships involving numbers or shapes, and use these to solve problems.

● Relate 2D shapes and 3D solids to drawings of them; describe, visualise, classify, draw and make the shapes.

● Draw and complete shapes with reflective symmetry and draw the reflection of a shape in a mirror line along one side.

1999

● Solve mathematical problems or puzzles, recognise simple patterns and relationships, generalise and predict. Suggest extensions by asking 'What if...?'

● Describe and extend number sequences.

● Investigate a general statement about familiar numbers or shapes by finding examples that satisfy it.

● Relate solid shapes to pictures of them.

● Classify and describe 3D and 2D shapes, including the hemisphere, prism, semi-circle, quadrilateral..., referring to properties such as reflective symmetry, the number or shapes of faces, the number of sides/edges and vertices, whether sides/edges are the same length, whether or not angles are right angles...

● Make and describe shapes and patterns, eg explore the different shapes that can be made from four cubes.

● Identify and sketch lines of symmetry in simple shapes, and recognise shapes with no lines of symmetry.

● Sketch the reflection of a simple shape in a mirror line along one edge.

Vocabulary

problem, solution, calculate, calculation, operation, inverse, answer, method, explain, reasoning, pattern, predict, estimate, approximate, triangle, square, rectangle, quadrilateral, pentagon, hexagon, octagon, cube, cuboid, pyramid, cone, cylinder, prism, face, edge, vertex, surface, solid, side, straight, curved, diagram, right-angled, line of symmetry, mirror line, reflection, symmetrical

Lesson 6 (Teach and reason)

Starter
Recall: Say together the 3-times table. Write the number sentences on the board, in order: 0 × 3 = 0; 1 × 3 = 3... Using the vocabulary of multiplication, invite the children to say the answers to questions such as: *What is 3 times 3? What is ___ multiplied by 3? What is 12 divided by 3?*

Main teaching activities
Whole class: Explain that you would like the children to continue to think about general statements about numbers. Write on the board: 'The difference between two even numbers is even'. Ask: *Is this true? Talk to your partner and write down four number sentences to show that this is true.* Invite the children to take turns to write their number sentences on the board, such as 8 - 4 = 4; 96 - 10 = 86... Invite the children to think about why this statement is true. They may find it helpful to model a simple number sentence, such as 6 - 4 = 2 using cubes.

Now repeat this for the difference between odd and even numbers. Write up: *The difference between an odd and an even number is...* Ask the children to work with their partner to decide how to complete the statement, then to find four examples to satisfy the statement. Again, invite the children to explain why the difference between an odd and an even number is always odd.

Paired work: Ask the children to consider the following statements, which should be written on the board:
- The difference between two odd numbers is always even.
- If you multiply numbers either way round the answer is the same.

Ask the children to decide whether the statements are true and to find six examples to satisfy each statement. Remind them that you may ask how they worked out their six examples so that they are ready to explain.

Review
Begin with the statement 'The difference between two odd numbers is always even.' Invite the children to take turns to write up on the board examples which show that the statement is true. Ask: *How did you work out this number sentence?* Encourage the children to explain this, using mathematical vocabulary. Ask the more confident children to explain why the statement is true. They may say that the difference between any two odd numbers, such as 5 and 7, is even, because they are two away from each other. This would be a good start to the discussion. Repeat for the second statement.

Differentiation
Less confident learners: Decide whether to work as a group to find examples to match the statements. Encourage the children to explain why the statements are true, using mathematical vocabulary. You may need to say their explanations in mathematical language for them if the children find this difficult.
More confident learners: Challenge the children to explain why these statements are true.

Lesson 7 (Teach and apply)

Starter
Revisit: Shuffle the three sets of 0-9 numeral cards and ask a child to select three cards. He or she orders the cards to make a three-digit number. Hold the cards up so that all can see. Repeat this to make another, different, three-digit number. Write each of these numbers on the board along an empty number line, so that the lower number is to the left, and the higher to the right at the end of the line. Invite the children to suggest numbers that will fit between and to take turns to write them on the board in their approximate place along the line. Repeat for other pairs of three-digit numbers.

Main teaching activities
Whole class: Explain that in this lesson children will be exploring the properties of 3D shapes. Introduce the vocabulary of 'corner', 'face', 'edge', 'end' and 'hollow' by showing shapes that exemplify the words. Invite the children to offer examples for the word 'solid' (often used in daily speech to mean 'good'). Write the vocabulary on the board.

Hand out the carrier bags and ask the children to describe the shape they can feel using some of today's vocabulary. Now ask them to sketch what they felt. Share afterwards the conventions for drawing 3D shapes by using dotted lines for edges you can't see. Ask the children to open the bags and check the shape that they drew with the model. Prompt them with questions such as: *How many faces are touching in each shape?* (Mostly three, but not always.) *Look down on the shape. How does it look now? Look at the shape from the front... side... What does it look like?*

Put one of the spare 4-cube models that was not placed into a carrier bag on the OHT. Ask the children to sketch what they see and to predict where any cubes that might be hidden are placed. Turn the shape to show a different view and repeat. Finally show the children all of the shape and encourage them to check their drawing. Repeat for the second spare shape.

Group work: The children now work in pairs. One child makes a shape with four interlocking cubes; their partner asks for the view to be sketched from the top, front and side and then using the sketches makes the shape. They check to see if it is correct, then swap over roles.

Review

Place a 5-cube shape that you have made onto the OHP. Challenge the children to describe what they see. Tell them that there are five cubes and that one of them is hidden. Ask: *Where do you think the hidden cube might be?* Provide the children with five cubes each and invite them to make the model as they think it is. Now change the orientation, showing a different view of the model on the OHP. Ask: *What shape can you see now? How do you need to change your model?* Repeat this for a different view. Discuss with the children that when looking at shapes from the front, back or side, we do not see all of the shape.

Lesson 8 (Teach and apply)

Starter
Revisit: Repeat the Starter from Lesson 7. This time ask the children to make all the three-digit numbers that they can with the three cards, order these on the number line, then fit another three-digit number between each pair of numbers on the number line.

Main teaching activities
Whole class: Explain that today the focus is on recognising images of 3D shapes. If possible, look at some of Kandinsky's work and invite the children to describe what they see in the pictures.

Place the OHT of general resource sheet 'Pictures of 3D shapes' onto the OHP. Ask the children to describe the shapes that they see and where they are placed. Invite a child to use the shapes in the box to make the model that they can see. Remove the OHT and ask the children to sketch the model. Replace the OHT and invite the children to check that their drawing is similar to that on the OHT. If not, ask for differences and explanations of why there are differences. These may be to do with the size of the shape models used.

Group work: Encourage the children to work in groups of four with a set of 3D shapes. They take turns to make a model, then they all sketch what is made. If they do this from different angles, they can compare what they have drawn and discuss if they could make the complete model from their sketches.

Review
Ask children from each group to put their models on view, and collect all of the sketches for these models. Give each group another group's sketches. Now invite the children to go from model to model, as a group, comparing the sketches that they have with the models. Challenge them to find the appropriate model for their sketch. Ask questions such as: *How did you recognise the model? What clues were there in the sketches? Is there anything else that could have been sketched to help?*

Differentiation
Less confident learners: You may wish to work with the children as a group, with you describing your hidden shape while the children sketch. Encourage them to use the vocabulary of shape in order to describe what they draw and what they see when you show them the hidden shape.
More confident learners: Challenge these children to complete all eight possible shapes made with four cubes.

Differentiation
Less confident learners: Decide whether to limit the range of shapes offered in order to simplify the models made.
More confident learners: Challenge the children to make more complex structures, particularly with 'hidden' shapes, then to compare sketches to see in which orientation the 'hidden' shape will show.

Lesson 9 (Teach and apply)

Starter

Recall: Explain to the children that you will say a tens number and that they are to say the number that when added to your number makes a total of 100. Begin by saying the tens numbers in order: 10, 20... with the children saying the complement to make 100, so that they hear the ascending and descending pattern of numbers, then repeat with the numbers out of order.

Main teaching activities

Whole class: Arrange to start in the hall. Ask the children to stand in a shape with a line of symmetry down the centre of their body. *What other shapes can you make with the imaginary vertical centre line?* The children now pair up with another child and each pair has a floor mat. Can they create a mirror image of their body shape with one hand touching? Can they create mirror images that have the following criteria: One foot and one hand on the floor? Makes a long thin shape? Has a right angle? Back in class, reveal the first shape on general resource sheet 'Symmetry'. Ask: *Where is the line of symmetry?* Write 'symmetry' on the board and point clearly along the line. Repeat this for the next shape, checking the lines with a safety mirror.
Paired work: Ask the children to work in twos. Provide them each with activity sheet 'Lines of symmetry' and ask them to check each picture carefully, to decide whether the shape is symmetrical, then sketch in the lines of symmetry.

Review

Ask the children to decide which capital letters have line/s of symmetry. Use this opportunity to check that the children can use the vocabulary of symmetry and understand that shapes can have none, one or more than one line of symmetry.

Differentiation

Less confident learners: Decide whether to work with the children in a group and encourage them to explain, using shape vocabulary, where the lines of symmetry are and how they know that.
More confident learners: Challenge the children to find other shapes with line symmetry and to sketch the shapes and mark in the lines of symmetry.

Lesson 10 (Teach and apply)

Starter

Recall: Repeat the Starter for Lesson 9, keeping the pace really sharp.

Main teaching activities

Whole class: Invite the children to make patterns with pegs and pegboards where the pattern has two lines of symmetry. Discuss how to use a mirror to check this by placing it along the horizontal and vertical lines and observe the reflection of half of the shape. More confident children may recognise that shapes can have diagonal lines of symmetry too.
Paired work: Ask the children to work in pairs. They both sketch half a shape, such as half a robot or half a butterfly, and check with a mirror whether or not their shape has a line of symmetry. If it has, they then sketch the reflection. Encourage the children to draw shapes that do have lines of symmetry.

Review

Invite children to draw their half of a shape on the board for others to copy and then draw the reflection.

Lessons 11-15

Preparation

Copy 'Smiley hundred square 2' onto card and cut out the different L-shapes.

Learning objectives

Starter

● Derive and recall all addition and subtraction facts for each number to 20, sums and differences of multiples of 10 and number pairs that total 100.

Unit 2 ▯ 3 weeks

You will need

Photocopiable pages
'Equivalent fractions' (page 75) for each child.

CD resources
Support and extension versions of 'Equivalent fractions'; 'Smiley hundred square 1' and 'Smiley hundred square 2' (see General resources).

Equipment
Beanbags; five or more 1-litre measuring jugs marked in millilitres; 20 or more empty plastic containers of different shapes but all geared to hold 1 litre; coloured water; ten or more empty transparent cola bottles holding 1 litre; containers that hold 250ml, 500ml and 750ml; metre rule, metre sticks marked in cm; interlocking cubes; counting stick; sticky labels and black pens, metre length strips of paper; counters.

- Read and write proper fractions (eg $3/7$, $9/10$), interpreting the denominator as the parts of a whole and the numerator as the number of parts; identify and estimate fractions of shapes; use diagrams to compare fractions and establish equivalents.
- Read, write and order whole numbers to at least 1000 and position them on a number line; count on from and back to zero in single-digit steps or multiples of 10.

Main teaching activities

2006
- Read and write proper fractions (eg $3/7$, $9/10$), interpreting the denominator as the parts of a whole and the numerator as the number of parts; identify and estimate fractions of shapes; use diagrams to compare fractions and establish equivalents.

1999
- Recognise unit fractions such as $1/2$, $1/3$, $1/4$, $1/5$, $1/10$ ... and use them to find fractions of shapes and numbers.
- Begin to recognise simple fractions that are several parts of a whole, such as $3/4$, $2/3$ or $3/10$.
- Compare familiar fractions, eg know that on the number line one half lies between one quarter and three quarters.
- Begin to recognise simple equivalent fractions, eg five tenths and one half, five fifths and one whole.
- Estimate a simple fraction.

Vocabulary

problem, solution, calculate, calculation, operation, inverse, answer, method, explain, reasoning, pattern, predict, estimate, approximate, add, subtract, multiply, divide, group, sum, total, difference, plus, minus, double, halve, multiple, part, fraction, one whole, one half, two halves, one quarter, two... three... four quarters

Lesson 11 (Teach and practise)

Starter

Revisit: Use the OHT of general resource sheet 'Smiley hundred square 1' and the L-shaped card from the resource sheet 'Smiley hundred square 2'. Cover up 37 faces, leaving the remainder 'clear'. Ask the children to calculate the number of faces that are covered. Ask: *How did you work out how many are covered? Is the number odd or even? How can you tell? What about the uncovered faces - is this an odd or even number?* The children should begin to notice that when the total of covered faces is even/odd, the other total of uncovered faces (the complement) is also even/odd. Repeat, using the other L-shapes from the 'Smiley hundred square 2' sheet.

Main teaching activities

Whole class: Invite the children to explain how many smiley faces would be in half the hundred square. Ask:
- *How many faces would be in a quarter?*
- *What about in a third? Why is this difficult?* (To be exact, one face would need to be split into three parts or the answer could be 33 r1 whole faces.)
- *What if you had 90 smiley faces, what would $1/3$ be then? What helps you to work this out?* (Knowing that 3 × 3 = 9, so 3 × 30 = 90.)
- *How could we calculate $2/3$ of the faces?*

Explain that fractions can be $2/3$, $3/4$ and so on. This means 'two equal parts out of three, three equal parts out of four'. Ask the children for their thoughts, before sharing out six beanbags between three children. Write on the board '$1/3$ of 6 equals 2'. Calculate with the class what $2/3$ of 6 would be.

Explain to the children that during the group work over the next two lessons, they are going to consider fractions in terms of measures (capacity and length). Split the class into two main groups for the next two lessons.

Group work: (Capacity) Ask the children to estimate how much they think each plastic container would hold in terms of litres and fractions of a litre, such as $^1/_2$, $^1/_4$... They use the measuring jugs to check their estimates. The water from each jug can then be poured into litre cola bottles for display and labelled by the children with the correct amount. Challenge the children to display the fractions in order of size.

(Length) Provide strips of paper and metre sticks. Ask the children to mark the following fractions onto a strip of paper: $^1/_2$ metre, $^1/_4$ metre, $^3/_4$ metre. Then ask them to think about how they might do the same for the fractions $^1/_3$ metre and $^2/_3$ metre. If time, they can repeat this for the fractions $^1/_5$ metre, $^2/_5$ metre, $^4/_5$ metre.

Review

For the capacity activity, ask questions such as:
- *What do you need to add to half a litre to get one whole litre?*
- *How many half litres are in two litres?*
  Invite the children to explain how they worked out their answers.
  For the length activity, invite children to explain how they found the fractions of length. Ask:
- *How many centimetres are there in $^1/_2$ of a metre? What about $^1/_4$? $^1/_5$?*
- *How close did you get to finding $^1/_3$ of a metre?*
- *What about $^1/_5$, $^2/_5$ of a metre? How did you discover this?*
  Discuss how the children recorded their findings on the strips of paper.

Differentiation

Less confident learners: This group would benefit from working with an adult for both activities. The adult should encourage the children to use appropriate language of measures and fractions as they explain their work.

More confident learners: This group uses fractions of one-tenth and multiples of this for the capacity activity. Challenge them to find more complex fractions of length, such as $^1/_8$, $^2/_8$, $^3/_8$ of a metre.

Lesson 12 (Teach and apply)

Starter

Recall: Use the Starter from Lesson 11 but extend by expecting the children to improve their ability to predict the evenness or oddness of the answer each time. Invite children to use the OHP of CD page 'Smiley hundred square 1' and the L-shaped cards to show other combination of numbers to 100.

Main teaching activities

Whole class: Provide the children with 30cm rulers, and ask them to calculate one-half, one-third, two-thirds and one-tenth of their 30cm ruler.
Paired work: Ask the children to draw 2D shapes and find which ones can be divided by folding exactly into halves, then quarters.

Review

Ask children to show which shapes they were able to divide exactly into half, then quarters. Ask: *How do you know?* Discuss how $^2/_4$ is equivalent to ½.

Lesson 13 (Teach and practise)

Starter

Reason: Write a list of numbers on the board, such as 20, 7, 4, 9, 15, 6 and 2. Ask: *Which of these numbers can be halved to make a whole number? How can you tell?* Now say any number between 1 and 20 and ask the children to say its double. Repeat this for any even number between 2 and 20.

Main teaching activities

Whole class: Explain that today the children will continue to think about fractions that are several parts of a whole, this time using quantities of counting apparatus. Invite a child to count out 30 cubes and ask: *What would $^1/_3$ of the cubes be? How can you tell? So what fraction would 20 cubes be?* Discuss how the children can divide by three in order to find $^1/_3$. Explain that if they find $^1/_3$ is 10, then $^2/_3$ would be 10 × 2. Repeat for 20 cubes and finding $^1/_5$, $^2/_5$ and so on.
Group work: Provide each pair with some counting apparatus. Ask them to count out 36 cubes and find the following fractions: $^1/_2$, $^1/_4$; $^1/_3$, $^2/_3$. They decide how to record what they find. They can repeat this for 50 cubes and

Unit 2 ▢ 3 weeks

Differentiation

Less confident learners: Decide whether to reduce the number of cubes to 24, then 30.
More confident learners: Challenge the children to work mentally to find the solutions, rather than by counting cubes. They should prepare to report back during the Review on how they did this.

finding $^1/_5$, $^2/_5$, $^4/_5$ and $^1/_{10}$, $^2/_{10}$, $^9/_{10}$.

Review

Invite the more confident children to explain how they worked mentally. Discuss the strategies that they used, which may include division, multiplication, repeated addition, and so on. You may find it helpful to model what the children report back with cubes. Ask questions such as:

● *What is $^1/_2$ of 12?*
● *So what would $^2/_4$ be?*
● *How did you work that out?*
● *What would $^4/_4$ be?*

Lesson 14 (Teach and reason)

Starter

Rehearse: Explain that you will say a number. Ask the children to write it in numerals on their whiteboards. When you say *Show me*, the children hold up their boards. Say, for example: 132, 246, 987, 205, 440 and 900.

Main teaching activities

Whole class: Draw a number line on the board, label one end 0 and the other 10 and ask a child to place 5 on the line. Now ask: *Where would 6 go? And where would $5^1/_2$ fit?* Repeat this for numbers such as $7^1/_2$, $1^1/_2$, $6^1/_2$...

Now explain to the class that they will be considering fractions that are worth the same but are written differently (equivalent fractions). On the board, draw a rectangle which is divided into four sections. Ask a child to colour in one of the sections, and another to choose another section to colour. Ask: *How many sections are there altogether? How many are coloured? So what fraction is coloured? Yes, two quarters or one half.* Write the fractions $^2/_4$ and $^1/_2$ next to the drawing on the board. Repeat this, colouring in different combinations of two of the four sections of the rectangle so that the children understand that even if this is done in a different way, still $^2/_4$ or $^1/_2$ has been coloured. Ask: *What fraction is not coloured? Say this fraction in two ways.* ($^1/_2$ and $^2/_4$)

Now show two interlocking cubes of different colours joined together. Ask: *What fraction is red? Blue?* ($^1/_2$) Repeat this for four ($^1/_2$, $^2/_4$), then eight ($^1/_2$, $^4/_8$), then ten ($^1/_2$, $^5/_{10}$) cubes. Point out that when the children have more than two cubes, but still an even number, they have a choice about how they join the two colours together. This results in different patterns but the overall result is the same - one half of the shape is red and one half is blue.

Paired work: Explain that you would like the children to work in pairs. Provide some equipment in two colours for the children to use to help them to make their patterns. Their challenge is to work with one resource to make patterns that show the equivalent fractions for $^1/_2$. Provide each child with a copy of activity sheet 'Equivalent fractions'. Suggest that they compare their work with their partner in order to consider different ways in which they can make the fraction patterns.

Differentiation

Less confident learners: There is a support version of the activity sheet which uses the equivalents $^1/_2$, $^2/_4$ and $^4/_8$.
More confident learners: There is an extension version of the sheet which challenges the children to find further equivalent fractions for $^1/_2$ and to find fractions that are not $^1/_2$.

Review

Invite the children to spend a couple of minutes comparing their results with others who completed the same version of the activity sheet. Now write the following sentence starters for the children to complete in pairs.

● It is true to say that one half...
● This fraction (show one of more confident children's work) cannot be worth the same as one half because...
● To work out one half of something...
● (For the more confident) An equivalent fraction...
Invite more confident children to explain what is meant by 'equivalent'.

Lesson 15 (Teach, apply and evaluate)

Starter
Rehearse: Repeat the Starter from Lesson 14, but ask the children to write the numbers in words. Include some more difficult numbers such as 408 or 560, as well as numbers such as 562 or 149.

Main teaching activities
Whole class: On the board, draw a rectangle divided into ten equal sections. Ask: *How many tenths can you see? Yes, ten. So how many fifths are there?* Point to two sections at a time and count the fifths. Agree that $5/5$ is the same as $10/10$, and that both of these are the same as one whole. Now colour in two sections and ask: *What fraction have I coloured? What other fraction could this be?* ($1/5$ or $2/10$) Repeat for colouring in another two sections ($2/5$ or $4/10$), then colour in one more section and ask: *What fraction is coloured?* Agree that this is $5/10$ or $1/2$, but that it is not a fraction of fifths because each fifth needs to have two sections coloured in.

Group work: Write some fractions related to tenths on the board, such as $4/10$, $2/5$, $8/10$, $1/5$... Ask the children to work in pairs to model the fractions using the apparatus from Lesson 14's paired work. Ask them to sketch their fractions on squared paper, to decide which fractions have equivalents and to write these in both forms.

Review
Invite the children to show their sketches for $4/10$. Discuss how the sketches all show the same number of sections coloured in but that the patterns are not the same. Say: *Tell me another fraction that is worth the same.* ($2/5$) Encourage the more confident children to suggest other equivalent fractions, such as $8/20$. Repeat for the other fractions.

Ask the children to discuss, in pairs, what they know about fractions. Invite those that you are targetting for assessment to give feedback to the rest of the class.

Differentiation
Less confident learners: Decide whether to work as a group to carry out this task. Encourage the children to use the vocabulary of fractions as they explain what they have made with the apparatus.

More confident learners: Challenge the children by asking them to find an equivalent fraction for each one that you write on the board. Remind them, if necessary, that, for example, $6/20$ is equivalent to $3/10$.

Name _____   Date _____

Spot the pattern

Write the missing numbers in these number patterns.

1. 2, 7, 12, ☐, ☐, ☐   **2.** 13, 16, 19, ☐, ☐, ☐

The rule is _____   The rule is _____

3. 2, 5, 8, ☐, ☐, ☐   **4.** 16, 21, 26, ☐, ☐, ☐

The rule is _____   The rule is _____

Write the rule for each of these patterns.

5. 11, 13, 15, 17, 19   **6.** 26, 29, 32, 35, 38

The rule is _____   The rule is _____

7. 34, 38, 42, 46, 50   **8.** 96, 91, 86, 81, 76

The rule is _____   The rule is _____

Now write your own sequence.

It must include the numbers 8 and 17.

Write the rule.

Name _____   Date _____

Sparky – Queen of the chickens (part 2)

Read the story.

Write the answers in the boxes.

Sparky and her 3 band players were not happy.

They were laying 5 double-yolker eggs each, every week.

How many eggs did they lay in 4 weeks? ⬜

_____

_____

The farmer was pleased.

He charged double price for double yolkers. Normally eggs cost 20p each.

How much would he get for 5 double yolkers? ⬜

_____

_____

Sparky found out the farmer was putting special double-yolker feed in their trays.

The feed cost him 30p each day.

So how many eggs did he have to sell in a week to earn more than the feed cost

him? ⬜

_____

_____

The farmer sold 6 double-yolker eggs on Monday,

4 on Tuesday and 5 on Wednesday.

How much money did he take? ⬜

_____

_____

Remember the feed cost him 30p each day.

How much did he have left after paying for the feed? ⬜

_____

_____

Name _____   Date _____

Equivalent fractions

Ask your teacher for some equipment in two different colours.

Use your equipment to show the following fractions.

$$\frac{1}{2} \qquad \frac{2}{4} \qquad \frac{4}{8} \qquad \frac{5}{10}$$

Now sketch your results in the correct box.

$\frac{1}{2}$	$\frac{2}{4}$
$\frac{4}{8}$	$\frac{5}{10}$

Write a sentence about your drawings using 'the same as'.

_____

_____

_____

Securing number facts, understanding shape

Lesson	Strands	Starter	Main teaching activities
1. Teach and apply	Use/apply	**Add or subtract mentally combinations of one-digit and two-digit numbers.**	Represent the information in a puzzle or problem using numbers, images or diagrams; use these to find a solution and present it in context, where appropriate using £.p notation or units of measure.
2. Teach and apply	Knowledge	As for Lesson 1	**Derive and recall all addition and subtraction facts for each number to 20, sums and differences of multiples of 10 and number pairs that total 100.**
3. Teach and apply	Knowledge	As for Lesson 1	As for Lesson 2
4. Teach and practise	Knowledge	Use knowledge of number operations and corresponding inverses, including doubling and halving, to estimate and check calculations.	Derive and recall multiplication facts for the 2-, 3-, 4-, 5-, 6- and 10-times tables and the corresponding division facts; recognise multiples of 2, 5 or 10 up to 1000.
5. Teach and practise	Knowledge	Use knowledge of number operations and corresponding inverses, including doubling and halving, to estimate and check calculations.	Use knowledge of number operations and corresponding inverses, including doubling and halving, to estimate and check calculations.
6. Teach and practise	Counting	Read, write and order whole numbers to at least 1000 and position them on a number line; count on from and back to zero in single-digit steps or multiples of 10.	Read and write proper fractions (eg $\frac{3}{7}$, $\frac{9}{10}$) interpreting the denominator as the parts of a whole and the numerator as the number of parts; identify and estimate fractions of shapes; use diagrams to compare fractions and establish equivalents.
7. Teach and practise	Counting	As for Lesson 6	As for Lesson 6
8. Teach and apply	Counting	As for Lesson 6	As for Lesson 6
9. Teach and apply	Counting Use/apply	As for Lesson 6	• Read and write proper fractions (eg $\frac{3}{7}$, $\frac{9}{10}$) interpreting the denominator as the parts of a whole and the numerator as the number of parts; identify and estimate fractions of shapes; use diagrams to compare fractions and establish equivalents. • Solve one-step and two-step problems involving numbers, money or measures, including time, choosing and carrying out appropriate calculations.
10. Teach and apply	Counting	Round two-digit or three-digit numbers to the nearest 10 or 100 and give estimates for their sums and differences.	Read and write proper fractions (eg $\frac{3}{7}$, $\frac{9}{10}$) interpreting the denominator as the parts of a whole and the numerator as the number of parts; identify and estimate fractions of shapes; use diagrams to compare fractions and establish equivalents.
11. Teach and practise	Use/apply	**Derive and recall all addition and subtraction facts for each number to 20, sums and differences of multiples of 10 and number pairs that total 100.**	Solve one-step and two-step problems involving numbers, money or measures, including time, choosing and carrying out appropriate calculations.
12. Teach and practise	Use/apply	As for Lesson 11	As for Lesson 11
13. Teach and apply	Shape	Derive and recall multiplication facts for the 2-, 3-, 4-, 5-, 6- and 10-times tables and the corresponding division facts; recognise multiples of 2, 5 or 10 up to 1000.	Relate 2D shapes and 3D solids to drawings of them; describe, visualise, classify, draw and make the shapes.
14. Teach and apply	Shape	As for Lesson 13	Use a set-square to draw right angles and to identify right angles in 2D shapes; compare angles with a right angle; recognise that a straight line is equivalent to two right angles.
15. Teach, apply and evaluate	Use/apply	As for Lesson 13	Identify patterns and relationships involving numbers or shapes, and use these to solve problems.

Unit 3 ▢ 3 weeks

Speaking and listening objective
● Develop and use specific vocabulary in different contexts.

Introduction
During this 15-lesson unit, encourage the children to discuss their work with a partner and with the whole class so that they have opportunities to use specific mathematics vocabulary in context. They extend their skills in using and applying mathematics by solving word problems, using what they know to investigate right-angled triangles. In this unit it is expected that children will have reasonable recall of the 2-, 3-, 4-, 5-, 6- and 10-times tables, and similarly they will be able to derive the related division facts. They are expected to have reasonable recall of addition and subtraction facts to 20, and to use these facts to derive others, including sums and differences of multiples of 10 and number pairs to make 100. They reinforce their understanding of fractions, and of 2D and 3D shape.

Using and applying mathematics
● Solve one-step and two-step problems involving numbers, money or measures, including time, choosing and carrying out appropriate calculations.
● Represent the information in a puzzle or problem using numbers, images or diagrams; use these to find a solution and present it in context, where appropriate using £.p notation or units of measure.
● Identify patterns and relationships involving numbers or shapes, and use these to solve problems.

Lessons 1-5

Preparation
Copy CD page 'Number problems' onto an OHT.

You will need
Photocopiable pages
'Fruity problems' (page 89), 'Finding differences' (page 90), 'Multiples of ten' (page 91) and 'Checking calculations' (page 92) for each child.
CD resources
Support and extension versions of 'Fruity problems', 'Multiples of ten' and 'Checking calculations'; 'Number problems' (see General resources). Interactive resource 'Number grid', set up to show a hundred square.

Learning objectives

Starter
● Add or subtract mentally combinations of one-digit and two-digit numbers.
● Use knowledge of number operations and corresponding inverses, including doubling and halving, to estimate and check calculations.

Main teaching activities
2006
● Represent the information in a puzzle or problem using numbers, images or diagrams; use these to find a solution and present it in context, where appropriate using £.p notation or units of measure.
● Derive and recall all addition and subtraction facts for each number to 20, sums and differences of multiples of 10 and number pairs that total 100.
● Derive and recall multiplication facts for the 2-, 3-, 4-, 5-, 6- and 10-times tables and the corresponding division facts; recognise multiples of 2, 5 or 10 up to 1000.
● Use knowledge of number operations and corresponding inverses, including doubling and halving, to estimate and check calculations.
1999
● Choose and use appropriate operations (including multiplication and division) to solve word problems, and appropriate ways of calculating: mental, mental with jottings, pencil and paper.
● Recognise all coins and notes. Understand and use £.p notation (for example, know that £3.06 is £3 and 6p).
● Know by heart: all addition and subtraction facts for each number to 20; all pairs of multiples of 100 with a total of 1000 (eg 300 + 700); all pairs of multiples of 5 with a total of 100 (eg 35 + 65).
● Derive quickly all number pairs that total 100 (eg 62 + 38, 75 + 25, 40 + 60).
● Know by heart multiplication facts for the 2-, 5- and 10-times tables; begin to know the 3- and 4-times tables. Derive quickly corresponding division facts.
● Recognise two-digit and three-digit multiples of 2, 5 or 10, and three-digit multiples of 50 and 100.
● Begin to know multiplication facts for the 6-times table.

▷ **Vocabulary**
problem, solution, calculate, calculation, operation, inverse, answer, method, explain, reasoning, pattern, predict, estimate, approximate, add, subtract, sum, total, difference, plus, minus, multiple

Lesson 1 (Teach and apply)

Starter
Reason: Ask the children to write the answers to these addition questions on their whiteboards. Say: *What is 43 + 30? 43 + 29? How did you work that out? What about 43 + 31?* Repeat for other examples, such as 56 + 40 and 37 + 50, so that the children have the opportunity to calculate by adding the multiple of 10 before adjusting by one for the subsequent questions.

Main teaching activities
Whole class: Explain that you would like the children to use the empty number line methods that they have learned as an aid to solving problems. Uncover the first example on the OHT of the general resource sheet 'Number problems'. Ask: *How shall we solve this?* Invite a child to draw an empty number line on the board and to write in the additions. Write the number sentence: 45 + 36 = 45 + 30 + 6 = 75 + 5 + 1 = 80 + 1 = 81.

Repeat this for the second question on the OHT. First ask the children to explain what sort of problem it is (subtraction) and then invite a child to draw an empty number line to show how the problem could be solved. You may wish to do this both by counting up and by compensation. For counting up, write up: 25 + 5 + 60 + 1 = 91, so 91 - 25 = 5 + 60 + 1 = 66.

Write also:
$$25 + 5 = 30$$
$$+ 60 = 90$$
$$+ 1 = 91$$
So 5 + 60 + 1 = 66.

For compensation, write: 91 - 25 = 91 - 30 + 5 = 61 + 5 = 66.
Individual work: Provide the activity sheet 'Fruity problems' for the children to complete individually.

Review
Choose another question from the OHT 'Number problems'. Invite a child to draw the empty number line and to explain what sort of problem it is. Work through the problem as a class and write up the equation. Then invite the children to suggest how they could check their answer.

Now say: *Pat had 40 pears. He sold some and had 15 left. Which of these is a number sentence that shows this?* Write these on the board:
□ - 15 = 40; 15 - □ = 40;
□ - 40 = 15; 40 - □ = 15.

Differentiation
Less confident learners: Decide whether to use the support version of the activity sheet which contains TU + TU and TU - TU only.
More confident learners: There is an extension version of the sheet which contains HTU + HTU and HTU - HTU only.

Lesson 2 (Teach and apply)

Starter
Reason: Repeat the Starter from Lesson 1, this time concentrating on subtraction. For example, ask: *What is 36 subtract 10? What is 42 subtract 14?* Invite the children to explain the mental methods that they chose.

Main teaching activities
Whole class: Explain that in today's lesson the children will recall pairs of numbers that total 100. Reveal the interactive resource 'Number grid', set up to show a hundred square. Ask the children to find the complement to 100 for each number that you point to. Begin with the multiples of 10, and cross out each pair of numbers with the electronic pen as the children find them. Then move to those which have a 5 in the unit place. Ask: *What do you need to look for to find its pair?* Agree that the other number must also end in a 5. Now look at the other numbers that are left. Ask: *If the number is odd what*

must its pair be? And if it is even, what must its pair be? Agree that odd + odd gives even, and even + even gives even. Complete the hundred square for finding the other pairs.

Write on the board 112 - 89 and ask: *How can we use what we know about totals to 100 to find the answer to this?* Draw an empty number line and model the calculation of: 89 + 11 = 100; 100 + 12 = 112. So, 112 - 89 = 11 + 12 = 23.

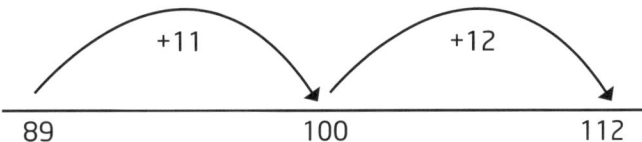

Repeat this for another example, such as 121 - 94, but this time ask the children to use mental methods and jottings, including the empty number line if this helps them. Ask the children to explain how they calculated the answer and what they needed to write down.

Paired work: Write some more examples on the board. Ask the children to work independently to find their answers and to record any jottings that were helpful. Encourage them to compare what they have done and to discuss how they calculated. Write up: 115 - 98, 123 - 87, 145 - 99, 136 - 89. Add more examples if there is time.

Review

Invite children from each ability group to explain how they found the answers for each calculation. Discuss which method seems best and why the children think that. Now ask: *How can we calculate 113 - 76? Where should we start?* Discuss the methods that the children suggest and the jottings that they need to make.

Differentiation

Less confident learners: Decide whether to work as a group to find the answers. If so, for each calculation encourage the children to work independently first to find the answer and to record their jottings. Then discuss how to find the answer and compare methods.

More confident learners: Challenge the children to work mentally as much as possible to find the answers.

Lesson 3 (Teach and apply)

Starter

Reason: Repeat the Starter activities from both Lessons 1 and 2. Encourage the children to explain each time how they calculated. They can make jottings where necessary.

Main teaching activities

Whole class: Provide further examples of finding differences, such as 123 - 94. Work through this example together.

Individual work: Ask the children to work independently to find solutions to the problems on the activity sheet 'Finding differences'. There is space for them to record their jottings.

Review

Invite children from each group to show how they solved the problem and discuss the word problems that the more confident children have written. Ask for each problem: *How did you work that out? Is there another way? Which way do you think is better? Why do you think that?*

Differentiation

Less confident learners: Encourage the children to work as a group to solve the problems.

More confident learners: Challenge the children to write word problems for each of the subtractions.

Lesson 4 (Teach and practise)

Starter

Recall: Explain that you will say a number. Ask the children to say its double. Begin with numbers 1–9, then teen numbers, then extend this to doubles of multiples of 10 to 100. Keep the pace sharp.

Main teaching activities

Whole class: Explain that in this lesson, children will multiply one-digit numbers by multiples of 10. Begin with: *I have 20 boxes of cakes. Each box*

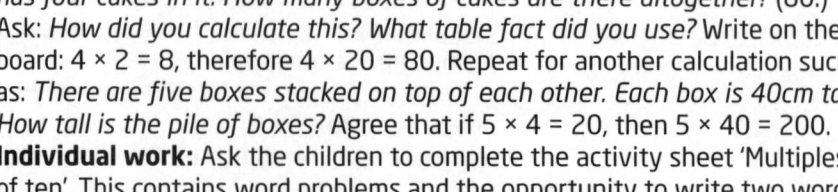

has four cakes in it. How many boxes of cakes are there altogether? (80.) Ask: *How did you calculate this? What table fact did you use?* Write on the board: 4 × 2 = 8, therefore 4 × 20 = 80. Repeat for another calculation such as: *There are five boxes stacked on top of each other. Each box is 40cm tall. How tall is the pile of boxes?* Agree that if 5 × 4 = 20, then 5 × 40 = 200.
Individual work: Ask the children to complete the activity sheet 'Multiples of ten'. This contains word problems and the opportunity to write two word problems for given equations.

Review

Ask for examples of word problems from each ability group. Ask the other children to say the answer, and how they worked it out. Ask: *What multiplied by 30 gives an answer of 120? How did you work that out?* Repeat for other examples, such as: *What is 4 multiplied by 80?*

Lesson 5 (Teach and practise)

Starter
Recall: Repeat the Starter from Lesson 4, this time asking for halves of even numbers to 40, and multiples of 10 to 200. Keep the pace sharp, and give a few seconds of thinking time.

Main teaching activities
Whole class: Explain that in this lesson the children will check their calculations by using addition for subtraction, multiplication for division, doubling for halving, and so on. Ask: *What is half of 36? How did you work that out?* Ask the children to write a sentence that uses the word 'double' and the numbers 36 and 18. Invite individuals to read out their sentences. Now write 37 – 18 = 15 and ask: *Is this correct? How can we check this?* Discuss how children can add 18 and 15. Ask: *Does this give 37? No. So find the correct answer by subtraction and check it by addition.* Repeat this for multiplication and division, such as 50 × 6 = 200.
Individual work: Provide copies of the activity sheet 'Checking calculations'. There are examples that use multiplication, division, addition, subtraction, halving and doubling.

Review
Mark the work quickly. The children can do this for themselves. Now invite children to identify any of the calculations that they found difficult, or had an incorrect answer for. Ask those who had the correct answer to explain how they found their answer. Now write on the board: *Half of 36 is 18; 36 – 19 = 16; 36 ÷ 9 = 4.* Ask: *Which of these calculations is wrong? How did you work that out?*

Differentiation
Less confident learners: There is a support version of the activity sheet where the multiplication is within 100.
More confident learners: There is an extension version of the sheet where the multiplication includes the 8-times table.

Differentiation
Less confident learners: Decide whether to provide the support version of the activity sheet where numbers are smaller. Encourage the children to use an empty number line as an aid to calculation for addition and subtraction, and doubling and halving.
More confident learners: There is an extension version of the sheet which includes more complex questions.

Lessons 6-10

Preparation
Make OHTs of CD pages 'Fraction number lines', 'Fraction cards' (cut out the fraction cards), 'Fraction shapes' and 'Estimates'.

You will need
Photocopiable pages
'Fraction estimates' (page 93) for each child.
CD resources
Support and extension versions of 'Fraction estimates'; 'Fraction number lines' 'Fraction cards', 'Fraction shapes', 'Estimates' and 'Number lines' (see General resources).

Learning objectives

Starter
● Read, write and order whole numbers to at least 1000 and position them on a number line; count on from and back to zero in single-digit steps or multiples of 10.
● Round two-digit or three-digit numbers to the nearest 10 or 100 and give estimates for their sums and differences.

Main teaching activities
2006
● Read and write proper fractions (eg $3/7$, $9/10$), interpreting the denominator as the parts of a whole and the numerator as the number of parts; identify and estimate fractions of shapes; use diagrams to compare fractions and establish equivalents.
1999
● Recognise unit fractions such as $1/2$, $1/3$, $1/4$, $1/5$, $1/10$... and use them to find fractions of shapes and numbers.
● Begin to recognise simple fractions that are several parts of a whole, such as $3/4$, $2/3$ or $3/10$.
● Compare familiar fractions, eg know that on the number line one half lies between one quarter and three quarters.
● Begin to recognise simple equivalent fractions, eg five tenths and one half, five fifths and one whole.
● Estimate a simple fraction.

Vocabulary
problem, solution, calculate, calculation, operation, inverse, answer, method, explain, reasoning, pattern, predict, estimate, approximate

Lesson 6 (Teach and practise)

Starter
Recall: Explain that you will say a number. Ask the children to write it in numerals on their whiteboards. When you say *Show me*, the children hold up their boards. Say, for example: 456, 923, 879, 978, 798. Ask: *What does the ___ digit stand for? What if we swapped over the tens and units digit. What would the number be then?*

Main teaching activities
Whole class: Explain that the work for this week is on fractions and that in this lesson the children will be placing fractions on a number line. Show the OHT 'Fraction number lines' and write on one number line 0 at the beginning and 1 at the end. Point to the mid-point of the line and ask: *What fraction is this?* Agree that it is $1/2$ and place that fraction card in place. Place the other fraction cards from resource sheet 'Fraction cards' around the edge of the OHT so that the children can see what these are. Ask: *What other cards could go here?* Praise those who suggest $2/4$ and $5/10$ and ask for explanations as to why these are correct. Place the quarter cards and tenth cards.

Mark a second number line from 6 to 7 and ask: *What number is half way between 6 and 7?* Write in 6 $1/2$. Point to other positions on the line and ask the children to say which fraction would go there. Now repeat this for fifths.

Draw a line on the board and ask the children to help you to put in all the fractions of fifths and tenths from 0 to 3. Do this systematically: 0, $1/3$, $2/3$, 1, 1 $2/3$... 3. When the line is complete, read it forwards and backwards several times until the children are confident. Cover the line over with some large sheets of paper and ask questions such as: *What number is between 1$1/3$*

and 2? What is between 2¹/₃ and 3? Tell me any number between 1 and 2. Write down the children's responses, then uncover the line so that they can check that the answers are true.

Paired work: Ask the children to work together with a copy of 'Fraction number lines'. Ask the children to take turns to choose a fraction denominator, such as fifths. Their partner chooses a start number. They mark the line in fifths from the start number. They repeat this for other fractions and start numbers, such as halves and quarters, thirds, sixths and tenths.

Review

Using the OHT of 'Fraction number lines', invite the children to write up their start and end numbers and to say which denominator they used. Challenge the other children to say which fractions go where. Ask: *Which of these fractions can you say in another way?* (eg ½ and ²/₄; ¹/₅ and ²/₁₀ and so on).

Lesson 7 (Teach and practise)

Starter
Recall: Repeat the Starter from Lesson 6, but ask the children to write the numbers in words. Include some more difficult numbers such as 408 or 560, as well as numbers such as 562 or 149.

Main teaching activities
Whole class: Show general resource sheet 'Fraction shapes', with all but the top shape covered. Ask the children to count how many squares make up this shape. (10.) Now invite a child to colour in quickly ¹/₁₀ of the shape. Repeat this for ¹/₅ using a different colour. Now ask a child to colour in half of the shape, using a different colour again. Ask: *How many squares will you need to colour? So what fraction has been coloured? What fraction is not coloured?* (¹/₅) Repeat this for another shape.

Individual work: Ask the children to draw a row of 20 squares, and to colour it as follows: *Twice as much of one colour as another; a maximum of four colours; one-tenth one colour; one-fifth another colour.*

Review
Invite children to explain how they coloured each row of 20 squares. Ask: *Which fraction did you colour first? Was it helpful to follow the instructions in order, or not? In what order did you colour the squares? Was that a good choice? Why/why not?*

Lesson 8 (Teach and apply)

Starter
Recall: Ask the children to count together, in tens or hundreds from any two- or three-digit number that you say. Say, for example: *Count on in tens from 63. Stop. Now count back in tens.* Repeat this for other starting numbers, and then for counting in hundreds.

Main teaching activities
Whole class: Explain that today you would like the children to compare two fractions and to say which is greater and which is less. Using the OHT 'Fraction number lines', invite a child to mark on the line 0 and 1 at the two ends, and then the position of ¹/₂. Invite another child to mark on ¹/₄. If necessary, remind the children that this will come mid-way between the points of ²/₁₀ and ³/₁₀. Now ask: *Which is greater: ¹/₂ or ¹/₄? How can you tell?* Repeat this for other fractions, such as ³/₄, and ask the children to describe its position on the number line in terms of halves and wholes.

Paired work: Ask the children to work in pairs. They will need copies of general resource sheet 'Fraction number lines' and ten counters. Ask the children to take turns to take some of the counters, and to write onto the number line what fraction they have. They also mark in the fraction that is

Differentiation
Less confident learners: Decide whether to work as a group and to start each denominator family from zero.
More confident learners: Challenge these children to try fraction families such as fifths and tenths; sixths and twelfths; quarters and eighths.

Differentiation
Less confident learners: Decide whether to work as a group. Discuss what each fraction will be.
More confident learners: Challenge these children to repeat the activity using 40 squares. Ask: *Was the activity still possible? What is that?*

Differentiation

Less confident learners: Decide whether to ask the children to work in tenths.
More confident learners: Challenge these children to draw their own fraction number lines, and to work with 12 counters. This will mean that they can work in twelfths, sixths, quarters and halves.

left. They then say which fraction is the greater. Encourage the children to use equivalent fractions, such as $5/10$ and $1/2$, wherever possible.

Review
Review together some of the fractions that the children made. Discuss how these can be put into simpler, equivalent forms, where appropriate. Draw an empty number line on the board and encourage the children to place their fractions appropriately.

Lesson 9 (Teach and apply)

Starter
Recall: Repeat the Starter from Lesson 8, this time start by counting back from a three-digit number until you say *Stop*, then forward again. Repeat this, asking the children to count around the class, until you say *Stop*, then forward again.

Main teaching activities
Whole class: Show the OHT of general resource sheet 'Estimates'. Ask the children to estimate what time the first clock shows. If children respond with an answer such as 2.28, ask them to estimate to the nearest quarter of an hour (about half past 2.) Repeat this for the next clock. Now look together at the first cake and ask for an estimate of what has been eaten. Say: *So how much is left?* Repeat this for the second cake.

Show the children the metre rule and ask an individual to point to a measurement that they choose, such as 86 cm. Now ask: *Where do you think half of this measurement will be?* Repeat this for other measurements.
Paired work: Ask the children to work in pairs and give them a number line each. If using general resource sheet 'Number lines', which mark decades, the children should write in their chosen number, such as 64, and mark the point on the line. They take turns to mark a point on their number line and ask their partner to estimate what half of that number would be and to mark its position on the line.

Differentiation

Less confident learners: The children may find this activity easier if they use a metre rule with all centimetres marked.
More confident learners: When the children are confident with this activity, challenge them to work mentally, without the aid of the number line.

Review
Using the counting stick, label the ends 0 and 100, and count in tens along the stick. Now ask the children to look carefully at where you place your finger, such as at approximately 86. Invite them to say the number and then to calculate where the halfway point would come (43). Repeat this for different numbers. When the children are confident, ask one child to point to a place on the stick and the others to say the approximate number. Now ask another child to point to the approximate halfway point, and to say what the number at that point would be.

Lesson 10 (Teach and apply)

Starter
Recall: Explain that you will say a two-digit number. Ask the children to round it up or down to the nearest 10. Invite the children to say the rule for rounding - that is, 1 to 4 round down; 5 to 9 round up. Choose numbers such as 28, 63 and 55. Repeat this for rounding to the nearest 100, using three-digit numbers this time.

Main teaching activities
Whole class: Put ten counters onto the OHP. Give the children time to count these, then turn off the OHP light and move some of the counters to one side. Explain that you will turn the light back on for just a moment. Ask the children to look at the counters still in the centre of the OHP and to estimate what fraction of the original quantity that is. Switch the light on for a couple of seconds (not long enough for counting!) and then turn it off again. Ask: *What fraction do you estimate is left?* Repeat this several times, before

increasing the quantity of counters to 20 and repeating. Encourage the children to use fractions of halves and quarters.

Individual work: Provide the children with a copy of activity page 'Fraction estimates'. Ask them to estimate the fractions that they can see, and to complete the sheet.

Review

Put about 40 counters onto the OHP. It may help to count these on for the children. Now, with the light on the OHP turned off, remove some of the counters to the edge of the screen, turn the light back on for a couple of seconds and ask for an estimate of the fraction left. Repeat this several times so that you have an assessment of their ability to estimate fractions of quantities.

Differentiation

Less confident learners: There is a simpler version of the activity sheet which uses a more limited range of fractions.
More confident learners: There is an extension version of the sheet which uses more complex fractions.

Lessons 11–15

Preparation
Make an OHT of activity sheet 'Shape templates'.

You will need
Photocopiable pages
'Measures word problems' (page 94).
CD resources
Support and extension versions of 'Measures word problems', core version of 'Shape templates'; 'Carroll diagram' for each child (see General resources).

Learning objectives

Starter
● Derive and recall all addition and subtraction facts for each number to 20, sums and differences of multiples of 10 and number pairs that total 100.
● Derive and recall multiplication facts for the 2-, 3-, 4-, 5-, 6- and 10-times tables and the corresponding division facts; recognise multiples of 2, 5 or 10 up to 1000.

Main teaching activities
2006
● Solve one-step and two-step problems involving numbers, money or measures, including time, choosing and carrying out appropriate calculations.
● Relate 2D shapes and 3D solids to drawings of them; describe, visualise, classify, draw and make the shapes.
● Use a set-square to draw right angles and to identify right angles in 2D shapes; compare angles with a right angle; recognise that a straight line is equivalent to two right angles.
● Identify patterns and relationships involving numbers or shapes, and use these to solve problems.
1999
● Solve word problems involving numbers in 'real life', money and measures, using one or more steps, including finding totals and giving change, and working out which coins to pay. Explain how the problem was solved.
● Relate solid shapes to pictures of them.
● Classify and describe 3D and 2D shapes, including the hemisphere, prism, semi-circle, quadrilateral... referring to properties such as reflective symmetry, the number or shapes of faces, the number of sides/edges and vertices, whether sides/edges are the same length, whether or not angles are right angles...
● Make and describe shapes and patterns, eg explore the different shapes that can be made from four cubes.
● Identify right angles in 2D shapes and the environment.
● Recognise that a straight line is equivalent to two right angles.
● Compare angles with a right angle.
● Solve mathematical problems or puzzles, recognise simple patterns and relationships, generalise and predict. Suggest extensions by asking 'What if...?'
● Describe and extend number sequences.
● Investigate a general statement about familiar numbers or shapes by finding examples that satisfy it.

Vocabulary
problem, solution, calculate, calculation, operation, inverse, answer, method, explain, reasoning, pattern, predict, estimate, approximate, triangle, square,

Securing number facts, understanding shape — BLOCK B

rectangle, quadrilateral, pentagon, hexagon, octagon, cube, cuboid, pyramid, cone, cylinder, prism, face, edge, vertex, surface, solid, side, straight, curved, diagram, right-angled

Lesson 11 (Teach and practise)

Starter
Reason: Explain to the class that you would like them to play a bingo-type game. Ask the children to choose three numbers which are multiples of 5 and less than 100, and to write these on their whiteboards. Explain that you will then say a number that is a multiple of 5, and if the children have written the number that adds to this to make 100 they can cross it out. For example, if you say 55 and they have 45, they can cross 45 out. The first child to cross out all of their numbers, wins.

Main teaching activities
Whole class: The purpose of the activities over the next three days is to develop word problem-solving strategies within the context of measures. The children should attempt each problem using resources provided. The emphasis is on them talking through and demonstrating the problem, rather than it being a pencil and paper exercise. To this end it is suggested that you have all measuring equipment available and assess how well the children select suitable equipment.

Begin with the following problem. Write it on the board and read it together: *A small apple weighs approximately 50g. How many apples approximately would you expect to have in a 1kg bag?* Ask questions such as:
● *How many apples approximately would weigh 100g? How did you work that out?*
● *So how many would weigh 200g? 400g? 80g?*
● *How many grams are there in a kilogram?*
● *How many apples would weigh about 1kg? Why is it hard to say exactly the number of apples?* (They are a non-uniform size.)

Repeat for another problem such as: *The ball of string contains 35 metres of string. How many people can each have a length of string of 5 metres?*
Individual work: Provide each child with a copy of the activity sheet 'Measures word problems'. Ask them to write the solutions to the problems and to show their working.

Review
Use the following problem with these measures written on the board: 1500m, 1600m, 1300m. *Three children entered a race. After 30 minutes, Runner One had run 1500m, Runner Two had run 1600m and Runner Three had run 1300m.*

Ask questions such as:
● *Who ran the fastest?* (Runner Two.) *How do you know?*
● *Who travelled the least distance?* (Runner Three.)
● *What is the total distance covered?* (4400m.) *What calculation do you need to do?* (Find the total.)
● *How many ways could you have found out the answer?*
● *What is 1400 metres in kilometres?* (1.4km) *How could you check it is the correct answer?*

Differentiation
Less confident learners: Decide whether to use the support version of the activity sheet with smaller numbers.
More confident learners: There is an extension version of the sheet available which involves larger numbers.

BLOCK B

Securing number facts, understanding shape

Lesson 12 (Teach and practise)

Starter
Reason: Repeat the bingo game from Lesson 11, but ask the children to write a different set of multiples of 5 on their whiteboards.

Main teaching activities
Whole class: Explain that you will ask the children to solve a word problem. Write the following problem on the board and read it together: *A farmer ploughs up 20kg of potatoes. He fills 10 sacks equally. How much does each sack hold? Then half of the sacks go to market. How many kilograms of potatoes are left?*

Ask: *How shall we begin to solve this problem?* Elicit from the children that the problem is in a number of parts: how much each sack holds; how many sacks go to market; how many sacks of potatoes the farmer keeps; what the total weight of those sacks is. Then ask:

● *What are the important mathematical words in this problem?* (equally, how much, half)
● *What is the first calculation needed?* (20 ÷ 10 = 2.)
● *What type of measurement is the first calculation? Is it a kilogram answer or a number of sacks?*
● *What is the second calculation?* (10 ÷ 2 = 5.) *So five sacks go to market. But the question asks how many kg of potatoes are left, so we need another calculation.* (5 × 2kg = 10kg.)

Paired work: Explain that you will write some word problems on the board. Ask the children to copy the problem into their jotters and, first of all, to underline the important mathematical words. Then ask them to break the problem down into what they need to find out, and to solve it. Write on the board:

1. *Seema buys four boxes of satsumas. Each box has 50 satsumas in it. She sells 100 of her satsumas at 6p each. How much money does she make?* (£6.) *Each satsuma weighs about 50 grams. How much do the satsumas she has left weigh altogether?* (5kg.)
2. *The swimming pool is 25 metres in length. Jodie swims on Monday and Friday. On Monday she swims 8 lengths. On Friday she swims twice as far as on Monday. How far does she swim altogether?* (600m.)

Review
Review the two problems from the board. Ask: *What are the important mathematical words here? What do we need to find out? What order should we do this in? What type of number operations do we need to use?* Then ask the more confident children to set their problems to the other children. (Do check these first and choose the ones that are suitable!) Ask similar questions as before to help the children to focus upon what is important in the problem and what they need to find out.

Differentiation
Less confident learners: Decide whether to work as a group to solve these (perhaps simplified) problems. Work together, identifying the mathematical vocabulary, and what has to be calculated.
More confident learners: When everyone has finished the problems, challenge them to invent their own problem. Explain that they will be asked to set this for others to solve during the plenary and that it must have at least two parts to it.

Lesson 13 (Teach and apply)

Starter
Recall: Explain that you will ask a multiplication question from the 2-, 3-, 4-, 5-, 6- or 10-times tables. Ask the children to say the answers together. Keep the pace of this sharp to encourage rapid recall of the table facts.

Main teaching activities
Whole class: Explain that today the children will be considering general statements about shapes and finding examples that fit. Ask the children to work in groups of between four and six, with a box of shape tiles in front of them. Explain that you are going to make a statement and each group must sort out their box of shapes, discarding those that do not fit the statements. Begin by saying: *The shape I am thinking of has four straight sides. All the sides are the same length. What shape is this?* (A square.)

Now ask: *Which shapes did you discard? Which did you keep when I said my shape has four straight sides?* (Rectangles and squares.) *How would you describe a rectangle?* Make a list of suggestions on the board, such as 'has four sides', 'all sides are straight', 'opposite sides are the same length' or 'all four angles are right angles'. From the list, make a Carroll diagram using 'Has four sides', 'Does not have four sides'; 'Opposite sides are the same length', 'Opposite sides are not the same length'. Ask the children to sort shapes into this diagram. Now say: *A square is a rectangle.* Invite the children to explain whether this is true (yes) and how they know. Ask: *Are all squares rectangles?* Repeat this, this time asking the children to consider the angles of their 2D shapes: are these larger, smaller or the same as a right angle? Discuss how these properties can be used to sort shapes using a Carroll diagram. Repeat this work using 3D shapes.

Paired work: Ask the children to sort shapes onto a Carroll diagram, choosing different criteria. Ask them to find different ways to do this, so provide several copies of the general resource sheet 'Carroll diagram'.

Review
Invite children from each ability group to give examples of their sorting. Now draw a Venn diagram onto the board. Choose one of the children's examples from their Carroll diagram and as a class, label the regions of the Venn diagram, and sort the shapes onto this diagram. Discuss the properties of the shapes in each region. Repeat this for another sorting.

Lesson 14 (Teach and apply)

Starter
Reason: Repeat the Starter from Lesson 13, this time for division facts, such as: *What is 36 divided by 6? If I shared 40 biscuits between five children how many would each receive?* Keep the pace reasonably sharp, giving time for thinking.

Main teaching activities
Whole class: Explain that in this lesson the children will explore the angles of shapes using a set square. On the board draw a square and ask: *Which angles are right angles? How can we tell?* Use the board set square to check the angles. Draw an isosceles triangle. Ask: *Are any of the angles right angles? Are any angles larger/smaller than a right angle? How can we check?* Invite a child to demonstrate how to check using the board set square. Now draw a straight line and demonstrate, with the set square, how the straight line is equivalent to two right angles.

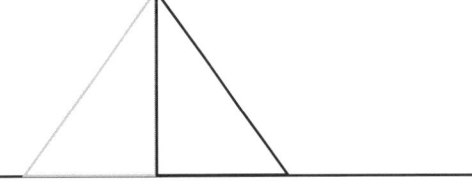

Paired work: Provide the children with set squares and a copy of general resource sheet 'Shape templates'. Ask the children to look at each shape and to check the angles. They mark each angle according to a code given on the sheet. When they have finished this, challenge them to use the set square and a ruler to draw a rectangle with sides of 8cm and 10cm.

Review
Using an OHT of the sheet 'Shape templates', review each shape and the angles. Invite children to demonstrate how they used their set square to check the angles. Discuss how they used a ruler and a set square to draw their rectangle. Ask: *Which shapes always have four right angles?*

Differentiation
Less confident learners: Work with this group, encouraging the children to use the vocabulary of shapes as they explain where shapes belong on the diagram.
More confident learners: Challenge these children to include more shapes, such as tetrahedrons.

Differentiation
Less confident learners: Encourage these children to use the vocabulary of shape in their discussions with their partner.
More confident learners: Challenge the children to draw a square, then one diagonal. Ask them to describe the two shapes they have made in terms of their angles.

Lesson 15 (Teach, apply and evaluate)

Starter

Reason: Repeat the Starters for Lessons 11 and 12, mixing together questions for both multiplication and division facts.

Main teaching activities

Whole class: Explain that in this lesson you would like the children to solve a shape problem. Begin by asking them about right-angled triangles: *How many angles do these have? How many are right angles? Why can there only be one right angle? What shape do two right angles make?*

Paired work: Ask the children to work individually but to compare what they are doing and to discuss their work together. Their task is to make two identical right-angled triangles using a ruler and set square. Now they find how many different shapes they can make by placing the triangles together edge to edge. Remind them that this means that the triangles cannot be joined just by a vertex. They record their work by sketching what they find. Remind them to make neat sketches to record their work.

Review

Discuss this activity together. Ask the children to take turns to give one of their solutions. They can draw this on the board. Ask them to describe the shape that they have made. Discuss if any of the shapes are the same; that is, if they were reflected in a mirror, or turned around, they would be the same. Ask the more confident children to explain how they know they have found all the possible solutions.

Now ask the children to discuss with their partner what they have learned in this series of lessons about shape.

Differentiation

Less confident learners: Decide whether to put the children together as a group and help them to make two identical triangles to begin.

More confident learners: Challenge the children to explain how they know, at the end of the activity, that they have found all possible solutions.

Name _____ Date _____

Fruity problems

Write the answers to these problems.

Use the empty number lines to help you.

Write a number sentence to show how you worked out your answer.

Answer

1. Claire buys 56 bananas. James buys 137 oranges.
How much fruit do they have altogether to give to Sam the giant?

Number line

_____

Answer

2. Sam the giant eats 136 mangoes and 65 peaches.
How much fruit has he eaten in total?

Number line

_____

Answer

3. The supermarket has 76 pumpkins. Sam the giant buys 48 of the
pumpkins. How many pumpkins are left in the supermarket?

Number line

_____

Answer

4. Sam the giant collects some of the pumpkin seeds to make a
necklace. He collects 93 seeds and uses 64 to make a necklace.
How many seeds does he have left?

Number line

_____

Name _____   Date _____

Finding differences

Write the answers to these calculations.

Show any jottings.

Subtraction	Jottings	Answer
1. 111 – 97		
2. 116 – 89		
3. 114 – 85		
4. 124 – 79		
5. 132 – 86		
6. 137 – 78		

Name _____   Date _____

Multiples of ten

Write the answers to these word problems.

Show your jottings.

Problem	Jottings	Answer
1. Mark gets 40p from his Grandma every week. He saves this for six weeks. How much money does he save?		
2. Jane collects six stickers every week. How many stickers has she collected after 50 weeks? How many stickers would Jane have if she collected them for a year?		
3. Summer buys 40 beads every week. She does this for three weeks. How many beads does she have?		
4. Each month Jon buys 50 football cards. How many cards does he have after four months?		

Calculate the answers to these multiplications.

Write a word problem for each calculation.

5. 7 x 30 = [ ] _____

_____

6. 9 x 40 = [ ] _____

_____

Name _____ Date _____

Checking calculations

Here is Simon's work.

Check his answers using a different calculation.

Write your calculation. Tick if Simon's answer is correct.

If his answer is wrong, put a cross and write the correct calculation.

Simon's work	Check calculation	Tick or cross	Write the correct calculation
1. 45 – 26 = 19			
2. 36 + 48 = 82			
3. 8 x 30 = 240			
4. 35 ÷ 5 = 7			
5. Half of 42 = 22			
6. Double 17 = 32			

Name _____ Date _____

Fraction estimates

Estimate and write the fractions that you can see.

Now answer these questions.

Approximately what fraction is:

110g of a kg    260ml of a litre    22 minutes of an hour

SCHOLASTIC **PHOTOCOPIABLE**

Name _____   Date _____

Measures word problems

Write the answers to these word problems.

Show your working out.

1. A large banana weighs about 200 grams. About how many large bananas weigh 1 kilogram? [   ]

   Working out

2. A bottle of cough medicine holds about 100ml of medicine. How many 5 millilitre spoonfuls can be poured from the bottle of medicine? [   ]

   Working out

3. Two rolls of carpet tape measure 37 metres and 56 metres long. What is their total length? [   ]

   What is the difference between their lengths? [   ]

   Working out

4. Dilshad went on a sponsored walk for charity. For every kilometre he walked, he earned £4. He earned £36 in total. How many kilometres did he walk? [   ]

   Working out

BLOCK B Securing number facts, understanding shape

Handling data and measures

Key aspects of learning
- Enquiry
- Problem solving
- Reasoning
- Information processing
- Social skills
- Communication

Expected prior learning
Check that children can already:
- collect and record the data needed to answer questions
- begin to organise results and solutions, and present data as block graphs and pictograms
- sort objects using lists, tables and diagrams
- explain decisions, methods and results in words, pictures or written form
- choose and use standard units (m, cm, kg, litre) to estimate and measure
- choose and use suitable instruments and equipment to measure and collect data
- recognise multiples of 10 and derive and recall the 10-times table
- read scales with numbered divisions and interpret the divisions shown
- identify and use units of time and work out time intervals
- begin to use ICT to organise and present data.

Objectives overview
The text in this diagram identifies the focus of mathematics learning within the block.

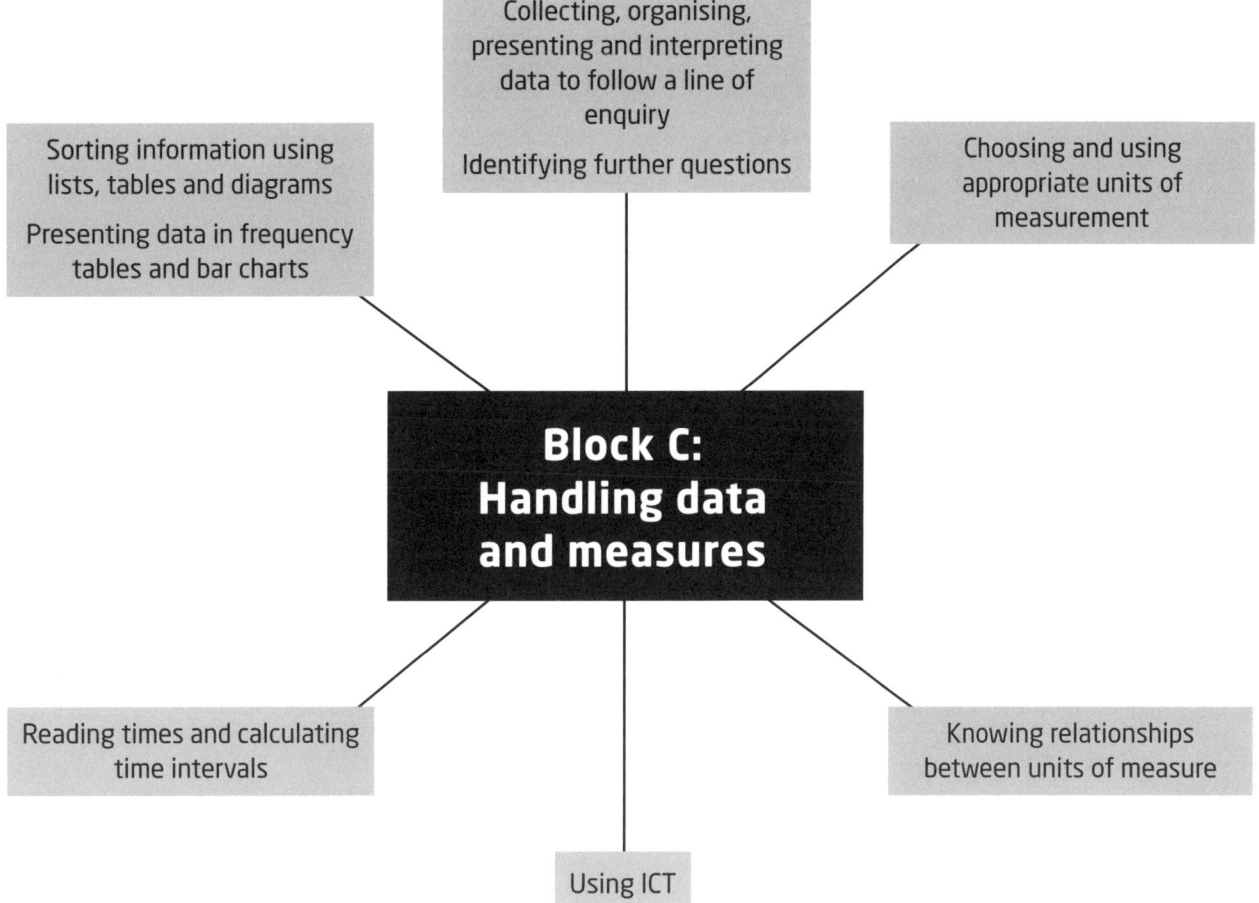

Collecting, organising, presenting and interpreting data to follow a line of enquiry

Identifying further questions

Sorting information using lists, tables and diagrams

Presenting data in frequency tables and bar charts

Choosing and using appropriate units of measurement

Block C: Handling data and measures

Reading times and calculating time intervals

Knowing relationships between units of measure

Using ICT

Unit 1 ▢ 2 weeks

Handling data and measures

BLOCK C

Handling data and measures

Speaking and listening objective
● Use talk to organise roles and actions when following a line of enquiry.

Introduction
In this ten-lesson unit, children decide on information to collect, record and organise, when sorting data onto Carroll and Venn diagrams. They work in pairs and groups for some activities, and should be encouraged to discuss who will take which roles and carry out what specific actions. Children collect data about their own measurements (height, hand span and so on). This should be kept safe for use again during the summer term.

Using and applying mathematics
● Follow a line of enquiry by deciding what information is important; make and use lists, tables and graphs to organise and interpret the information.

Lesson	Strands	Starter	Main teaching activities
1. Teach and practise	Measure	Use knowledge of number operations including doubling and halving.	Know the relationships between kilometres and metres, metres and centimetres, kilograms and grams, litres and millilitres; choose and use appropriate units to estimate, measure and record measurements.
2. Teach and practise	Measure	As for Lesson 1	**Read, to the nearest division and half-division, scales that are numbered or partially numbered; use the information to measure and draw to a suitable degree of accuracy.**
3. Teach and practise	Measure	Derive and recall multiplication facts for the 2-, 5- and 10-times tables and the corresponding division facts.	As for Lesson 2
4. Teach and apply	Measure	Read, write and order whole numbers to at least 1000.	Know the relationships between kilometres and metres, metres and centimetres, kilograms and grams, litres and millilitres; choose and use appropriate units to estimate, measure and record measurements.
5. Teach, practise and evaluate	Measure	As for Lesson 4	As for Lesson 4
6. Teach and apply	Data	Derive and recall multiplication facts for the 2-, 3-, 4-, 5-, 6- and 10-times tables and the corresponding division facts.	**Use Venn diagrams or Carroll diagrams to sort data and objects using more than one criterion.**
7. Teach and apply	Data	As for Lesson 6	As for Lesson 6
8. Teach and practise	Data	As for Lesson 6	As for Lesson 6
9. Teach and apply	Data	As for Lesson 6	Answer a question by collecting, organising and interpreting data; use tally charts, frequency tables, pictograms and bar charts to represent results and illustrate observations; use ICT to create a simple bar chart.
10. Teach, apply and evaluate	Data	As for Lesson 6	As for Lesson 9

Lessons 1-5

Preparation

Using CD page 'Number fans', make a number fan for each child; copy CD pages 'Reading scales' and 'Lines to measure' onto OHTs, or enlarge to A3; copy CD pages 'Three-digit numbers' and 'Three-digit number words' onto card to make teaching sets.

You will need

Photocopiable pages
'Measuring scales' (page 105) for each child.

CD resources
'Measuring lengths'; 'Number fans', 'Reading scales', 'Lines to measure', 'Three-digit numbers' and 'Three-digit number words' (see General resources). Interactive resource: 'Number line'.

Equipment
Metre stick marked in 10cm increments; counting stick; string (approximately 1.5m long); shape templates; measuring devices (including rulers, tape measures, etc).

Learning objectives

Starter

- Use knowledge of number operations including doubling and halving.
- Derive and recall multiplication facts for the 2-, 5- and 10-times tables and the corresponding division facts.
- Read, write and order whole numbers to at least 1000.

Main teaching activities

2006

- Know the relationships between kilometres and metres, metres and centimetres, kilograms and grams, litres and millilitres; choose and use appropriate units to estimate, measure and record measurements.
- Read to the nearest division and half-division, scales that are numbered or partially numbered; use the information to measure and draw to a suitable degree of accuracy.

1999

- Measure and compare using standard units (km, m, cm, kg, g, l, ml).
- Know the relationships between kilometres and metres, metres and centimetres, kilograms and grams, litres and millilitres.
- Begin to use decimal notation for metres and centimetres.
- Suggest suitable units and measuring equipment to estimate or measure length, mass or capacity.
- Read scales to the nearest division (labelled or unlabelled); record estimates and measurements to the nearest whole or half unit (eg 'about 3.5 kg'), or in mixed units (eg '3 m and 20 cm').
- Use a ruler to draw and measure lines to the nearest half centimeter.

Vocabulary

problem, enquiry, solution, calculate, calculation, method, explain, reasoning, reason, metric unit, standard unit, millimetre (mm), centimetre (cm), metre (m), kilogram (kg), gram (g), litre (l), millilitre (ml), ruler, tape measure, length, width, height, depth

Lesson 1 (Teach and practise)

Starter

Recall: Explain that you will say a number and that you would like the children to show you the double of that number using their number fans. Use numbers between 1 and 25.

Main teaching activities

Whole class: Write on the board '1 kilometre', and ask: *How many metres in a kilometre?* Agree that there are 1000. Ask: *So how many metres in half a kilometre?* Repeat this for the number of centimetres in metres. Ask: *How many centimetres in two metres... half a metre... two and a half metres?*

Now repeat this for millimetres in a given number of centimetres. Ask the children to look carefully at the rulers and to note that each centimetre is marked in millimetres as well. Discuss how, when measuring, the measurement will be approximate because it is not possible to be 'dead accurate'.

Group work: Invite the children to work in groups of four and to write lists of what they could measure in: kilometres; metres, centimetres and millimetres. For this activity, it is suggested that the children work in mixed ability groups. Observe how the children interact, the development of their social skills, and how well they use talk within the group situation.

BLOCK C

Handling data and measures

Review

Review the group lists; invite other groups to say whether they agree with suggestions and to explain their thinking. Explain that in the United Kingdom we still measure road distances in miles, but in Europe they use kilometres, and that a kilometre is just over half a mile in length.

Lesson 2 (Teach and practise)

Starter

Recall: Repeat the Starter for Lesson 1, this time asking for halves of even numbers between 2 and 50.

Main teaching activities

Whole class: Using the interactive resource 'Number line', label one end '0' and the other '100'. Explain that you would like the children to estimate what should go at points on the line. Point to the mid-point of the line and ask: *Which number do you think will go here?* Invite a child to write in their answer. Repeat for other positions along the line, working in approximate decades. Draw another line like the first. This time mark positions which are not quite decades. Invite the children to write in their estimates and to explain how they made their decisions.

Use a metre stick which is marked in 10cm increments. Point to positions on the metre stick, first to decade markings, then to positions that are not 'exact' decades. Ask the children to give an estimate of what the reading would be. Put up an OHT of general resource sheet 'Reading scales'. Invite the children to look at the ruler. With a whiteboard pen, put an arrow above the 15cm position and invite the children to say what the reading is, and why. Repeat for other positions. Repeat this for the dial scale, then for the litre jug. Each time, invite a child to explain how they made their reading.

Group work: Provide each child with a copy of the activity sheet 'Measuring scales'. Ask the children to look carefully at each picture and to write in their estimate of the reading from the scale. Explain that for the dial scales they can write their answer as, for example, '1kg and 500g' or '1.5kg'.

Review

Show the children a counting stick and label the ends of the stick – for example, '0' and '100'. Ask the children to estimate the number at the point where you touch the stick. At first point to the decades, then point between the decades, and challenge the children to decide what to estimate and to explain their thinking. Extend this, by re-labelling the ends of the stick '0' and '1000', so that the intermediate points are in hundreds. Ask: *What number do you think this point is? Why do you think that? Write that number on the board for me.*

Differentiation

Less confident learners: Decide whether to work with these children as a group. Use an enlarged version of the 'Measuring scales' and discuss each picture so that the children have the opportunity to take turns to make their reading.

More confident learners: When the children have finished the 'Measuring scales' sheet, ask them to work with a partner. They take turns to draw a line and mark the beginning and end of it with numbers, then mark a point on the line. Their partner estimates the reading on the scale.

Lesson 3 (Teach and practise)

Starter

Recall: Write on the board three numbers that make a multiplication or division fact in the 2-times table, such as 2, 6 and 10. Ask the children to put up their hands to give you one of the facts and write this on the board. Repeat this until all four facts have been written. Continue with other sets of three numbers for the 2-, 5- and 10-times tables. Keep the pace sharp.

Main teaching activities

Whole class: Hold up a piece of string that measures approximately 1.5 metres and ask: *How long do you think this string is?* Invite some suggestions and write these on the board. Now invite suggestions of which measuring equipment would be best for measuring the string, such as a tape measure. Invite two children to come to the front and measure the string. Ask: *How long is it? How close was this to our estimate? How will you record this?* On the board write '3 metres 50 centimetres' and explain

SCHOLASTIC

that this can be written in another way. Write '3.5 metres'. Explain that the decimal point separates the whole metres from parts of a metre, and that the '.5' represents 50cm, or half of a metre. Repeat this for the other lengths of string. Each time, invite a child to record the measurement on the board.

Now show how to measure with reasonable accuracy using a ruler. Explain that the measurement begins at the beginning of the marks on the ruler, not at the edge of the ruler. Using an OHT of general resource sheet 'Lines to measure' and a clear plastic ruler, demonstrate how to measure. Show where the ruler is placed against the line and how to read the measurement. Repeat for the other lines on the sheet, asking a child to make the measurement this time and explain, where necessary, that half way between two centimetres is .5 of a centimetre, or 5 millimetres. Write a measurement on the board, such as 5.5cm and 5cm 5mm. Record each measurement against the line using an OHT pen.

Now, using a new, blank OHT sheet, demonstrate how to draw a line of a given length, such as 6cm. Repeat this, this time inviting a child to demonstrate.

Individual work: Provide paper and pencils and ask the children to draw lines of the following lengths: 10cm, 5cm, 8cm, 13cm, 9.5cm and 3.5cm. Check that everyone is using the ruler appropriately. Now ask the children to swap their work with the person sitting next to them to check the lengths of the lines by measuring.

Paired work: Ask the children each to draw a line on a sheet of paper. They swap papers with their partners, measure the line and write its measurement, then their partner checks that they agree. Ask them to do this six times, each drawing three lines which are whole centimetres in length, and three lines which have a half centimetre in the length, such as 8.5cm.

Review

Draw a line (for example, 9.5cm in length) on a blank OHT and invite a child to measure it. Ask the other children to watch carefully and to check where the ruler is placed against the line, and what they think the length is. Ask the child to record the length on the board. Now invite the children to explain the following:
- *Which part of the ruler is not used for measuring? Why is that?*
- *Where do we place the ruler against the line?*
- *How would we record six and a half centimetres?*
- *What is another way to say .5 of a centimetre?*

Differentiation

Less confident learners: Check that the children understand how to use the ruler appropriately. If they are unsure, simplify the task by providing rulers marked just in centimetres to begin with, so that they measure and draw lines of whole centimetres in length.
More confident learners: Invite the children to draw around a shape template, such as a rectangle or pentagon. Ask them to estimate first the total length around the shape, then to measure each side and to calculate the total length.

Lesson 4 (Teach and apply)

Starter
Recall: Explain that you will hold up a card with a number on it. Ask the children to read the number aloud. Use cards from general resource sheets 'Three-digit numbers' and 'Three-digit number words', so that the children practise reading three-digit numbers and number words.

Main teaching activities
Whole class: Explain that you would like the children to solve some measurement problems. Begin by asking them to work in small groups of about four to look at the items on the tray and to decide which of these measure more than 20cm, which measure less, and which measure about 20cm. Suggest that they make a group list to show their estimates. Review the sorting that the children have done and ask: *How did you decide which items you estimated were more than/less than/about 20cm?* Encourage the children to explain their thinking. Now ask them to use rulers to check their sorting. Ask: *Did you make a good estimate?*
Paired work: Working in pairs, ask the children to begin with the first of these measuring activities, and to try the second one if time allows.
1. Choose a measuring device to estimate and measure the hand span, around the wrist, and arm length of a partner. Measure and record, to the

BLOCK C Handling data and measures

nearest half centimetre. Decide which of the partners has the wider hand span, longer arm, larger wrist.

2. Find ten things in the classroom that are estimated to be about 30cm in length. Check by measuring and record each measure to the nearest half centimetre.

Review

Ask: *Who had the longer arm? Did this match your estimate?* Ask each pair to compare their results with another pair and to order the results for hand span from widest to narrowest. Invite a group of four to write up the hand span measurements, in order, on the board and ask the other children to check that they agree with the ordering. If children have found items of about 30cm in length, invite individuals to measure one of their choices to show how close their estimate was.

Lesson 5 (Teach, practise and evaluate)

Starter

Recall: Ask the children to record on their whiteboard the three-digit numbers that you suggest. Say whether you would like the children to record their answer in numerals or words.

Main teaching activities

Whole class: Review recording to the nearest half centimetre, and how to write this as a decimal fraction of a centimetre.

Individual work: Ask the children to complete the activity sheet 'Measuring lengths' individually.

Review

Ask questions such as:
● *Which measurement do we use to measure distances in the United Kingdom? In Europe?*
● *How would you write the measurement eight and a half centimetres?*
● *How do you think you would record three and a half metres?*
● *How much, in centimetres, is 3.5 metres?*
● *How many centimetres do you think there are in 3.05 metres?* (If necessary, explain that the .05 means five centimetres, or five out of 100 centimetres.)

Ask those children that you are targetting for assessment what they have learned about measuring in this series of lessons.

Lessons 6-10

Learning objectives

Starter

● Derive and recall multiplication facts for the 2-, 3-, 4-, 5-, 6- and 10-times tables and the corresponding division facts.

Main teaching activities

2006

● Use Venn diagrams or Carroll diagrams to sort data and objects using more than one criterion.
● Answer a question by collecting, organising and interpreting data; use tally charts, frequency tables, pictograms and bar charts to represent results and illustrate observations; use ICT to create a simple bar chart.

1999

● Solve a given problem by organising and interpreting numerical data in Venn and Carroll diagrams (two criteria).
● Solve a given problem by organising and interpreting numerical data in

---

Differentiation

Less confident learners: Decide whether to work as a group at this activity, and check the children's measuring skills for reasonable accuracy.
More confident learners: Encourage the children to work quickly but accurately, and to complete both activities.

Differentiation

The activity sheet is not differentiated so you may wish to work with the less confident children as a group.

Preparation

Copy sets of 0-9 digit cards using CD page 'Numeral cards 0-20'.

You will need
CD resources
'Multiplication facts for 2-, 5- and 10-times tables' and 'Numeral cards 0-20' (see General resources).
Equipment
Sets of 2D shapes; Blu-Tack; rulers marked in mm; measuring tapes; metre sticks; database (eg NNS database); a computer for each group.

simple lists, tables and graphs, eg simple frequency tables; pictograms; bar charts; Venn and Carroll diagrams (one criterion).

Vocabulary
problem, enquiry, solution, calculate, calculation, method, explain, reasoning, reason, predict, collect, organise, compare, sort, classify, represent, interpret, effect, information, data, survey, table, frequency table, block graph, bar chart, Carroll diagram, Venn diagram, label, title

Lesson 6 (Teach and apply)

Starter
Recall: Explain that you will hold up a multiplication fact for the 2-, 5- or 10-times table. Ask the children to say the answer. Repeat this, this time asking a division fact that is derived from the multiplication. For example, for 5 × 2 you might ask: *What is 10 divided by 2?* Keep the pace sharp.

Main teaching activities
Whole class: Explain that today the children will learn how to make a simple Carroll diagram. On the board draw a two-region Carroll diagram and write the title above it: 'All even numbers from 20 to 40', with regions labelled 'even' and 'not even'. Ask: *What numbers will go in the 'even' box? What will go into the 'not even' box?* Write in the suggested numbers: 20, 22, 24... 40 in the 'even' box and 21, 23... 39 in the 'not even' box.

Repeat this for another simple Carroll diagram for sorting, for example: 'All numbers with a 9 as a digit from 1 to 30', so that 9, 19, 29 are in the '9 digit' region and the 'not 9 digit' region contains the other numbers. Explain that 'not' will always be included in the heading for the second region in a Carroll diagram.

Group work: Ask the children to work in pairs. They will need two sets of 0–9 digit cards prepared using general resource sheet 'Numeral cards 0–20'. Ask them to draw a two-region Carroll diagram on squared paper, with the title 'Multiples of 2, 5 and 10'. Then they head one region 'even' and the other 'not even'. The pair takes turns to take two cards and to make a TU number which they then sort onto the Carroll diagram. Ask the children to keep a list of numbers which will not fit. Remind them that they can choose the ordering of their two digits.

Differentiation
Less confident learners: Work with this group. The activity can be undertaken as a group task, and the recording completed on a large sheet of paper, with children taking turns to decide where to write their number.
More confident learners: Challenge these children to choose three cards each time and to make three-digit numbers to sort into the diagram.

Review
Invite the children to discuss what they have done and to give examples of numbers that would not fit. Ask: *Why would these numbers not fit on your chart?* Encourage them to use vocabulary such as 'multiple': 'These numbers are not a multiple of 2, 5 or 10'. More confident children may be able to explain why: 'Multiples of 2 have an even units digit; multiples of 5 have a 5 or 0 units digit, and multiples of 10 have a 0 units digit'.

Lesson 7 (Teach and apply)

Starter
Recall: Repeat the Starter for Lesson 6, this time for 3-times table facts.

Main teaching activities
Whole class: On the board draw a two-region Carroll diagram, write in the title 'Shapes' and the region headings of 'squares' and 'not squares'. Ask a child to pick up a shape from the box of 2D shapes and ask: *Where will this shape fit?* Fix the shape to the diagram using Blu-Tack. Repeat this for other shapes. Discuss how all the squares are together, and the other shapes, which are not squares, are together.
Paired work: Provide the children with sets of mixed shapes. Ask them to decide how to sort these onto a Carroll diagram. They could sort them into four different two-region diagrams, for example: 'triangles' and 'not

BLOCK C

Handling data and measures

Differentiation

Less confident learners: Decide whether to limit the range of shapes for these children to, for example, circles, triangles, rectangles and pentagons.
More confident learners: Challenge the children to draw six different Carroll diagrams.

triangles'; 'has 4 sides', 'does not have 4 sides' and so on. Suggest that they begin by considering the properties of the shapes in their box and how these could be sorted.

Review

Invite the children to make up their own regions for a Carroll diagram and to sort their shapes accordingly.

Lesson 8 (Teach and practise)

Starter

Recall and derive: Explain that you will ask a multiplication fact from the 4-times table. Ask the children to give the answer, and then to find a corresponding division fact. For example, for 6 × 4 the children give the answer of 24, then suggest a division fact such as 24 ÷ 4 = 6 or 24 ÷ 6 = 4. If children are unsure, write the facts on the board with relevant division facts beside the multiplication one.

Main teaching activities

Group work: Introduce the two-region Venn diagram with the region headings 'Multiples of 3' and 'Multiples of 4'.

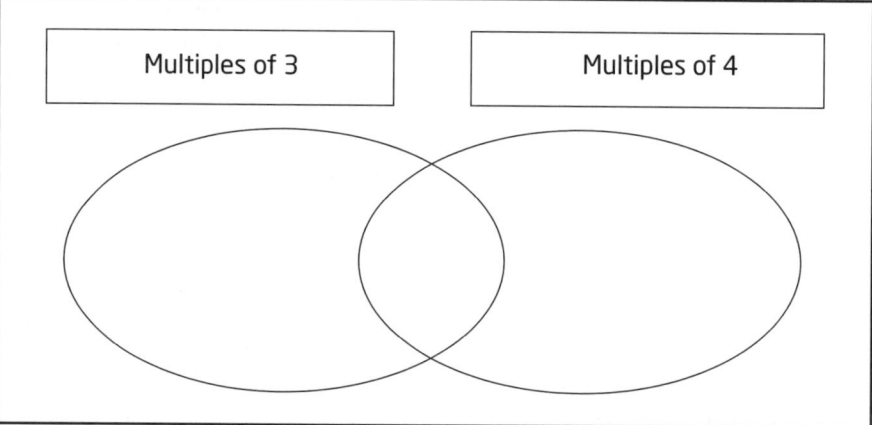

Discuss where the multiples of 3 go, where the multiples of 4 go, and what will go into the overlapping section. (The intersection contains numbers which are both multiples of 3 and of 4.) Then ask the children to sort the numbers from 1 to 50 onto the Venn diagram. Ask: *Where does the number 15 fit? Why? Where does 26 fit? Why?* Discuss how numbers that will not fit into either circle go into the outer area. Repeat this for another two-region Venn diagram, with the criteria 'Even numbers' and 'Multiples of 3', again for the numbers 1 to 50.
Paired work: Ask the children to work in pairs. They draw their own two-region Venn diagram and sort the numbers 1 to 50 for the criteria 'Multiples of 2' and 'Multiples of 3'. Then they make another Venn diagram choosing their own two criteria.

Review

Invite the more confident children to show their own Venn diagram and explain why they chose their criteria, and how they made their decisions on placing the numbers. Draw another Venn diagram, with the criteria 'Greater than 15' and 'Multiples of 4'. Ask the children to help to place the numbers 1 to 30 onto the diagram. Ask, for example: *Where does 6 go? Where does 28 fit? What about 17?* Ask for an explanation of which numbers would fit in the intersection.

Differentiation

Less confident learners: Decide whether to work with these children as a group. Encourage them to explain for each number that is placed why it belongs in its specific place.
More confident learners: Ask the children to be prepared to show their own Venn diagram and explain why they chose their criteria, and how they made their decisions on placing the numbers.

Lesson 9 (Teach and apply)

Starter

Recall: Repeat the Starter from Lesson 6, this time for the 6-times table facts and division facts.

Main teaching activities

Whole class: Explain that today the children will learn how to make a simple frequency table. On the board, write a list of favourite pets which the children suggest, such as cats, dogs, and so on. Now ask the children to vote for their favourite pet. Explain that they can have just one vote each. Count how many votes each pet receives and add this information to the frequency table.

Now ask questions about the frequency table data, such as: *Which is the most/least popular pet? How can you tell? Which had fewer than/more than ___ votes? How would the table change if you all had two votes? Who might find it useful to know which are the children's favourite pets? What are the three most popular choices?*

Group work: Ask the children to work in mixed-ability groups of six to eight. Explain that each group will have the task of making a frequency table for data for their group, working on large sheets of sugar paper. Ask the children to decide what they would like to find out and to agree on the questions they need to ask and how they will record the responses. If they need help with ideas for information gathering they could ask:
- the number of brothers and sisters in each family in the group
- the number of letters in first names in family members
- favourite sports
- favourite TV shows.

Each group should prepare a short presentation of their findings for the others to see, and to ask and answer questions on the data.

Review

Invite one of the groups to explain what information the children decided to collect, and the criteria that they wrote for collecting the information. Show the information to the class. Invite the children to ask questions about the information. If they are hesitant, model the questions, such as: *How many more ___ than ___ were there? Which was most/least popular? What if there were three more ___ in ___ . Which would be the most/least popular then?* Repeat this for the other groups.

Lesson 10 (Teach, apply and evaluate)

Starter

Recall: Explain that today the children will be asked for multiplication and division facts from the 2-, 3-, 4-, 5-, 6- and 10-times tables. Keep the pace sharp. Decide whether to put the class into teams and for the teams to take turns in answering the questions. Keep a score so, for example, the first team to win 10 points is the winning team.

Main teaching activities

Whole class: Explain to the children that today they will enter data into a database. Explain that you would like the children to collect the following information which you write on the board: their height, shoe size, length of foot, hand span. Ask: *How do you think you will collect this information? What sort of recording will you need to do? Can you find these things out working alone? Why not?* Check that the children understand that they will need to work cooperatively, especially to, for example, measure their heights. Ask: *What sort of measuring equipment will you need?* Discuss which equipment will be suitable for which measurements, and why.

Group work: Ask the children to work in mixed ability groups of four to six children. Explain that the first thing they should do is to plan how they will

Differentiation

With mixed-ability groups, ensure that the less confident children are encouraged by the others to take an active part. The more confident children may try to take over the activity and this should be discouraged. When working as a mixed-ability group, this is the opportunity for children to develop their social skills as well as their mathematical understanding.

BLOCK C

Handling data and measures

work; next they should decide how they will collect the information. For measurements that need to be taken, ask the children to estimate before they begin measuring.

As the children work, observe how the children in each group organise themselves, and who takes which role and how that is arranged. Demonstrate how to enter data into the database by choosing one group's data set for 'height'. Agree which child's data will be entered for each colour. Ask for suggestions for how the data should be titled and demonstrate how to enter this. Show how to make a bar chart from the data.

Now ask each group to enter their data into the computer for their heights. Remind the children to keep a record of which colour refers to which child.

Review

Choose one of the databases produced by the groups and show this to the whole class. Ask questions such as:
- *Which child is tallest/shortest?*
- *How many children are shorter/taller than 125cm? How do you know?*
- *What is the difference in heights between the tallest and shortest child?*
- *How many children have heights between 120cm and 130cm? How did you work this out?*

Over time, provide opportunities for each group to make another database from their data and as a group to interrogate their database and keep a written record of the questions they asked and their answers.

Ask each child to make a prediction about their own measurements and how much they think these will alter by the summer term. All of this work needs to be kept safe for the summer term.

Invite those children that you are targetting for assessment to say what they have learned about handling data in this series of lessons.

Name _____   Date _____

Measuring scales

Look at the arrows on these scales.

Write in your estimate of the measurement in the first answer box.

Write what length is shown between the arrows in the second answer box.

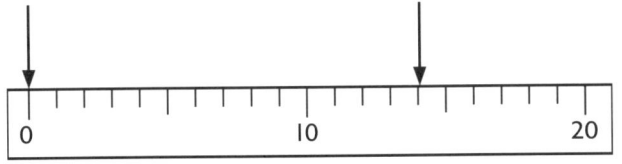

1. [cm] [cm]

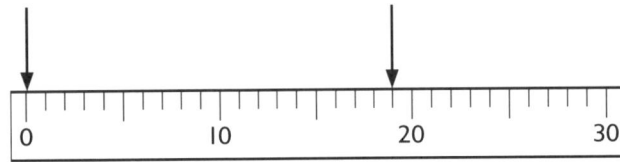

2. [cm] [cm]

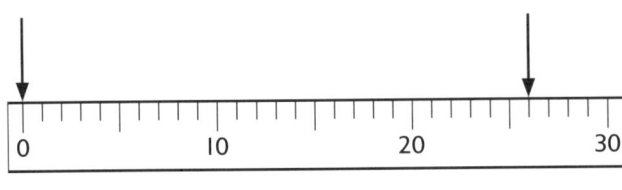

3. [cm] [cm]

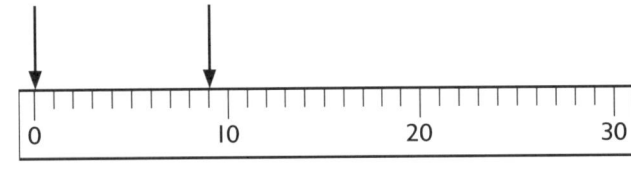

4. [cm] [cm]

Write the weight shown on each scale.

5. 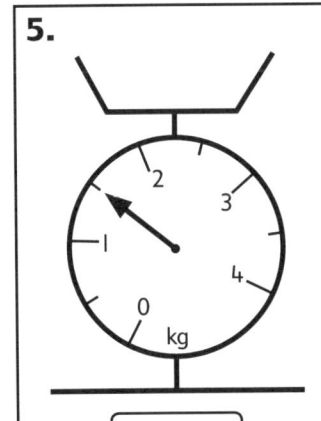	**6.** 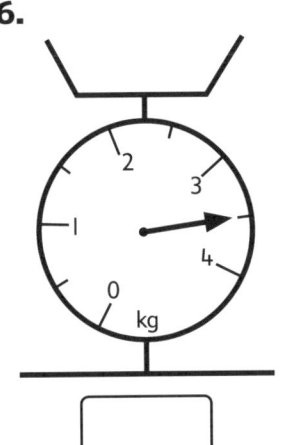	**7.** 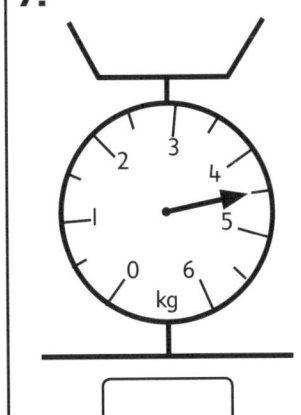	**8.** 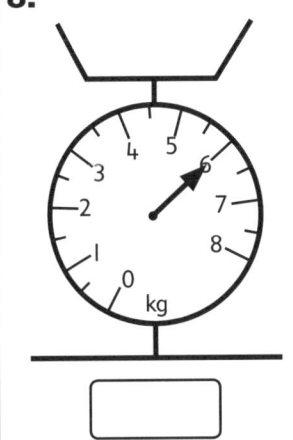
[ ]	[ ]	[ ]	[ ]

Write how much water is in each jug.

9. 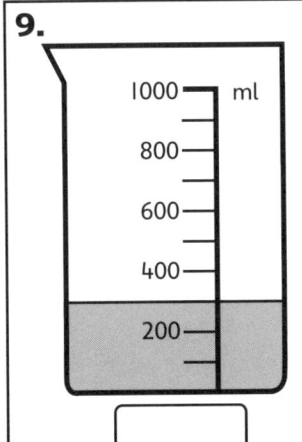	**10.** 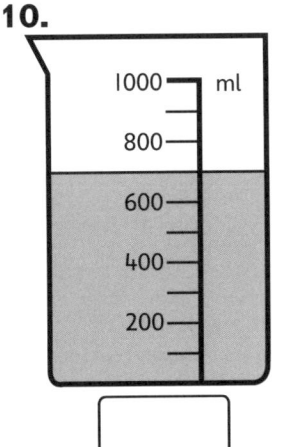	**11.** 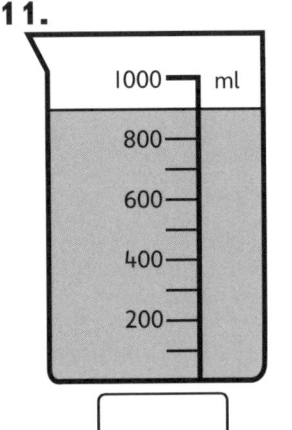	**12.** 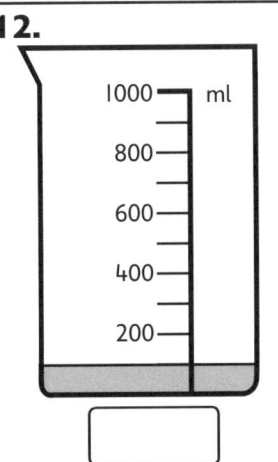
[ ]	[ ]	[ ]	[ ]

BLOCK C

Handling data and measures

Handling data and measures

Speaking and listening objective
- Identify the presentational features used to communicate the main points.

Introduction
In this ten-lesson unit, children report on their work, making their communication succinct and clear. They develop their skills in handling data. They build on their skills in measuring, whilst concentrating on mass for this unit. They continue to develop their skills in telling the time and calculate intervals of time. They make Venn and Carroll diagrams, and use these to sort numbers, including multiples. They make bar charts of data that they have collected themselves.

Using and applying mathematics
- Follow a line of enquiry by deciding what information is important; make and use lists, tables and graphs to organise and interpret the information.

Lesson	Strand	Starter	Main teaching activities
1. Review	Measure	Derive and recall multiplication facts for the 2-, 3-, 4-, 5-, 6- and 10-times tables and the corresponding division facts; recognise multiples of 2, 5 or 10 up to 1000.	Know the relationships between kilometres and metres, metres and centimetres, kilograms and grams, litres and millilitres; choose and use appropriate units to estimate, measure and record measurements.
2. Teach and apply	Measure	As for Lesson 1	**Read, to the nearest division and half-division, scales that are numbered or partially numbered; use the information to measure and draw to a suitable degree of accuracy.**
3. Teach and apply	Measure	As for Lesson 1	As for Lesson 2
4. Teach and apply	Measure	**Partition three-digit numbers into multiples of 100, 10 and 1 in different ways.**	Read the time on a 12-hour digital clock and to the nearest 5 minutes on an analogue clock; calculate time intervals and find start or end times for a given time interval.
5. Teach, apply and evaluate	Measure Data	As for Lesson 4	• Read the time on a 12-hour digital clock and to the nearest 5 minutes on an analogue clock; calculate time intervals and find start or end times for a given time interval. • Answer a question by collecting, organising and interpreting data; use tally charts, frequency tables, pictograms and bar charts to represent results and illustrate observations; use ICT to create a simple bar chart.
6. Review	Data	As for Lesson 4	**Use Venn diagrams or Carroll diagrams to sort data and objects using more than one criterion.**
7. Teach and apply	Data	As for Lesson 4	Answer a question by collecting, organising and interpreting data; use tally charts, frequency tables, pictograms and bar charts to represent results and illustrate observations; use ICT to create a simple bar chart.
8. Teach and practise	Data	As for Lesson 4	As for Lesson 7
9. Teach and practise	Data	As for Lesson 4	As for Lesson 7
10. Teach, apply and evaluate	Data	Derive and recall multiplication facts for the 2-, 3-, 4-, 5-, 6- and 10-times tables and the corresponding division facts; recognise multiples of 2, 5 or 10 up to 1000.	**Use Venn diagrams or Carroll diagrams to sort data and objects using more than one criterion.**

Unit 2 ▢ 2 weeks

Lessons 1-5

Preparation
Set the scale for the ITP Thermometer to read in ones from -10°C to 40°C; copy three sets of digit cards 0-9 using CD page 'Numeral cards 0-20'.

You will need
Photocopiable pages
'Weighing scales' (page 116) and 'Thermometers' (page 117) for each child.
CD resources
Support and extension versions of 'Weighing scales' and 'Thermometers'; core versions of 'Beat the clock' and 'Passing time'; 'Numeral cards 0-20' (see General resources). ITP Thermometer.
Equipment
Various types of weighing instruments including pan balances and weights, dial scales, and digital scales; strong paper bag; strong bags containing, for example, potatoes, which weigh amounts such as 500g, 1kg, 1.5kg... up to 4kg; NNS animation for mass; dial scale; analogue teaching clock; 12-hour digital clock; computer and graph program.

Learning objectives

Starter
● Derive and recall multiplication facts for the 2-, 3-, 4-, 5-, 6- and 10-times tables and the corresponding division facts; recognise multiples of 2, 5 or 10 up to 1000.
● Partition three-digit numbers into multiples of one hundred, ten and one in different ways.

Main teaching activities
2006
● Know the relationships between kilometres and metres, metres and centimetres, kilograms and grams, litres and millilitres; choose and use appropriate units to estimate, measure and record measurements.
● Read, to the nearest division and half-division, scales that are numbered or partially numbered; use the information to measure and draw to a suitable degree of accuracy.
● Read the time on a 12-hour digital clock and to the nearest five minutes on an analogue clock; calculate time intervals and find start or end times for a given time interval.
● Answer a question by collecting, organising and interpreting data; use tally charts, frequency tables, pictograms and bar charts to represent results and illustrate observations; use ICT to create a simple bar chart.
1999
● Measure and compare using standard units (km, m, cm, kg, g, l, ml).
● Know the relationships between kilometres and metres, metres and centimetres, kilograms and grams, litres and millilitres.
● Begin to use decimal notation for metres and centimetres.
● Suggest suitable units and measuring equipment to estimate or measure length, mass or capacity.
● Read scales to the nearest division (labelled or unlabelled); record estimates and measurements to the nearest whole or half unit (eg 'about 3.5 kg'), or in mixed units (eg '3 m and 20 cm').
● Use a ruler to draw and measure lines to the nearest half centimeter.
● Read the time to 5 minutes on an analogue clock and 12-hour digital clock; use the notation 9:40.
● Solve a given problem by organising and interpreting numerical data in simple lists, tables and graphs, eg simple frequency tables; pictograms; bar charts; Venn and Carroll diagrams (one criterion).

Vocabulary
problem, enquiry, solution, calculate, calculation, method, explain, reasoning, reason, predict, pattern, relationship, collect, organise, compare, sort, classify, represent, interpret, effect, bar chart, metric unit, standard unit, kilogram (kg), gram (g), balance, scales, time, clock, minute, hour, before, after, start time, end time, how long...?

Lesson 1 (Review)

Starter
Reason: Explain that you will say a number between 1 and 19. Ask the children to respond by saying its double. Keep the pace of this sharp.

Main teaching activities
Whole class: Use bags of potatoes or similar to estimate with the children weights of more than 1kg. Let the children feel a 1kg bag of sugar to get a good idea first. Show them how to express 1½kg as 1.5kg. Write on the

BLOCK C

Handling data and measures

board: 1kg 500g = 1½kg = 1.5kg. Repeat with other examples involving 500g, such as 2500g, 5500g, and so on.

Group work: Ask the children to work in groups of four. They begin at their own table, pass the bag of potatoes around the group to estimate its weight, then check by weighing. They record the weight in grams, in kilograms and grams, and as a decimal fraction of a kilogram. For example, for 2500g they write 2500g, 2kg 500g, 2.5kg. On your signal, the groups move to a different table and repeat this activity, until every group has estimated, weighed and written their results for each bag of potatoes.

Review
On the board draw this spidergram:

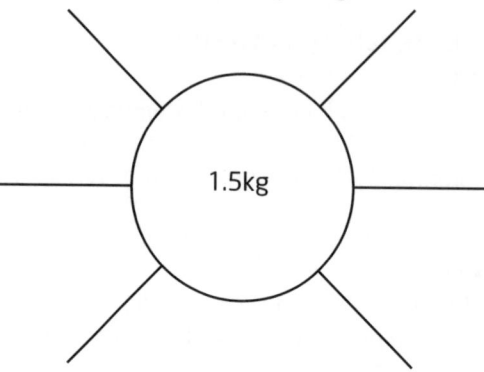

Ask the children: *How many different ways can I write 1.5kg?* (In words, as 'g', as a fraction, and so on.) Write all their ideas onto the diagram, discussing the ease/complexity of each one. Ask the children to decide which one they prefer and which they have seen used most frequently. Now review the estimates, weights and ways in which the potato weights were recorded. Invite a child to record each bag of potatoes' weight on the board as a decimal fraction of a kilogram. Now challenge the children to put these in weight order, beginning with the lightest. If the more confident children have totalled the weights of the potatoes, review this as a group. Ask: *If all the potatoes were in one sack, do you think you could lift them? Would this be sensible?* (Probably not, because of their weight.) Ask: *What measuring instruments would you use to find the weight of an orange... the weight of a person?*

Differentiation
Less confident learners: If the children need help with the recording of decimal fractions, move around the room with this group, offering support with estimating, weighing and recording.
More confident learners: Challenge the children to work out the total of the weight of all of the potatoes.

Lesson 2 (Teach and apply)

Starter
Reason: Repeat the Starter for Lesson 1, this time asking for halves of even numbers from 2 to 40. Keep the pace sharp.

Main teaching activities
Whole class: Explain that today is about being able to weigh accurately and read from different types of scales. Use the NNS animation to show the children how to read a kitchen scale accurately. Ask: *What happens when the weights are increased? What happens if you take some weight away?* Show the class how to adjust the reading arrow to zero on a dial scale. Use the NNS animation to show adding 50g and 50g. Ask: *In what other ways could you make 100g?*

Individual work: Provide a copy of the activity sheet 'Weighing scales' for the children to complete. They are asked to draw in the reading arrow on the dial scales for given weights, then to round the readings on more scales to the nearest 100g.

Differentiation
Less confident learners: There is a support version of the sheet which uses 10g intervals and rounding to the nearest 10g.
More confident learners: There is an extension version of the sheet with more challenging readings and roundings.

Review
Review the core version of 'Weighing scales' together. Ask: *Where will the reading arrow point for ___ weight? How would you round this weight to the nearest 100g?*

Lesson 3 (Teach and apply)

Starter

Reason: Repeat the Starters for Lessons 1 and 2, mixing doubling and halving questions. Extend the range of numbers to up to 100.

Main teaching activities

Whole class: Reveal the ITP Thermometer. Ask: *What is the smallest temperature that can be read with this thermometer? What is the largest temperature?* If children are unsure about negative numbers, explain that it is possible to count back beyond zero. Practise this together, as you point to each division on the scale. Now set the liquid in the thermometer to 10°C and ask: *What is the reading on the thermometer? How do you know that?* Repeat for other readings, such as 20°C, 15°C, -5°C, and so on. Now re-set the thermometer scale to read in steps of 2°C. Ask: *What does each division on the scale read now? How did you work that out?* Ask the children to read other temperatures that you set, including negative ones. Now ask: *If the temperature is -2°C when you get up and 10°C by lunchtime, how much has the temperature increased?* Discuss how to find the answer. Model the problem using the on-screen thermometer, and count up from -2°C.

Individual work: Provide each child with a copy of activity sheet 'Thermometers'. Ask the children to write the temperatures marked on the thermometers and then to solve the temperature problems.

Review

Ask individual children from each ability group to explain how they solved one of the word problems. Ask questions such as: *How did you find the difference? Did anyone use a different method? Which method do you think was better? Why do you think that?*

Differentiation

Less confident learners: Decide whether to provide the support version of the sheet with thermometers marked with temperatures above zero and scales marked in 1°C increments.
More confident learners: There is an extension version of the sheet with temperatures marked in 2°C and 5°C increments.

Lesson 4 (Teach and apply)

Starter

Recall: Shuffle the three sets of numeral cards. Take three cards and ask a child to make a three-digit number from the numerals and write it on the board as numerals. Invite the children to write this number in words on their whiteboards and to hold these up for you to see when you say *Show me*. Invite another child to make another three-digit number from the original cards and repeat until all six possible numbers have been made, written on the board by you in numerals and by the children as words. (For example, for 1, 2, 3: 123; 132; 213; 231; 312; 321.) Repeat for another set of three digits.

Main teaching activities

Whole class: The main emphasis for this lesson is to know the parts that make up a full day and how we tend to mark these times collectively in most parts of Britain. You may wish to pursue cross-curricular links with cultural expectations – for example, use of prayer punctuating the day for Muslims. Gather assessment information by asking questions such as:

● *How many hours does the average person sleep every night?* (8 hours.)
● *What time do you go to bed/get up each day?*
● *What kinds of things tend to happen before lunch?* (Going to school, breakfast, walking the dog...)
● *What kinds of things happen after lunch?* (People relax after eating...)
  Relate each of these events to time, before inviting a child to set the hands on the analogue clock to show that time, whilst another child writes the time in digital format on the board. Explain about 'am' (*ante meridian* or before noon) and 'pm' (*post meridian* or after noon). Write 'am' and 'pm' on the board and say: *am begins at 12 o'clock midnight; pm begins at 12 o'clock noon.* Suggest events during the day and ask for an approximate time for these and whether these will be 'am' or 'pm' events, such as: *At what time do we have morning/afternoon break? At what time do you go home from*

BLOCK C

Handling data and measures

▪SCHOLASTIC

school? Record these times as digital time on the board. Discuss how we write, for example 3:40, but say *twenty to four.* Repeat this for other 'past the hour times', showing each one on an analogue clock, saying it as a 'past the hour' time, and recording it digitally.

Group work: This is in two distinct parts. Provide copies of the activity sheet 'Beat the clock'. The children have ten minutes to see how many of the digital times they can write on the analogue clock face, and vice versa. Then provide the activity sheet 'Passing time' and ask the children to work in pairs to discuss the times and what they did yesterday.

Review

Discuss what the children have done since they woke up today. Ask:
● *What were you doing at 8.30am?*
● *What did you do next?*
● *Do you think you will be doing the same thing at 8.30am tomorrow?*

On the board write 'am', 'pm', 'yesterday', 'today' and 'tomorrow' and invite the children to suggest sentences which use this vocabulary. Practise reading the times from a large clock face for the following times: 2.20, 4.35, 5.55, 10.15. Assess whether most of the children are able to use past and to the hour accurately. Ask the children to time their journey to school by noting the time when they leave home and again when they arrive at school. This information will be needed for Lesson 5.

Lesson 5 (Teach, apply and evaluate)

Starter
Recall: Repeat the Starter for Lesson 4, using different sets of three digits.

Main teaching activities
Whole class: Within a small group, ask the children to compare the time taken for their journey to school. Explain that they must calculate the difference between the time they left home and the time they arrived at school. Ask them to check their neighbour's calculation. Provide strips of squared paper and ask the children to count one square for each minute that it took them to reach school. They cut off the rest of the paper. So, if it took them 20 minutes to reach school their piece of paper will be 20cm in length. Within small groups they compare their strips and order them for length and thus for time taken.

Now discuss as a whole class how the longer the strip of paper, the more time it took to get to school. Make a class bar chart with the strips, and ask the children to stick their strips onto the chart in order of length (eg shortest first). Agree on a title for the bar chart and discuss how the axes should be labelled, then label them. Alternatively, use a computer graphing program and input the data from the children's strips.

Individual work: Write some questions about the class bar graph onto the board, such as:
● *Who had the journey that took the most/least time?*
● *What is the difference between the shortest/longest journey times?*
● *How many children take longer than ten minutes to get to school?*
Ask the children to work in mixed ability groups to answer these questions.

Review
Invite individual children to give answers to the questions on the board. Ask: *How did Meg's answer help you to understand?* Ask further questions of the bar chart such as: *Do the children with the shorter journey time walk to school? How can we find this out?* Then ask: *Was this a good way to find the answer? How could we improve this?*

Invite the children to discuss in pairs what they have learned about measuring in this series of lessons.

Differentiation
Less confident learners: Decide whether to concentrate on telling the time in five-minute intervals. The activity sheet 'Beat the clock' can be completed as a group activity, using teaching analogue and digital clocks for setting the hands or the digits for each question. Encourage the children to say the time for each question.
More confident learners: If these children finish more quickly, challenge them to write what they do on a typical Saturday, with the times written as 'am' or 'pm'.

Differentiation
The children are working in mixed ability groups. Check that the less confident children are making an appropriate contribution in their group and that the more confident children do not dominate the group.

Lessons 6-10

Preparation
Enlarge CD pages 'Data handling vocabulary' and 'Pencils' to A3; copy CD page 'Three-digit numbers' onto card and cut up to make a teaching set.

You will need
CD resources
Core, support and extension versions of 'Footwear fun'; 'Data handling vocabulary', 'Venn diagrams', 'Three-digit numbers', 'Bar chart', 'Pencils' and 'Carroll diagrams' (see General resources).
Equipment
Sticky notes.

Learning objectives

Starter
● Partition three-digit numbers into multiples of 100, 10 and 1 in different ways.
● Derive and recall multiplication facts for the 2-, 3-, 4-, 5-, 6- and 10-times tables and the corresponding division facts; recognise multiples of 2, 5 or 10 up to 1000.

Main teaching activities
2006
● Use Venn diagrams or Carroll diagrams to sort data and objects using more than one criterion.
● Answer a question by collecting, organising and interpreting data; use tally charts, frequency tables, pictograms and bar charts to represent results and illustrate observations; use ICT to create a simple bar chart.
1999
● Solve a given problem by organising and interpreting numerical data in Venn and Carroll diagrams (two criteria).
● Solve a given problem by organising and interpreting numerical data in simple lists, tables and graphs, eg simple frequency tables; pictograms; bar charts; Venn and Carroll diagrams (one criterion).

Vocabulary
problem, enquiry, solution, calculate, calculation, method, explain, reasoning, reason, predict, pattern, relationship, collect, organise, compare, sort, classify, represent, interpret, effect, information, data, survey, table, frequency table, block graph, bar chart, Carroll diagram, Venn diagram, axis, axes, horizontal axis, vertical axis, label, title, scale, interval, division, how often?, how frequently?, more/less, most/least, most/least popular, most/least frequent, greatest/least value

Lesson 6 (Review)

Starter
Recall: Explain that you will write a number on the board using figures. Ask the children to read the number aloud when you hold up your hand. The children will read the number as you write, so hold up your hand as soon as you have finished writing in order to check that they read quickly and accurately. Write numbers such as 123, 560, 807, 900 and 999. Repeat, this time writing different, but similar, numbers as words.

Main teaching activities
Whole class: Ask the children what they can remember about handling data and write specific data-handling vocabulary that the children use on the board. There is a lot of new vocabulary this week, so display the A3 enlargement of general resource sheet 'Data handling vocabulary' for the children to refer to during the week. Make a point of sharing the vocabulary and highlighting words as you use them.

Introduce the idea of Venn diagrams by sketching the diagram shown here. Ask the boys quickly to sort the girls into the two groups of 'Have ponytails' and 'Do not have ponytails', and write this information in the diagram. Discuss which piece of sorted information goes where, and how this can be recorded by, for example, drawing a stick picture for each girl, or by putting their initials into the appropriate place on the diagram.

Collect data from the class for the following criteria and make

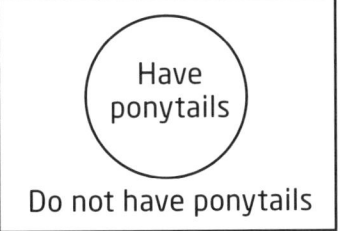

a Venn diagram for each result. (Note: It is quicker to give each child a sticky note upon which they write their initials. Then, when a question is asked, they place their sticky note in the correct place on the diagram.)

- *Who has/does not have any red on their clothes?*
- *Who ate/did not eat toast this morning?*
- *Who walked/did not walk to school today?*
- *Who likes/dislikes swimming?*

Now choose one of the Venn diagrams and ask: *How many children like/ dislike swimming? How can you tell? How many girls like swimming? Is that easy to find out? Why/Why not?*

Ask the children to sit in a circle and remove one shoe. The children place their shoe in front of them so everyone can see it. Invite the class to guess your criterion/rule for choosing your group of shoes. As you select shoes place them in the centre of the circle, encouraging the children to look closely at them but also to look at the ones you don't pick. Here are some suggestions for criteria:

- The shoes all have laces/buckles/Velcro.
- The shoes all have a bit of red/blue/white.
- The shoes all belong to girls/boys.
- The shoes are all types of trainer.
- The shoes are made from patent/suede/other.
- The shoes are all turned on their side/upside down.

Once you have given the children plenty of ideas for sorting the shoes, ask for a volunteer to make a group with their own sorting criteria. (Individuals may need some whispered encouragement for the first few tries!)

Group work: Ask the children to work in groups of about four. Give each child a copy of the general resource sheet 'Venn diagrams'. Encourage them to fill in the labels according to their own sort criteria and to write the initials of the children to whom the shoe belongs. Ask them to discuss how they could sort their shoes into the two sets of 'Have ___' and 'Do not have ___'. Challenge the children to find four different ways of sorting their shoes.

Review

Discuss the interesting criteria that children have come up with. Invite each group to show, by copying their Venn diagram on the board, one of their ways of sorting. Invite the rest of the class to ask questions about the sorting, such as: *How many had ___? Was this everyone in your group? Can you tell whether the person was male or female? How? Why not?*

If the more confident children have undertaken the two-region challenge, decide whether to discuss their work now during the Review, or whether to find another time just for this group. This decision will depend upon the confidence of the other children in the class with making and using Venn diagrams.

Lesson 7 (Teach and apply)

Starter

Recall: Repeat the Starter for Lesson 6, but this time, ask the children to write down the numbers that you say, firstly as figures, then as words. Include numbers such as 608 and 990, so that the children think about the position of the zero digit and its place value. Include some four-digit numbers, such as 1051 and 1003, to challenge the more able.

Main teaching activities

Whole class: Ask the children how many different types of footwear they can think of and make a list, such as: Wellingtons, slippers, tap dancing shoes, riding boots, ballroom dancing shoes, ice skates, walking boots, 'best shoes', trainers, flip flops, sandals. Ask questions such as:

- *Which footwear is easy to walk in?*
- *Which footwear is most suitable for wearing in the rain?*
- *Which footwear do you prefer?*

Differentiation

Less confident learners: Give the children a starting criterion such as 'Have laces' and 'Do not have laces'. Now challenge the children to think of three more ways of sorting their shoes.
More confident learners: When the children have finished the task of sorting by one criterion, challenge them to sort by two, such as 'Have laces' and 'Are black'. Show them how to make a two-region Venn diagram. Discuss what goes into the intersection of the Venn diagram, and what will go outside the two circles.

Make a table of their votes surrounding each question, for example: 25 children thought walking boots were easiest to walk in; 30 children thought trainers; 3 children thought riding boots; 2 children disagreed that riding boots were comfortable to walk in.

Referring to the answers, show the class how to represent their information in a sentence like this: *Most of the class think that walking boots and trainers are the easiest footwear to walk in. Three people thought that riding boots were also comfortable to walk in. Two people disagreed and thought that riding shoes were not very comfortable for walking in.*

Ask the class if they can work out how many children are in the class simply by reading the information. (They can't!) Whilst no precise answer can be given, they can deduce that it is around 30 as we have written 'most' of the children in our sentences. Encourage the children to think about what the information DOES NOT tell them, as well as what it does tell them.

Individual work: Provide copies of the activity sheet 'Footwear fun'. Ask the children to read the information in the table carefully, and then to complete the sentences about the families.

Review

Ask the children to explain their deductions from the activity sheet 'Footwear fun'. Of course, there is no conclusive proof for their interpretations, just likelihoods. Ask questions such as: *How did you decide that? Who thinks something different? Why do you think that?* You may like, at the end of the lesson, to give the children the following extra information about the families, then ask: *What information could we not tell from the table?*

Extra information

The Davies family: 2 adults, 3 children aged 14, 19 and 21. The family like walking. They live on a farm in a wet part of the country, so need Wellingtons. They like to go hill walking. One person is a keen cyclist; this happens to be the father who has size 11 feet. The extra pair of Wellingtons is size 4. These are kept for a cousin who visits often. The children aren't allowed to wear trainers to school.

The Williams family: 2 adults, 3 children aged 6, 6 and 14. The family likes to wear slippers on their new carpet. The twins have just starter to roller skate. The adults and teenager sometimes go walking. They are digging up their garden so they all have to wear Wellingtons often. However, Dad has a hole in his and has thrown them away.

Ask the more confident children to share what they had decided they couldn't definitely tell from the chart. For example, exactly how many people lived in the house; what style of trainer/shoe they would have; whether they preferred lace-ups.

Differentiation

Less confident learners: There is a support version of the activity sheet which contains information and sentences to be completed about just one family.
More confident learners: The extension version of the sheet for these children contains data in tables, then space for the children to write their own sentences about the families and their footwear.

Lesson 8 (Teach and practise)

Starter

Reason: Explain that you will give a three-digit number card (from general resource sheet 'Three-digit numbers') to each of three children. Ask them to stand at the front of the class, out of number order. Invite another child to reorder the group holding the cards so that the numbers are in order, starting with the smallest number. Repeat this for other sets of three cards and different children.

Main teaching activities

Whole class: Explain that today the children will be collecting data, putting it into a frequency table, then making a bar chart from the data in their table. Ask them to collect data for their group about their favourite pair of shoes at home. Say: *Find out the colour of these shoes.* Ask the children to collect this data, then explain that the data will be combined in order to make a frequency table for the whole class. On the board make the following frequency table:

Colour	Votes
Black	12
Brown	10
Blue	4
Green	1
Red	2

When the table is completed, ask questions about the data, such as: *How many children have blue shoes as their favourite? Which is more popular: green or blue? Which colour had fewer/more than six votes?* Explain that this data can be put into a bar graph. Either using a computer graphing program or drawing the graph on the board, show the children how to compile a simple bar graph, where the vertical axis is labelled in ones. Ask the children to compare the two ways of displaying the information. Ask the same questions as of the frequency table data, but encourage the children to use the bar chart to answer.

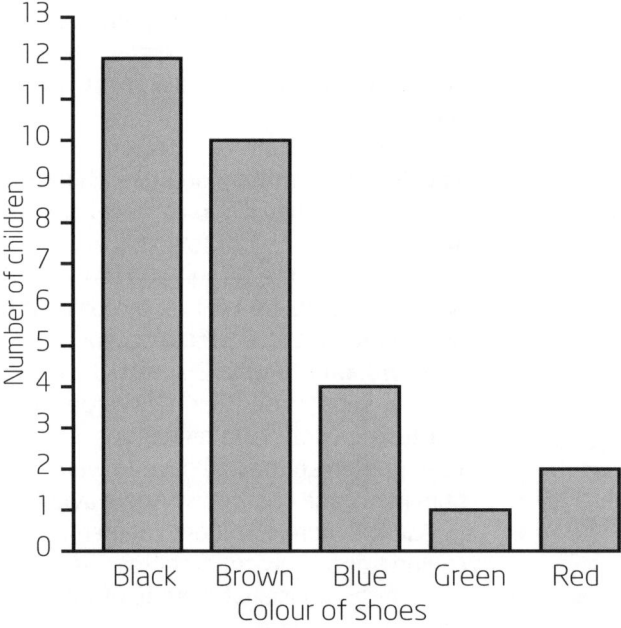

Group work: Ask the children to work in mixed-ability groups of about four. Explain that you would like them to collect data about the types of shoes that they have; both what they are wearing today and what they have at home. Suggest that each child can list up to five pairs of footwear. Explain that you would like them to construct a frequency table and a bar chart for the information that they collect. Provide the general resource sheet 'Bar chart' for the children to use to record their bar chart. Remind them to label the chart and its axes. Ask them to make their own frequency chart.

Differentiation

Less confident learners: Check that the children are contributing to the work. Encourage them to use the vocabulary of handling data as they discuss what they are doing in their group.
More confident learners: Encourage the children to ask questions of the other children in their group about the data that they collect.

Review

Choose one of the groups' frequency tables and bar charts and show it to the class. Ask questions about the data, for example: *How many more/fewer than ___ are there? How many shoes are there altogether? How did you work that out? So how many shoes in total do you think ___ has? Can you tell that from this data?* Repeat for other groups.

Lesson 9 (Teach and practise)

Starter
Recall: Repeat the Starter from Lesson 8, this time asking for the three numbers in both ascending then descending order.

Main teaching activities
Whole class: Display the data for general resource sheet 'Pencils' and ask questions such as: *In which years were most/least pencils bought? Why do you think there were so few bought in 2005?* (This may have been an accumulation of spares.) *Do you think this is a lot of pencils for a school with 210 pupils? Why do you think that?*

Paired work: Now ask the children to work in mixed-ability pairs to create a bar chart to show how many pencils were bought each year. Then ask them to write some questions that they could ask the rest of the class from the data in their bar chart. You may wish some children to use computer software to design and complete their bar chart.

Differentiation
Check that the less confident learners are contributing fully to their group's work and that the more confident learners do not dominate their group's work.

Review
Invite pairs of children to ask their questions of the others. Ask: *Is it possible to answer this? What else could we ask? What information does the bar chart not provide?*

Lesson 10 (Teach, apply and evaluate)

Starter
Recall: Explain that you will ask some multiplication and division questions from the 2-, 3-, 4-, 5-, 6- and 10-times tables. Include a range of vocabulary, such as: *What is 3 multiplied by 6? What is 7 times 2? What is 40 divided by 5? If I share 24 marbles between three people, how many does each get?*

Main teaching activities
Whole class: Draw a two-region Carroll diagram on the board. Label the regions 'Even' and 'Not Even' and title it 'Multiples of 3 up to 30'. Ask: *Where will 6 fit? And 15?* Ask the children to work in pairs to draw their own Carroll diagram and to complete the sorting. Regroup and take turns to say where each number will fit. Discuss, for example, where 24…, 27… will fit. Now draw a four-region Carroll diagram and label the regions:

	Multiple of 4	Not a multiple of 4
Multiple of 2		
Not a multiple of 2		

Label the diagram 'Numbers 1 to 20'. Work together as a class to decide where each number fits in the diagram. When the chart is complete ask questions such as: *What sort of numbers are in the box for 'Not a multiple of 4' and 'Not a multiple of 2'?* Agree that these are all odd numbers. Ask: *What is special about the numbers that go into the top left-hand box?* Agree that all of these are multiples of 4.

Paired work: Provide each child with a copy of 'Carroll diagram'. Ask them to sort the numbers 1 to 50 into the following boxes: Multiple of 5; Not a multiple of 5; Multiple of 3; Not a multiple of 3.

Differentiation
Less confident learners: Decide whether to work with this group. It may help to list the multiples of 5, then the multiples of 3.
More confident learners: When they have finished this sorting, challenge them to sort multiples of 6 and multiples of 4 in the same way.

Review
Draw a four-region Carroll diagram on the board and label it with: Multiple of 5; Not a multiple of 5; Multiple of 3; Not a multiple of 3; and a title of 'Numbers 1 to 50'. When all of the numbers are sorted, ask questions such as: *What sort of numbers go here? Where do you think 60 would fit? What about 61… 62? Why do you think that?*

Ask the children what they have learned about handling data this week.

BLOCK C

Handling data and measures

Unit C2 — Lesson 2

Name _____   Date _____

Weighing scales

Draw in the missing arrows to show the weight.

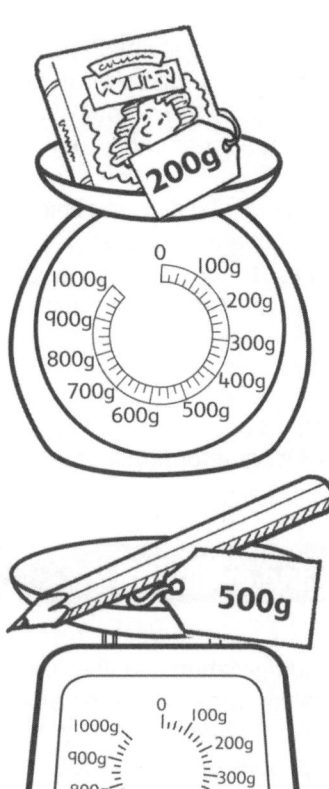

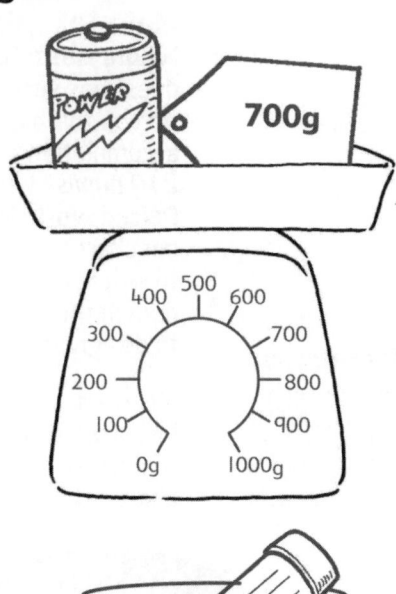

Now read these scales and write the weights to the nearest 100g.

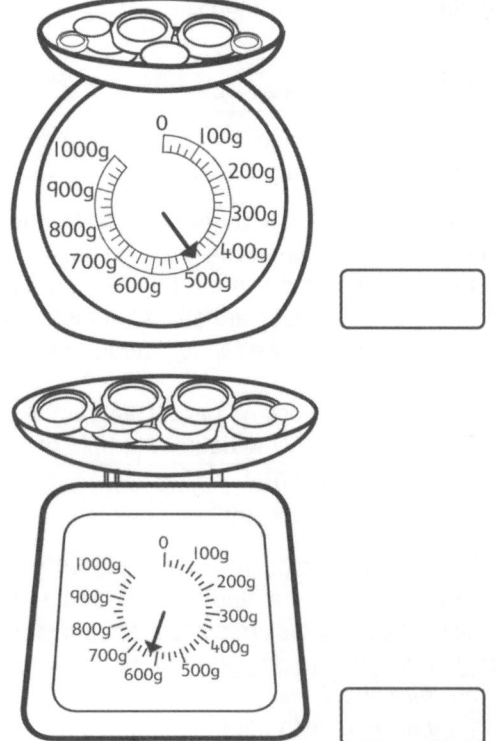

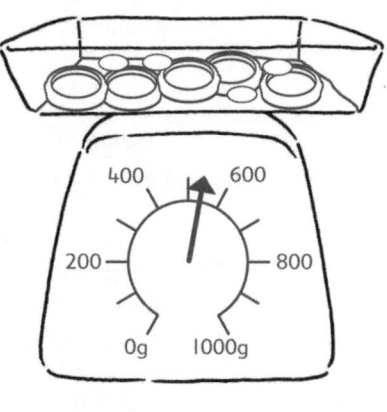

100 MATHS FRAMEWORK LESSONS · YEAR 3

BLOCK C — Handling data and measures

Name _____   Date _____

Thermometers

Read the thermometer scales and write the temperatures.

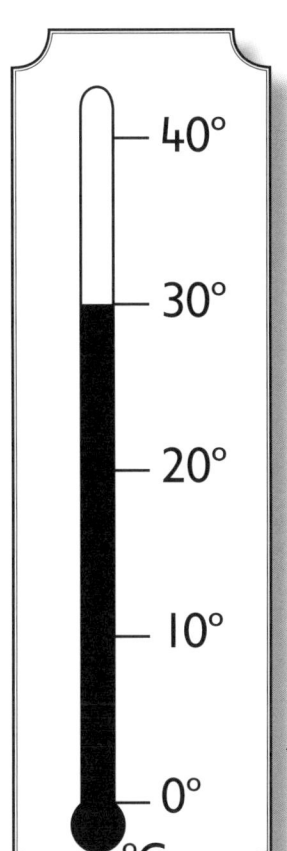 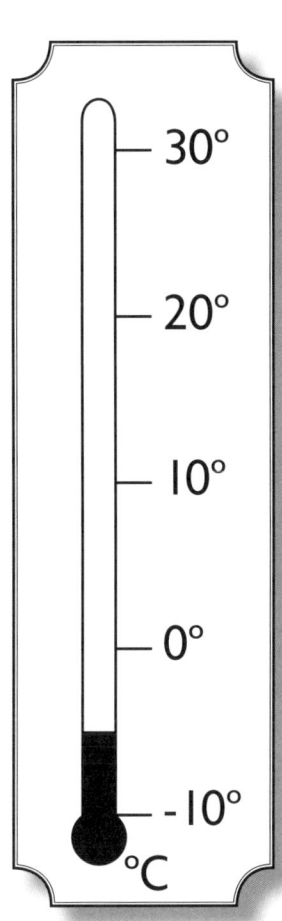 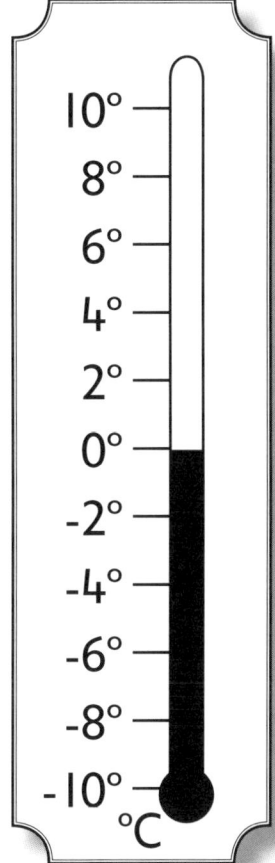 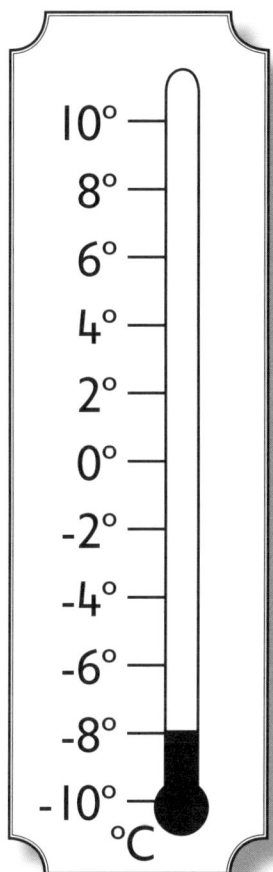

1. _____ **2.** _____ **3.** _____ **4.** _____

Write the answers to these problems.

5. The temperature outside is 6°C at 7.30am in the morning.

At midday the temperature is 13°C.

How much has the temperature increased? _____

6. The temperature in the classroom is 20°C.

The temperature outside is −5°C.

What is the difference between the temperatures? _____

BLOCK C

Handling data and measures

Handling data and measures

Lesson	Strand	Starter	Main teaching activities
1. Teach and practise	Measure	Read, write and order whole numbers to at least 1000 and position them on a number line; count on from and back to zero in single-digit steps or multiples of 10.	Know the relationships between kilometres and metres, metres and centimetres, kilograms and grams, litres and millilitres; choose and use appropriate units to estimate, measure and record measurements.
2. Teach and practise	Measure	As for Lesson 1	• Know the relationships between kilometres and metres, metres and centimetres, kilograms and grams, litres and millilitres; choose and use appropriate units to estimate, measure and record measurements. • **Read, to the nearest division and half-division, scales that are numbered or partially numbered; use the information to measure and draw to a suitable degree of accuracy.**
3. Teach and practise	Measure	Derive and recall multiplication facts for the 2-, 3-, 4-, 5-, 6- and 10-times tables and the corresponding division facts.	As for Lesson 2
4. Teach and practise	Measure	As for Lesson 3	As for Lesson 2
5. Teach, apply and evaluate	Measure	Know the relationships between kilometres and metres, metres and centimetres, kilograms and grams, litres and millilitres; choose and use appropriate units to estimate, measure and record measurements.	As for Lesson 2
6. Teach and practise	Data	**Derive and recall all addition and subtraction facts for each number to 20.**	Answer a question by collecting, organising and interpreting data; use tally charts, frequency tables, pictograms and bar charts to represent results and illustrate observations; use ICT to create a simple bar chart.
7. Teach and practise	Data	As for Lesson 6	As for Lesson 6
8. Teach and apply	Data	As for Lesson 6	As for Lesson 6
9. Teach and apply	Data	**Derive and recall sums and differences of multiples of 10 and number pairs that total 100.**	As for Lesson 6
10. Teach, apply and evaluate	Data	As for Lesson 9	As for Lesson 6

Unit 3 ▢ 2 weeks

Speaking and listening objective
● Explain a process or present information, ensuring items are clearly sequenced, relevant details are included and accounts ended effectively.

Introduction

In this ten-lesson unit, children are encouraged to work cooperatively in groups and to present their information. They ask questions about their data of the rest of the class so that they become more fluent with the relevant vocabulary. They develop their data handling skills, including using a scale for bar charts and using tallies and frequencies. For measures, they further develop their understanding of capacity, including understanding the relationship between the units.

Using and applying mathematics

● Follow a line of enquiry by deciding what information is important; make and use lists, tables and graphs to organise and interpret the information.
● Describe and explain methods, choices and solutions to puzzles and problems, orally and in writing, using pictures and diagrams.

Lessons 1-5

Preparation
Copy CD pages 'Capacity' and 'Making a measuring jug' onto an OHT; copy and make sets of cards using CD page 'Round the world cards' (for the children and an enlarged teaching set); copy and make cards from CD page 'Measurements'.

You will need

CD resources
'Capacity', 'Round the world cards' and 'Making a measuring jug' for each child, 'Round the world blanks' for each more confident child, 'Measurements' (see General resources).

Equipment
Containers from 50ml to 4 litres; water; medicine spoons; five plastic bottles with three-digit capacity; five commercial containers with labels covered; small individual cartons of fruit juice and cans of cola; containers with smaller amounts measured in ml; teapot, cup, plastic bucket; 1-litre measuring jugs; labels.

Learning objectives

Starter
● Read, write and order whole numbers to at least 1000 and position them on a number line; count on from and back to zero in single-digit steps or multiples of 10.
● Derive and recall multiplication facts for the 2-, 3-, 4-, 5-, 6- and 10-times tables and the corresponding division facts.
● Know the relationships between kilometres and metres, metres and centimetres, kilograms and grams, litres and millilitres; choose and use appropriate units to estimate, measure and record measurements.

Main teaching activities
2006
● Know the relationships between kilometres and metres, metres and centimetres, kilograms and grams, litres and millilitres; choose and use appropriate units to estimate, measure and record measurements.
● Read, to the nearest division and half-division, scales that are numbered or partially numbered; use the information to measure and draw to a suitable degree of accuracy.
1999
● Measure and compare using standard units (km, m, cm, kg, g, l, ml).
● Know the relationships between kilometres and metres, metres and centimetres, kilograms and grams, litres and millilitres.
● Begin to use decimal notation for metres and centimetres.
● Suggest suitable units and measuring equipment to estimate or measure length, mass or capacity.
● Read scales to the nearest division (labelled or unlabelled); record estimates and measurements to the nearest whole or half unit (eg 'about 3.5 kg'), or in mixed units (eg '3 m and 20 cm').
● Use a ruler to draw and measure lines to the nearest half centimetre.

Vocabulary

problem, enquiry, solution, calculate, calculation, method, explain, reasoning, reason, predict, pattern, relationship, collect, organise, compare, sort, classify, represent, interpret, effect, litr e (l), millilitre (ml), capacity

Lesson 1 (Teach and practise)

Starter
Rehearse: Ask the children to count with you in fifties to 500 and back. Repeat, extending the count to 1000. Now explain that you will say the number in the count and you would like the children to say its double. Begin with 50, so that the children say 100, then 100 (and 200), 150 (and 300) and so on. If necessary, remind the children that they can use the doubles of 5, 10, 15, and so on, to help them derive these facts.

Main teaching activities
Whole class: Begin by asking the children to give examples of capacity vocabulary, such as 'fill', 'empty' and 'litre'. Write the suggestions on the board. Now ask the children to write down as many facts as they can recall about capacity in about three minutes.

Now explain that this week the focus will be on capacity. Ask questions such as:
- *How many millilitres are there in a litre?* (1000)
- *How many are there in half a litre? A quarter of a litre?*
- *How many ways can you find of writing half a litre?* ($\frac{1}{2}$l, 500ml, 0.5l, half a litre.)
- *How could you write 1 litre 250ml?* (1.25l, 1250ml, 1$\frac{1}{4}$l, one and a quarter litres)
- *What size of jug would you need to measure milk for a baby's bottle? Oil for a car? Bottled water?*

Now ask:
- *Which is larger: 1500ml or one and a half litres? How do you know?*
- *What might you buy in litre containers?*

Show the OHT of the general resource sheet 'Capacity'. Ask individual children to mark the following measurements on different jugs: 100ml, 50ml, 1100ml and 240ml. (It will not be possible to do this on all jugs.) Ask the children on which jugs it is easy to do this, which is more difficult, and why.

Group work: Ask the children to work in threes. They cut out the 'Round the world cards' and shuffle them. Then the child with the 'Start' card reads what is on his/her card. The player with the answer reads their card, and so on.

Review
Using the enlarged set of 'Round the world cards', ask a child to come to the front of the class and hold any of the cards. Now ask another child to hold the next card. For each card, ask the child holding it to read out its measure. Determine where the smallest card will be placed, and ask how the two cards should be ordered. Continue until all 15 cards are held in an ordered line. Invite the children who are still sitting to suggest equivalent measurements for any of the cards, and write their suggestions on the board. For example, a quarter of a litre is 250ml, and 0.25l.

Differentiation
Less confident learners: Begin with all the cards being dealt out and on show to start. Repeat this until the children are confident and can play the game in groups of three without adult intervention.
More confident learners: When the children have mastered the original game, they can use the general resource sheet 'Round the world blanks' to make their own game for another group to use.

Lesson 2 (Teach and practise)

Starter
Rehearse: Repeat the Starter for Lesson 1, but increase the pace so that the children are kept on their toes!

Main teaching activities
Whole class: Use the 'Round the world cards' with the whole class as a warm-up activity. The children should have one card between two or three. They jump up when they have the answer and sit down straight afterwards. Encourage the children to build up their speed in completing the task.

Explain that the focus today is on being able to measure liquids accurately using a variety of measuring equipment. Display the OHT of general resource sheet 'Capacity' and ask children to point to where a particular measurement would be for each jug, such as 50ml, 100ml, 250ml, 0.5l and so on.

Teach the children to look for clues to help them work out the scale of the jugs they are using, such as:
- *Look for any markings, especially numbers.*
- *Where is zero? Where is the 'full' mark?*
- *Estimate how much you think the container would hold. Do you think this is more than a litre of milk or less?*

Group work: Set up a carousel of activities, which the children can all attempt during this and the next two lessons. The activities are suitable for mixed-ability groups.

A. Make a measuring jug: Provide the children with general resource sheet 'Making a measuring jug', gummed labels for writing the calibrations onto the containers, a variety of uncalibrated containers, each of which will hold at least 2 litres and two 1-litre measuring jugs. Ask the children to calibrate some containers to show the following measurements: ½l, 1l, 1½l and 2l.

B. Round the world containers: Work with this group. Using the 'Round the world cards' the children find containers which they think will hold the amount on each card. They use a measuring jug to fill the container with the required amount of water, then place the appropriate 'Round the world card' beside the container. They then order all 15 measurements. You may wish to subdivide the children working at this activity into three groups, so that each group has five cards. Then the groups come together to order all their containers from holding the least to the most.

C. How much does it hold? Provide this group with a selection of containers with the capacity covered over. They estimate and then measure how much they think the label describes the container as holding. Discuss the space left at the top of containers that is there to avoid spillage.

Review

Review one of the activities during this and the subsequent two lessons:

A. Make a measuring jug: Ask the children to explain what they had to do, what they found easy, and anything that was difficult. Discuss how they calibrated their containers. Discuss how accurate they think these calibrated containers will be, and why. How could they calibrate a container in 100ml increments and 50ml increments?

B. Round the world containers: Invite the children to explain what they had to do, what they found easy and anything they found difficult, and why it was difficult. Ask: *How did you order the containers?* Show the children the containers and discuss how a variety of shapes affects the level of water.

C. How much does it hold? Invite the children to explain what they did, what they found easy, and anything they found difficult, and why. Uncover the commercial labels so that the contents are visible and invite a child to read how much the container would hold. Discuss how close this amount is to the children's estimates and measures. Discuss why there may well be differences, such as did the children fill the container to the same point as the manufacturer would? Ask for suggestions as to why the manufacturer would not fill the containers right to the top. (To save spillages when opening the container and to allow space for the contents to expand.)

Differentiation

Less confident learners: Ensure that it is easy to read the measuring jugs given to these children for each activity.
More confident learners: Challenge these children to record their answers in a variety of equivalent ways, building on the work of Lesson 1. This group can work with 4l containers (such as plastic milk cartons) for activity A. However, use smaller measuring containers for activity C such as 25ml.

BLOCK C

Handling data and measures

Lesson 3 (Teach and practise)

Starter

Rehearse: Write 'How many ▢ in ▢?' on the board so that the children can generate some questions. Ask them to write a number sentence on their whiteboards, using their knowledge of the 2-, 5- and 10-times tables. Once every child has written a question, invite one to stand up to ask the class their question. The first person to offer the correct answer wins one point. (You might like to split the class into two halves and accumulate points.)

Main teaching activities

Whole class: Use the OHT of general resource sheet 'Capacity' and invite the children to estimate measurements. Draw in lines to represent the water level, ensuring they fall between the calibration marks, such as about 220ml. Invite the children to estimate the amount and to explain their estimate.
Group work: Continue with the carousel of activities from Lesson 2.

Review

Discuss one of the activities, using the suggestions in Lesson 2.

Lesson 4 (Teach and practise)

Starter

Recall: Repeat the Starter for Lesson 3, but this time make this more of a game. Ask the teams to answer by having the correct number of children standing; for example, a child asks how many fives in 45, so the first team to have nine children standing wins a point. (This takes a bit of non-competitive practising first.) Then review equivalents with the children such as: *Which is greater, 600ml or 0.5l? How do you know? How else might you record 0.5 litre?*

Main teaching activities

Whole class: Continue with the carousel of activities from Lesson 2.

Review

Discuss one of the activities using the suggestions in Lesson 2.

Lesson 5 (Teach, apply and evaluate)

Starter

Rehearse: Have a selection of plastic bottles/cartons of liquid with the three-digit capacity enlarged and stuck on the side. Turn the bottles so the children don't see the capacity at first. Ask a child to choose three of the bottles and invite the others to suggest how the bottles should be ordered for capacity. Now turn the bottles so that the children can read the capacities. Ask: *Are the bottles correctly ordered?* Repeat this for other choices of three bottles.

Main teaching activities

Whole class: Show the children a medicine spoon or teaspoon, a small carton of fruit juice and a can of cola. For each item, cover the ml measure and have two measurement cards taken from the general resource sheet 'Measurements'. To play in two teams, one team starts and, if they make a mistake, the other team can take over. Add more items to the game as you feel necessary. The team who gets to the last item and guesses correctly is the 'winner'. You can extend this game to include three labels for each item.

Now invite the children to suggest what would be suitable units and measuring equipment for measuring the capacity of each of the containers when empty. Discuss the suitability of each suggestion.

Unit 3  2 weeks

Review

Play 'Guess my capacity'. You will need a teapot, a cup and a plastic bucket. Each child writes their estimate for the capacity on their whiteboard. You choose the three nearest results of the teapot to come out. If no one is spot on with their estimate, they are each allowed to ask you one question before estimating again. Whoever is nearest this time wins a point. Continue with the other items. For each item ask: *Which measuring container would you use to measure that? Why is that a good choice? What have you learned about measuring capacity?*

Lessons 6-10

Preparation

Copy CD pages 'Data collection', 'Graphs' and 'Sunflowers' onto an OHT.

You will need

Photocopiable pages
'Using scales' (page 127) and 'Sunflowers' (page 128).

CD resources
Support and extension versions of 'Using scales'; 'Data collection' and 'Sunflowers' for the teacher's/LSA's reference and for each child, 'Graphs' (see General resources).

Equipment
Data handling package for the computer; the work that was kept from Block C, Unit 1, Lesson 9; database (eg NNS database); a computer for each group.

Learning objectives

Starter

● Derive and recall all addition and subtraction facts for each number to 20 and sums and differences of multiples of 10 and number pairs that total 100.

Main teaching activities

2006
● Answer a question by collecting, organising and interpreting data; use tally charts, frequency tables, pictograms and bar charts to represent results and illustrate observations; use ICT to create a simple bar chart.

1999
● Solve a given problem by organising and interpreting numerical data in simple lists, table and graphs, eg simple frequency tables; pictograms; bar charts; Venn and Carroll diagrams (one criterion).

Vocabulary

problem, enquiry, solution, calculate, calculation, method, explain, reasoning, reason, predict, pattern, relationship, collect, organise, compare, sort, classify, represent, interpret, effect, information, data, survey, questionnaire, table, frequency table, block graph, bar chart, axis, axes, horizontal axis, vertical axis, label, title, scale, interval, division, how often?, how frequently?, more/less, most/least, most/least popular, most/least frequent, greatest/least value, approximately, close, about the same as, ten times, hundred times

Lesson 6 (Teach and practise)

Starter

Recall: Explain to the children that you will say a number and that you want them to put up their hands when they have thought of an addition fact with that number as the answer. Say, for example, 18, and allow the class up to five seconds of thinking time. Then ask for answers.

Main teaching activities

Whole class: This lesson and the next focus on developing the skill of constructing appropriate lists, tables and graphs. Show the children the OHT of 'Data collection'. Ask:
● *What do you think this list is all about?*
● *How could we group the items?*
● *Can we work out how many children are in the class?*
● *Which category is the best to use to tell us how many children are in the class?* (Ways of getting to school.)
● *Why wouldn't the pets category be helpful?* (We can't be sure whether it tells about pets we have, would like or whether some children have more than one pet.)
● *What can we do about the tally marks to make things easier?* (Write in numbers.)

Handling data and measures

Now think of titles for each list, for example 'The numbers and type of pets in 3H', 'Our favourite colours' and 'How we travel to school'. Then work with the children to total the scores for each one. Ask the class to reason why the colours and the travelling lists will have the same total. Rearrange the data with the class to make frequency tables:

Cats	9
Rabbits	6
Dogs	4
Hamsters	11

Red	5
Yellow	5
Green	10
Blue	10

Bus	12
Car	2
Bike	6
Walk	10

Ask questions such as: *How many children walk/cycle to school? Which pet appears to be the most popular? How would the data change if we said who would like a dog/cat? Would this data be different in another class? Why?*

Remind the children that data like these can be put into graphs. Show the OHT of 'Graphs' and discuss the scale, headings of the columns, the title, and what can be deduced from the graphs.

Paired work: Provide each child with a copy of general resource sheet 'Data collection', and some squared paper. Ask them to work together to make sensible frequency tables for the data, then to make a bar chart and a pictogram for each of their frequency tables.

Review

Invite the less confident children to show their poster, and compare the different data presentations. Ask: *Which do you prefer for this data: a pictogram or a bar chart? Why?* Now ask the more confident children to show what they produced using the computer package. Encourage the children to explain how they input the data, and which display was easier to make and why.

Lesson 7 (Teach and practise)

Starter

Recall: Repeat the Starter from Lesson 6. This time, however, ask the children to give a subtraction fact for the number that you say. (The number is the result of the subtraction.) Keep the pace sharp.

Main teaching activities

Whole class: Explain that today is all about working to a scale. Count together in twos from 0 to 20, and explain that when working to a scale, each step along the scale stands for, in this case, two things.

Uncover the bar chart from the OHT of 'Sunflowers' and ask the children to look at it carefully. Explain that this is a bar graph. Point to the scale and explain that the scale increases by two each time. Ask questions such as: *How many sunflowers are about 150cm tall? How many are taller than that? How did you work that out? How many sunflowers are taller than 160cm but shorter than 200cm?*

Now reveal the second half of OHT 'Sunflowers', which shows the same data as a pictogram. Ask the children to look carefully at this and explain the scale: that one sunflower icon represents two sunflowers.

Individual work: Ask the children to work individually to draw a bar chart and a pictogram for the information given on the activity sheet 'Using scales'. They are asked to use one square, or icon, to represent two. Invite two children to use the computer graphing package to carry out this work.

Review

Ask the two children who drew their graphs on large sheets of paper to show the rest of the class what they did. Ask questions about the information in the bar chart, such as: *Which fruit was the most popular? How can you tell this? How many children like pears?* And for the pictogram: *What does one picture represent? So how many children ate meat feast pizza?*

Differentiation

Less confident learners: Work with this group to produce a giant pictogram and bar chart for later use.

More confident learners: Allow this group to work in pairs using a computer graphing package to present their data.

Differentiation

Less confident learners: There is a support version of the activity sheet which uses scales of 1:1.

More confident learners: There is an extension version of the activity sheet which uses scales of 5:1 and 10:1.

Lesson 8 (Teach and apply)

Starter
Recall: Combine the Starters for Lessons 6 and 7, so that for a given number, children give both addition, then subtraction, facts for it.

Main teaching activities
Group work: Ask the children to work in mixed-ability groups of about eight and decide what information they will collect about their group. Ask them to devise a data collection chart, frequency table, and then to put their data onto both a pictogram and a bar chart, using a 2:1 scale.

Review
Invite each group to display their work for others to see, and ask questions about the data.

Lesson 9 (Teach and apply)

Starter
Rehearse: Explain that you will say a multiple of 10, and then ask the children to say the multiple of 10 which will add to yours to make 100. For example, if you say 30, the children will say 70. Keep the pace sharp.

Main teaching activities
Whole class: Remind the children of the work that they did on their personal measurements in Block C, Unit 1, Lesson 10. Give this work to the children and ask them to read through what they did and the conclusions that they drew. Ask: *Do you think that your prediction about your measurements now will be accurate?*

Now show the bar chart that the class made in the previous lesson. Discuss how each block could represent two and demonstrate this by drawing a diagram onto the board, showing one of the bars from the previous chart.
Group work: Ask the children to work in groups as they did before. They re-measure their height, shoe size, length of foot and hand span, first estimating how much the difference will be from the previous measurements. They record their measurements. Now ask the children to make a group record on a chart. Then each group takes turns to enter their data for their heights into the database. They should use a scale of one block represents two. When this is complete, print out the chart from each of the data sets, ie from Unit 1 and from this unit. Provide each child with a copy of both sets of data.

Review
Ask the children to compare the two sets of data from the two lessons. Ask questions such as: *How many children have grown more than 2cm since we first did this work? How many are still the same height? How tall is the tallest child in the class? How tall was the tallest before Christmas? What is the difference in the two heights? Do you think these two measurements belong to the same child? Why do you think that?* Over time repeat this for the other measurements that the children have taken.

Differentiation
The children can work in mixed-ability groups for this task. Check that the more confident children do not dominate the group's work and that the less confident are making a valid contribution.

Lesson 10 (Teach, apply and evaluate)

Starter

Rehearse: Repeat the Starter from Lesson 9, this time asking for multiples of 5 which total 100. So, if you say 85 the children will say 15. Give just a few seconds of thinking time to keep the pace of this sharp.

Main teaching activities

Whole class: Draw a simple chart on the board to collect shoe size.

Shoe size	Tally	Frequency
2		
3		
4		

Begin by asking five children to come to the board in turn and to draw a stroke opposite their shoe size. Explain that the stroke is called a tally mark. Continue until against one shoe size there are four strokes. Explain that the next person with this shoe size puts a line through the strokes and that four strokes and line through it represents 5. Continue until everyone has had a turn. Now ask the children to total each set of tally marks. Write the totals. Explain that the last column, headed 'Frequency', shows how often this event occurred, or how many there were. Now ask: *How many people have size ___ shoe? Which is the most popular shoe size? How can you tell this? What is the largest shoe size? How many people take this size of shoe?*

Group work: Give each group a different task to make a tally chart from this list: foot length; hand span; height. (The children will already have this data from Lesson 9.)

Ask each group to make a tally chart and to collect the data from everyone in the class onto one chart. They will need to cooperate as a group in order to carry out this work. Their charts will need to be large enough for everyone to see in the Review, so suggest to the children that they produce a good chart on a large sheet of sugar paper and use thick felt pens so that the data is easily readable.

Review

Invite a group to display their chart. Now invite the group to ask questions about their chart to the rest of the class. For example, about foot length they could ask: *How long is the longest foot? What is the difference in length between the longest and shortest foot? How many children have a foot longer/shorter than ___ .* If the children find asking these questions difficult, model some for them. Repeat this for the other groups' work.

Ask the children to discuss in pairs what they have learned about handling data from this series of lessons. Invite those that you are targetting for assessment to give feedback.

Differentiation

The children can work in mixed-ability groups for this task. Check that the more confident children do not dominate the group's work and that the less confident are making a valid contribution.

Name _____   Date _____

Using scales

Draw a bar chart using this information.

The scale is one square per child.

There are 10 children who like to eat apples.
There are 7 children who like to eat bananas.
There are 12 children who like to eat oranges.
There are 9 children who like to eat pears.

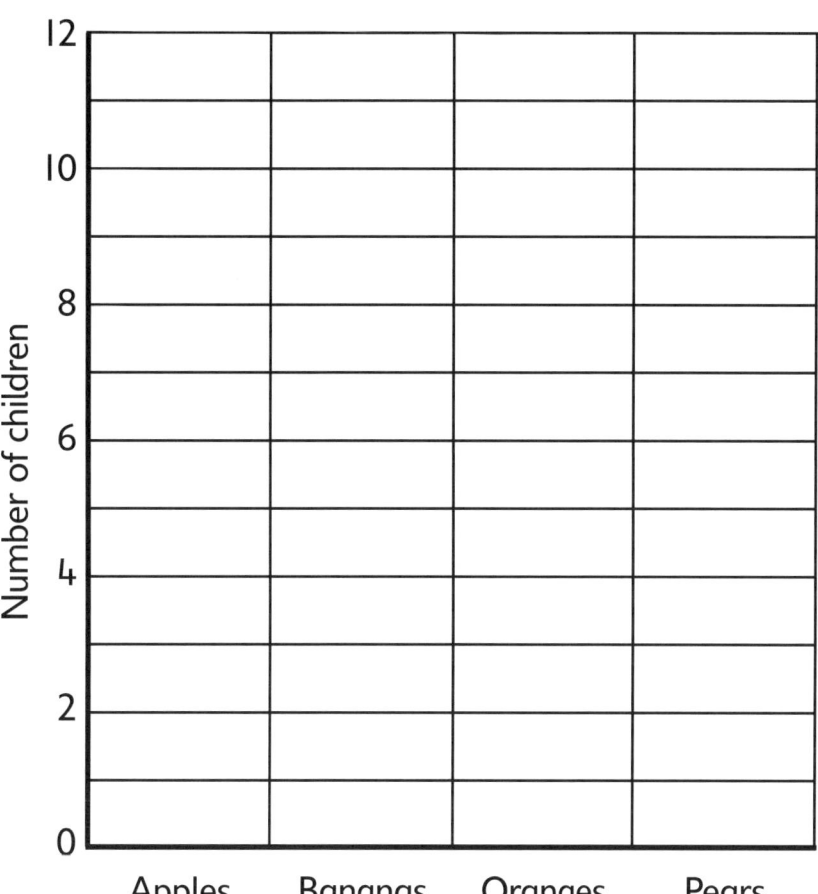

Draw a pictogram using this information.

Use one picture to represent two children.

10 children ate pepperoni pizza.
7 children ate meat feast pizza.
9 children ate prawn pizza.
11 children ate vegetarian pizza.

= 2 children

Number of children

Pepperoni   Meat feast   Prawn   Vegetarian

Name _____   Date _____

Sunflowers

Bar graph
Class 3's sunflowers

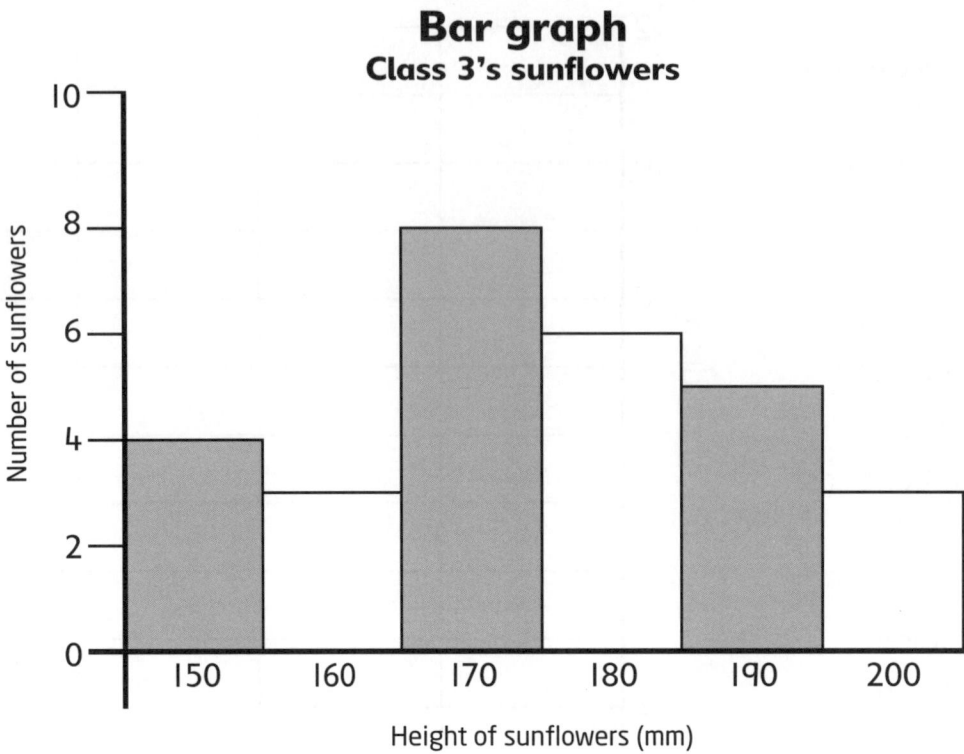

Height of sunflowers (mm)

Pictogram

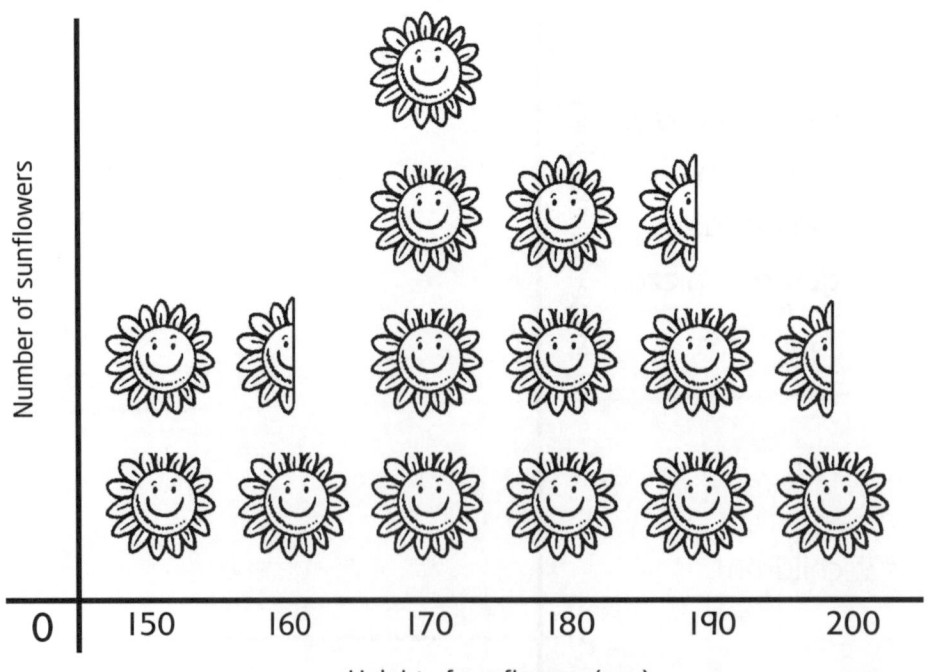

Height of sunflowers (mm)

BLOCK C

Handling data and measures

Calculating, measuring and understanding shape

Key aspects of learning
- Problem solving
- Reasoning
- Creative thinking
- Information processing
- Managing feeling
- Communication
- Empathy

Expected prior learning
Check that children can already:
- identify the operations needed in simple one-step word problems
- recognise and use the value of coins and measures of length, weight and capacity
- read numbered and unnumbered divisions on simple scales
- add and subtract mentally a one-digit number to or from a two-digit number
- record informally the addition and subtraction of two-digit numbers
- recognise simple fractions and find halves and quarters of numbers and quantities
- understand multiplication as repeated addition and division as repeated subtraction
- use symbols to record simple number sentences
- follow instructions using vocabulary related to position, direction and movement
- recognise and use right angles to describe turns and corners of shapes.

Objectives overview
The text in this diagram identifies the focus of mathematics learning within the block.

Solving problems and representing information; set solutions in the context of the problem

Developing written methods of calculation for all four operations

Finding unit fractions of numbers and quantities

Using measures and scales

Comparing angles with right angles

Block D: Calculating, measuring and understanding shape

Understanding multiplication and division as inverse operations

Using inverses to estimate and check calculations

Using the vocabulary of position, direction and movement

Unit 1 ▭ 2 weeks

Calculating, measuring and understanding shape

Speaking and listening objective

- Follow an explanation or set of instructions, noting and interpreting the language associated with position, direction and movement.

Introduction

In this ten-lesson unit, children solve one- and two-step problems for addition and subtraction of one- and two-digit numbers, fractions and for measures. They listen carefully to instructions, and this should be emphasised for Lessons 7 and 8 for position, direction and movement, where they will need to interpret the vocabulary. Children may need reminding that forward movements on a graph or chart should be interpreted as 'up' and backward movements as 'down'.

Using and applying mathematics

- Solve one- and two-step problems involving numbers, money or measures, including time, choosing and carrying out appropriate calculations.

Lesson	Strands	Starter	Main teaching activities
1. Teach and practise	Calculate	**Derive and recall all addition and subtraction facts for each number to 20.**	**Add or subtract mentally combinations of one-digit and two-digit numbers.**
2. Teach and practise	Calculate	As for Lesson 1	As for Lesson 1
3. Teach and apply	Calculate	As for Lesson 1	Find unit fractions of numbers and quantities (eg ½, $^1/_3$, ¼ and $^1/_6$ of 12 litres.
4. Teach and apply	Calculate	As for Lesson 1	As for Lesson 3
5. Teach, apply and evaluate	Use/apply	As for Lesson 1	Solve one-step and two-step problems involving numbers, money or measures, including time, choosing and carrying out appropriate calculations.
6. Teach and practise	Measure	Derive and recall multiplication facts for the 2-, 3-, 4-, 5-, 6- and 10-times tables and the corresponding division facts.	Read the time on a 12-hour digital clock and to the nearest five minutes on an analogue clock; calculate time intervals and find start or end times for a given time interval.
7. Teach and practise	Shape	As for Lesson 6	Read and record the vocabulary of position, direction and movement, using the four compass directions to describe movement about a grid.
8. Teach and practise	Shape	As for Lesson 6	As for Lesson 7
9. Teach and apply	Measure	As for Lesson 6	• Know the relationships between... kilograms and grams; choose and use appropriate units to estimate, measure and record measurements. • **Read to the nearest division and half-division, scales that are numbered or partially numbered; use the information to measure and draw to a suitable degree of accuracy.** • Solve one-step and two-step problems involving measures..., choosing and carrying out appropriate calculations.
10. Teach, apply and evaluate	Measure	As for Lesson 6	As for Lesson 9

Unit 1 2 weeks

Lessons 1-5

Preparation
Copy two sets of 0-9 numeral cards from CD page 'Numeral cards 0-20' for each pair. Make an OHP copy of the activity sheet 'How much?'.

You will need
Photocopiable pages
'Working mentally' (page 19) and 'How much?' (page 139).
CD resources
Support and extension versions of 'Working mentally'; 'Numeral cards 0-20' (see General resources). Interactive resources: 'Number line' and 'Number sentence builder'.
Equipment
Strips of card; elastic bands; interlocking cubes in red and blue; squared paper.

Learning objectives

Starter
- Derive and recall all addition and subtraction facts for each number to 20.

Main teaching activities
2006
- Add or subtract mentally combinations of one-digit and two-digit numbers.
- Find unit fractions of numbers and quantities (eg $\frac{1}{2}$, $\frac{1}{3}$, $\frac{1}{4}$ and $\frac{1}{6}$ of 12 litres.
- Solve one-step and two-step problems involving numbers, money or measures, including time, choosing and carrying out appropriate calculations.

1999
- Use mental calculation strategies - several objectives, including: use known number facts and place value to add/subtract mentally; add and subtract mentally a 'near multiple of 10'; add mentally three or four small numbers; find a difference by counting up.
- Recognise unit fractions such as $\frac{1}{2}$, $\frac{1}{3}$, $\frac{1}{4}$, $\frac{1}{5}$, $\frac{1}{10}$... and use them to find fractions of shapes and numbers.
- Solve word problems involving numbers in 'real life', money and measures, using one or more steps, including finding totals and giving change, and working out which coins to pay with. Explain how the problem was solved.

Vocabulary
problems, solution, methods, sign, operation, symbol, number sentence, equation, mental calculation, written calculation, informal method, jottings, diagrams, add, plus, total, subtract, take away, minus, difference, fraction, part, equal parts, one whole, one half, one third, one quarter, one fifth, one sixth, one tenth

Lesson 1 (Teach and practise)

Starter
Recall: Explain that you will say a number, from zero to 10. Ask the children to write on their whiteboards all four number sentences that include that number and 10. For example, if you say 6, they write 6 + 4 = 10; 4 + 6 = 10; 10 - 4 = 6; 10 - 6 = 4. When you say *Show me* they hold up their boards for you to check. Keep the pace sharp.

Main teaching activities
Whole class: The interactive resource 'Number line' can be used for this teaching activity. Explain that today the children will use the mental strategy of putting the larger number first in order to count on. On the board, write 5 + 26 and ask: *How should we begin to do this mentally?* Accept the suggestion of rewriting the sentence as 26 + 5. Draw a number line as follows:

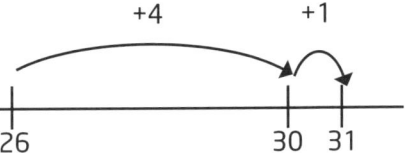

When the children have understood the modelling using an empty number line, provide further examples of adding a single-digit to a TU number, such as 7 + 38, 8 + 63, and so on.

Now draw another empty number line, and write the subtraction 36 – 9. Invite the children to explain how they could use an empty number line to help them:

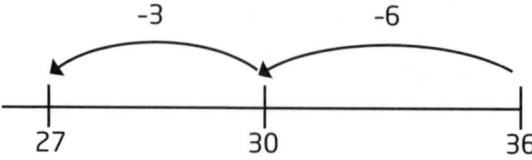

Agree that they can count back 6 to 30, then 3 more to 27, because 3 + 6 = 9. Repeat this method for further examples.

On the board, write an addition sentence, such as 65 + 10 and ask: *How could we use the number line to work this out?* The children may suggest 65 + 5 + 5, or 65 and count on 10. Both are acceptable. Model these and write up the answer: 65 + 10 = 75. Now say: *If 65 + 10 = 75, what would 75 subtract 10 equal? How did you work that out? What other addition and subtraction sentences can you make from the numbers 65, 10 and 75?* Write up the children's suggestions of 10 + 65 = 75 and 75 – 65 = 10. Repeat this for other addition and subtraction sentences, such as 27 + 30. Encourage the children to work mentally where possible, by counting along a mental number line to add/subtract 30.

Group work: Ask the children to work in pairs. Give each pair two sets of 0–9 numeral cards and ask them to shuffle the cards together. One of them takes two cards, generates a TU number; the other takes a single card. They write an addition sentence, putting the larger number first and counting on mentally to find the answer. Ask them to generate ten such questions, shuffling the cards after each one. Then they take turns to take two cards to make a TU number and take one more card, to which they add a zero to make a decade number. Again, they write the addition sentence and calculate mentally. Again, ask them to generate ten such questions

Review

Invite children from each ability group to write up one of their number sentences (without the answer) on the board. Ask the class: *How can we solve this?* Invite the children to explain how they calculated the answer. Write on the board 45 – ☐ = 27. Ask the children to explain how they would solve this by counting, using an empty number line to model the answer.

Differentiation

Less confident learners: Suggest to the children that they make 'TU add U' sentences, and draw a blank number line if they need help.

More confident learners: Challenge these children to calculate addition sentences using HTU and decade numbers.

Lesson 2 (Teach and practise)

Starter

Recall: Repeat the Starter for Lesson 1, this time for complements of 20. If you say 16, the children write 16 + 4 = 20; 4 + 16 = 20; 20 – 4 = 16; 20 – 16 = 4.

Main teaching activities

Whole class: Explain to the class that today they will be adding and subtracting to/from a two-digit number, crossing the tens boundary. Using the interactive resource 'Number sentence builder', begin with subtracting a single-digit number from a teens number, such as 16 – 7. Explain that this can be done in two steps: 16 – 6 – 1, so that the calculation could be written as 16 – 6 – 1 = 10 – 1 = 9. Repeat this for other examples, such as 13 – 7, 15 – 8, 14 – 9. Now ask the children to respond to questions that you write on the board such as: 14 – 8 = ☐; 14 – ☐ = 6; ☐ – 8 = 6. Discuss how, if you know one fact, others can be found.

Now write on the board: 57 + 6 = ☐ and explain that this can be calculated by crossing the tens boundary: 57 + 6 = 57 + 3 + 3 = 60 + 3 = 63. Repeat for further examples, such as 45 + 8, asking the children to work mentally and to explain what they did. Write the mental calculation on the board for everyone to see. Repeat this for subtraction, such as 53 – 8. Then ask the children to work mentally to complete questions that you write on the board: $47 + 6 = \square$; $47 + \square = 53$; $\square + 6 = 53$; and $74 - 7 = \square$; $74 - \square = 67$; $\square - 7 = 67$.

Individual work: Provide each child with a copy of the activity sheet 'Working mentally' to complete.

Review

Divide the class into two teams and choose captains. Ask the captains to come to the front. Explain that each team will, in turn, be given a number question to solve, and that the captain will decide who answers. However, the captain must ask a different person each time! Keep a score on the board for correct answers, and the first team to score ten points wins. Ask questions such as: *What is 15 subtract 7? What is 67 + 8? 92 - 5? 54 - 8?* When one team has gained ten points, ask: *What strategies did you find helpful to work out the answers?*

Lesson 3 (Teach and apply)

Starter

Recall: Combine the Starters from Lessons 1 and 2 (using complements to 10 and 20). Again, keep the pace sharp. If children take longer over answering a question, invite them to explain how they worked out the answer.

Main teaching activities

Whole class: Ask the children to suggest fraction vocabulary, and write down their suggestions. Now ask the children to sketch, on their whiteboards, what they think 'one half' looks like. Use some of their examples to illustrate that a half can be half of any shape (circles are very likely to be drawn). Consider with the children that 'half' can also represent part of a number greater than/less than 1:

I can place all of the numbers on a number line:

0    $\frac{1}{2}$ 1 $1\frac{1}{2}$ 2...

Provide each child with a strip of card and an elastic band. Ask them to place their elastic bands onto the card strip to show 'half way between' for the following examples: 0 and 1 ($\frac{1}{2}$), 0 and 10 (5), 0 and 20 (10), 30 and 50 (40). Then prompt the children to think of 0 to 10 and then put the elastic band where they think 5 would be. Then ask where $5\frac{1}{2}$ would be, noting that $5\frac{1}{2}$ is between 5 and 6. Consolidate all the half numbers between zero and 10. Emphasise that fractions are numbers too and that they are always there on the number line, having their own place.

Now provide each table with some interlocking cubes. Ask the children to count out given quantities. Say, for example: *Count out six cubes. How many will half of 6 be? How many would $\frac{1}{3}$ be?* Write the fraction and the quantity on the board so that the children see how the unit fraction is written each time. Repeat this for different quantities and fractions, to include $\frac{1}{2}$, $\frac{1}{3}$, $\frac{1}{4}$, $\frac{1}{5}$, $\frac{1}{6}$ and $\frac{1}{10}$.

Group work: Ask the children to work in pairs. They count out 20 cubes. Ask them to find out what $\frac{1}{2}$, $\frac{1}{4}$, $\frac{1}{5}$, $\frac{1}{10}$ of 20 would be. Now ask them to find if it is possible to make exactly $\frac{1}{3}$ of 20, and if not, to find a number near to 20 where it is possible to find exactly $\frac{1}{3}$, then repeat this for $\frac{1}{6}$. Ask the children to decide for themselves how to record their work.

Review

Invite the children to report their findings for the number 20. Ask: *Can you find exactly $\frac{1}{3}$ of 20? Why not?* Children may well have found $\frac{1}{3}$ of 21 or 18 and $\frac{1}{6}$ of 18 or 24. Invite the more confident children to report their findings for the number 60. Encourage them to explain why it is possible to find all of the requested fractions of 60. (They will need to realise that 60 can be divided exactly by 2, 3, 4, 5 and 10.)

Differentiation

Less confident learners: Decide whether to use the support version of the activity sheet for this group, which contains addition and subtraction for crossing 10 and 20.
More confident learners: You may like to use the extension version of the activity sheet which includes some examples of crossing hundreds.

Differentiation

Less confident learners: Decide whether to work with this group and record each fraction, and how many, on the board.
More confident learners: Challenge this group to explore the quantity 60 in the same way, and to report back what they discover during the Review.

Calculating, measuring and understanding shape

BLOCK D

Lesson 4 (Teach and apply)

Starter
Recall: Repeat the Starter for Lesson 3. This time, arrange the class into four teams. For the number that you say, each team will give one of the addition or subtraction sentences. Keep the pace of this sharp.

Main teaching activities
Whole class: Write the number 30 on the board. Ask: *What is half of 30? How did you work that out? What is half of 20? And what is half of 10?* Explain that 5 is $\frac{1}{4}$ of 20.

Write on the board: $\frac{1}{2} + \frac{1}{2} = 1$. Draw a rectangle on the board and divide it into three unequal parts. Ask: *Are these sections thirds? Why not?* Discuss how fractions are always about equal parts. Repeat with a rectangle divided into four unequal parts so that children recognise that fractions refer to equal parts of a whole.

Paired work: Provide each pair with squared paper. Ask them to find different ways of colouring in a rectangle made from 20 squares: $\frac{1}{2}$ red and $\frac{1}{2}$ blue; $\frac{1}{4}$ red, $\frac{1}{4}$ blue and $\frac{1}{2}$ yellow. Invite them to find five different ways of showing each of these fraction colourings. Repeat this for a rectangle made from 24 squares, showing $\frac{1}{6}$ and $\frac{1}{3}$ in the same way.

Review
Ask: *How can we find $\frac{1}{2}$ of a number? Or $\frac{1}{4}$? Or $\frac{1}{3}$?* Invite the children to suggest ways of doing this, such as dividing by 2, 3, or 4. Now invite a pair to show their set of colouring for $\frac{1}{2}$ red and $\frac{1}{2}$ blue. Ask: *Do all of these show half? How can you check?* Repeat this for $\frac{1}{4}$. If there is time, invite the more confident to show their colourings of $\frac{1}{3}$ and $\frac{1}{4}$ of 24.

Differentiation
Less confident learners: Decide whether to reduce the number of squares to be coloured to 8 or 12 in order to increase the opportunities of successfully making the fractions.
More confident learners: Challenge these children to make a rectangle of 24 squares. Ask them to find different ways of colouring $\frac{1}{3}$ in blue (eight squares) and $\frac{1}{4}$ in red (six squares).

Lesson 5 (Teach, apply and evaluate)

Starter
Recall: Repeat the Starter of Lesson 4, including any addition or subtraction up to 20. For example, ask for the four number sentences which are linked by $12 + 6$ ($12 + 6 = 18$; $6 + 12 = 18$; $18 - 12 = 6$; $18 - 6 = 12$). Ask each team to give one of the number sentences.

Main teaching activities
Whole class: Explain that in this lesson the children will solve one- and two-step problems using addition and subtraction of one- and two-digit numbers, and finding fractions of quantities and numbers.

Reveal the first problem from the activity sheet 'How much?'. Read the question together, aloud. Now ask: *What do we have to find out? How much money does Paul have? How much does he spend? How can we work this out?* Draw an empty number line on the board to show $50 - 7 = 43$, by counting back from 50. Repeat this for questions 2 and 3, noting that there is unnecessary information about price in question 3. Question 4 is a two-step problem. Ask: *What do we have to find out?* Agree that the children need to total the costs first, then find the difference between the total and how much Cheung spends. Use an empty number line to model the first part of the question: $20 + 10 + 5 = 35$; then another empty number line to model $35 - 8$. This time bridge back through the ten: $35 - 5 - 3 = 30 - 3 = 27$.

Individual work: Provide copies of the activity sheet 'How much?' and ask the children to solve the questions on the sheet. Explain that they need to show their working and that this can include an empty number line.

Review
Review the activity sheet together. Ask: *How did you solve this problem?* Invite children to demonstrate how they calculated, and how they used an empty number line to help them. Ask: *What strategies have you learned to help you with addition and subtraction?*

Differentiation
Less confident learners: Decide whether to use the copy of the activity sheet which contains money questions to 20p.
More confident learners: There is an activity sheet which contains more challenging questions, with unnecessary information.

Lessons 6-10

Preparation

Photocopy CD page 'Analogue clock face' onto card. Ask the children to cut these out and make up their clock faces using paper fasteners to fit the hands.

You will need

Photocopiable pages

'Digital times' (page 140) and 'Find the treasure' (page 141) for each child.

CD resources

'Two-egg cake'; 'Analogue clock face' and 'Grid coordinates' for each child/pair; 'Dial' for OHT (see General resources).

Equipment

Analogue teaching clock, digital clock face; sheets of paper with 'North', 'South', 'East' and 'West' written on them; tray; strong carrier bag and food items such as cans, packs of teabags, so that there is a total weight of about 1.5kg; various types of weighing instruments, including pan balances and weights, dial scales, and digital scales; strong paper bag; strong bags containing, for example, potatoes, which weigh amounts such as 500g, 1kg, 1.5kg... up to 4kg.

Learning objectives

Starter

- Derive and recall multiplication facts for the 2-, 3-, 4-, 5-, 6- and 10-times tables and the corresponding division facts.

Main teaching activities

2006

- Read the time on a 12-hour digital clock and to the nearest five minutes on an analogue clock; calculate time intervals and find start or end times for a given time interval
- Read and record the vocabulary of position, direction and movement, using the four compass directions to describe movement about a grid.
- Know the relationships between... kilograms and grams; choose and use appropriate units to estimate, measure and record measurements.
- Read to the nearest division and half-division, scales that are numbered or partially numbered; use the information to measure and draw to a suitable degree of accuracy.
- Solve one-step and two-step problems involving measures..., choosing and carrying out appropriate calculations.

1999

- Read the time to 5 minutes on an analogue clock and 12-hour digital clock; use the notation 9:40.
- Solve word problems involving measures.
- Read the time to the nearest minute from a 12-hour digital clock.
- Read and begin to write the vocabulary related to position, direction and movement, eg describe and find the position of a square on a grid of squares with the rows and columns labelled.
- Recognise and use the four compass directions N, S, E, W.
- Measure and compare using standard units (km, m, cm, kg, g, l, ml).
- Know the relationships between kilometres and metres, metres and centimetres, kilograms and grams, litres and millilitres.
- Begin to use decimal notation for metres and centimetres.
- Suggest suitable units and measuring equipment to estimate or measure length, mass or capacity.
- Read scales to the nearest division (labelled or unlabelled); record estimates and measurements to the nearest whole or half unit (eg 'about 3.5 kg'), or in mixed units (eg '3 m and 20 cm').
- Use a ruler to draw and measure lines to the nearest half centimetre.

Vocabulary

problems, solution, methods, sign, operation, symbol, number sentence, equation, mental calculation, written calculation, informal method, jottings, diagrams, add, plus, total, subtract, take away, minus, difference, fraction, part, equal parts, one whole, one half, one third, one quarter, one fifth, one sixth, one tenth

Lesson 6 (Teach and practise)

Starter

Recall: Explain that you will say a number, such as 15, which is an answer to a multiple of 5. Ask the children to write down the multiples (3 × 5) on their whiteboards and, when you say *Show me*, to hold these up. Repeat this for multiples of 2, then multiples of 10 and for the corresponding division facts.

Main teaching activities

Whole class: Show an analogue teaching clock. Ask: *How many minutes are*

there in an hour? Move the minute hand forward from 12 and encourage the children to count in leaps of five up to 60. Now set the hands of the clock to, for example, ten past five and ask: *What time does the clock show? Where does the hour hand point? And the minute hand? So how do you know that the minute hand shows ten minutes past the hour?* Repeat this for other five-minute intervals, such as 5.20, 7.15, 8.45. Now discuss how to read 'minutes to the hour', such as 8.40. Explain that this is 20 minutes to the next hour, nine. Repeat this for all of the five-minute intervals to the next hour.

On the board write a digital time such as 7.30 and ask: *What time is this?* Elicit the responses of both 7.30 and half past seven. Repeat this for 'quarter past' and 'quarter to' times. Now introduce the other five-minute intervals written as digital time, such as 4.05, 2.10, 7.40, 9.50. Explain that the way in which we write time is the same way in which digital clocks and watches show digital time. Children who have their own digital watch could show this to a neighbour at this point, if you wish.

Using the analogue teaching clock, set the times to five-minute intervals of your choice, such as 2.05 or 6.20. Then invite the children to use their whiteboards to write down the digital time, and to hold up their boards when you say *Show me*.

Group work: Provide each child with a copy of activity sheet 'Digital times', which asks them to write the digital equivalent for different analogue times.

Review

Ask children to work in pairs to write on a whiteboard a digital time (using multiples of five minutes only) that would appear before midday, such as 9:05. One child of each pair comes out and holds up their time for the class to see. Those children still sitting direct you to move the children until they are standing in time order, with the earliest time on the left to the latest on the right. Ask the children:
● *What helped you to sort this out?*
● *How many minutes are there in every hour?*
● *What other facts do you know now from this lesson that might help at another time?*

Use a large digital clock face. Set the digital clock in turn to these times: 10:15, 08:20, 12:45, 06:50. Ask the children to set their 'Analogue clock face' to these times. When you say *Show me*, they hold up their clock face for you to check. If you have time, invite the more confident children to say their favourite TV programmes and to set both the analogue and digital clock faces to start and finish times for the other children to read. Challenge the more confident children to state how long each programme lasts.

Differentiation

Less confident learners: Work with this group. Provide each child with the 'Analogue clock face' so that they can set the time shown on the activity sheet. If they are unsure of the 'minutes to' times, count from half past: 30, 25... to the clock minute hand, to find the minutes, then agree what the next hour would be. Ask the children to count around the clock in five-minute intervals in order to find the digital time.
More confident learners: When the children have completed the activity sheet, ask them to write down their favourite TV programmes. They should draw or stamp two clock faces next to each other, and show the start and finish times as analogue times, then write the digital times underneath.

Lesson 7 (Teach and practise)

Starter
Recall: Repeat the Starter from Lesson 1 for 3-times table facts and corresponding division facts.

Main teaching activities
Whole class: Explain that today the children will be learning about the four compass directions. Show them the sheets pinned up on the wall and ask them to point to each one as you say its name. On the board, write 'North', 'South', 'East' and 'West' and their shortened form of N, S, E and W. Show the children how to read coordinates from a grid using an OHT of general resource sheet 'Grid coordinates'. Explain that the convention is to read along the horizontal axis first and then up the vertical axis. Demonstrate this to show that the word 'ant' is at E5 (for example). Now explain that hidden on the grid there are some more words. Divide the class into two teams, each with a captain who will choose someone to suggest the coordinates of a square. If a correct square is chosen, write a word into that square and award that team a point. Continue until one team has won five points.

Paired work: Give each pair of children several copies of 'Grid coordinates' and explain how to play 'Hunt the cat'. Explain that each of them draws in a cat and four mice on their own grids, but does not show their partner what they have done. They take turns to say a coordinate for a square. Their partner either says 'Found cat', 'Mouse' or 'Miss!' The children should mark in which squares they choose with a cross, and mark in 'Cat' or 'Mouse' when they find one of those squares. The winner is the one who finds all of his/her partner's cat and mice first.

Review

Show the children the OHT of 'Grid coordinates' again. Mark a square with a cross and a different square with a circle. Invite children to suggest how they can move from one square to another by describing the route as, for example, 'Two squares west and two squares north'. Repeat this for other pairs of squares, using the vocabulary of both compass points and of coordinates.

Differentiation
Less confident learners: Group the children in fours so one pair makes the choices and one pair checks the correct finds.
More confident learners: Challenge this group by suggesting that they draw in the cat and mice, but to extend beyond one square each time. Now they need to find all the squares which contain each animal.

Lesson 8 (Teach and practise)

Starter
Recall: Repeat the Starter from Lesson 7, this time asking for multiplication and division facts from the 4-times table, and review coordinates and compass point directions.

Main teaching activities
Whole class: Provide each pair with a copy of the activity sheet 'Find the treasure'. Ask them to write a list of movements to get from the ship to the treasure on the island. Remind the children that they should give the direction using compass directions and the square to move to using coordinates. Challenge the more confident children to draw their own Treasure Island on squared paper, and to write how to find the treasure using both coordinates and compass points. Work with the less confident children to complete the task.

Review
Use an acetate of 'Find the treasure' and mark the treasure in a different position. Invite individual children to say the moves and to use an OHT pen to mark in the moves on the acetate to assess their understanding of both coordinates and compass points.

Lesson 9 (Teach and apply)

Starter
Recall: Repeat the Starter for Lesson 7, this time for multiplication and related division facts from the 6-times table.

Main teaching activities
Whole class: Show the OHT made from general resource sheet 'Dial'. Explain it is the dial on some scales. Mark zero at one end and 500g at the other. Draw the needle in different positions and ask the children to read the mass shown. Ask questions such as:
- *What is each division worth? How did you work that out?*
- *Can you think of an item that might have a mass near 100g?*
- *Can you think of an item that would force me off the end of my 0-500g scale?*

Change the range of the dial to 500g to 1000g, and repeat the activity and questions. Check that the children understand that 1 kilogram weighs the same as 1000 grams. Write this on the board, and the shortened forms of kilogram (kg) and gram (g).

You may like to address the issue of 'mass' and 'weight' by explaining that scales measure mass. Mass remains constant, but weight is a force and can change according to the force of gravity. Our mass is the same on Earth and on the Moon, for example, but our weight is less on the Moon because there is one-sixth as much gravity there.

Now ask the children to look at the mass measuring equipment that you have put out. Ask them to check that the dial scales are correctly set and that the pans are in equilibrium, and to alter them if not.

Group work: Choose from this circus of activities and give the children, working in groups, time to try each one.

1. Provide the activity sheet 'Two-egg cake'. Ask the children to work in pairs to complete this sheet.

2. The children can work in groups of three or four for this activity. Provide a range of food items and a shopping bag on a tray. Ask the children to pack the bag so that it weighs about 1kg. Encourage them to estimate first, then to check by balancing. Suggest that they find different ways of doing this, and let them decide how to record their work on paper.

3. The children can work in groups of three or four for this activity. Ask them to pack a paper bag with classroom items that weigh about 300g. The children can collect their own items, and should estimate first before checking by weighing. Suggest that they find different ways of doing this, and let them decide how to record their work on paper.

Review

Here are three possible Reviews, one for each of the activities:

1. Discuss with the children that this really is a recipe that has been used for a long time. Ask: *Why do you think people used this recipe?* (It was probably handed down, from parent to child, and is very easy to remember. Perhaps, too, with little or no education, this was an easy way of remembering what would work.) Ask the children who have completed this activity to explain how they worked out the new weights for the ingredients. Discuss how much is needed for six, then 12, people each to have cake. Finally, ask: *How much would we need of each ingredient if only three people wanted cake?*

2. Ask for suggestions of how to fill the bag. *How close to 1kg did you get? How many different ways did you find to do this? How did you record your work?* Discuss the merits of the different ways of recording. Some children may have drawn pictures; others may have shown totals of weights. Ask which way gives most information (probably showing weights so that items could be substituted to find a new way of making 1kg). Invite the more confident children to explain the differences between the net weight printed on the packs and their actual weight. (The packaging – the net weight refers to the contents of the pack.)

3. Ask the children to explain how they found their totals. Discuss how close to their target of 300g they were. Again, invite the children to discuss how they recorded their work and how effective this was.

Differentiation

The children can work in mixed-ability groups for these tasks. As they work, ensure that the less confident children are taking an active role and contributing to the work. Challenge the more confident children to work out the difference between the net weights of the packs of food in the second activity, compared with their gross weight, and to explain why these are different to the other children during the Review.

Lesson 10 (Teach, apply and evaluate)

Starter

Ask multiplication and division facts for the 2-, 3-, 4-, 5-, 6- and 10-times tables. Keep the pace sharp.

Main teaching activities

Whole class: Invite the children to suggest things that they would expect to weigh in grams, and things that they would expect to weigh in kilograms, listing the items on the board. Choose from the activities for Lesson 9 for the group work.

Review

Ask questions about how much children would expect items to weigh, such as: *Would you expect an apple to weigh about 100g or 1kg?* Use the Review for your chosen activity from Lesson 9. Invite the children to say what they have learned about direction and measuring.

Name _____   Date _____

How much?

Sheet of problems that can be used with interactive whiteboard or enlarged to A3 for flipchart.

1. Paul buys a 7p lolly. He pays with a 50p piece.
How much change does he get?

_____

2. Avis buys a bar of chocolate for 60p. She eats one fifth of
her bar of chocolate. It had twenty squares of chocolate.
How many squares are left?

_____

3. Beena has 80p to spend. She spends a quarter of her
money. How much money does she have left?

_____

4. Cheung has some coins. He has a 20p, 10p and 5p.
He buys a chew for 8p. How much change does he receive?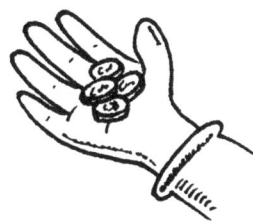

_____

■SCHOLASTIC **PHOTOCOPIABLE**

Calculating, measuring and understanding shape

BLOCK D

Name _____   Date _____

Digital times

Look at the clocks below. Write the times they show as digital times. The first one has been done for you.

Remember, the clock is a 12-hour clock only.

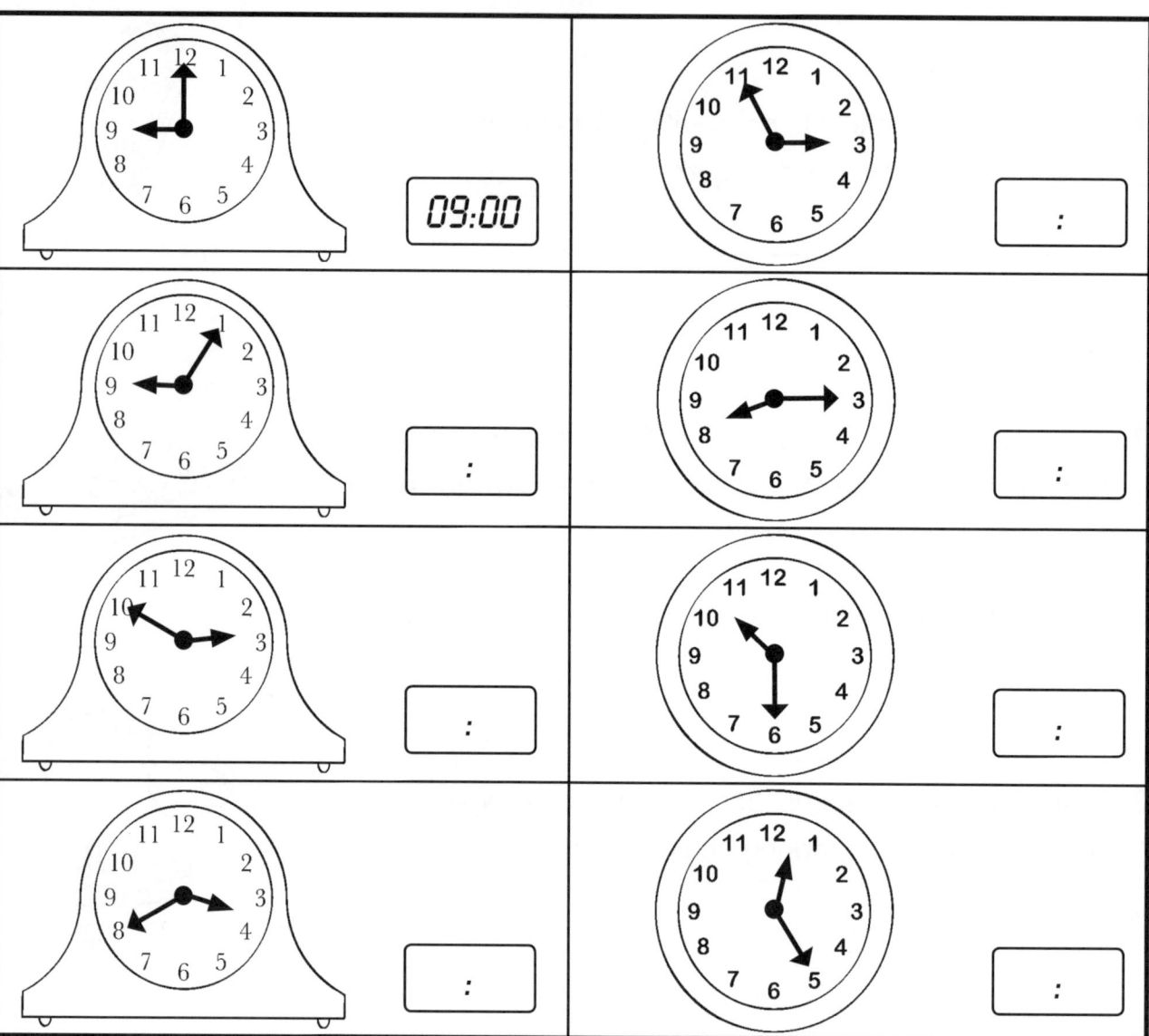

Now draw and write your own analogue clock and matching digital time.

Name _____   Date _____

Find the treasure

Find a route from the ship to the treasure.

Write down your moves using coordinates and compass point directions.

Now put a cross elsewhere on the island.

This is where more treasure is buried.

Write the moves from the ship to

the extra treasure.

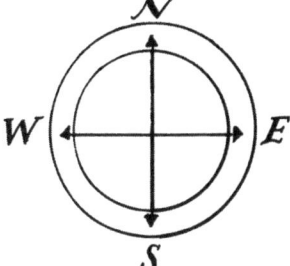

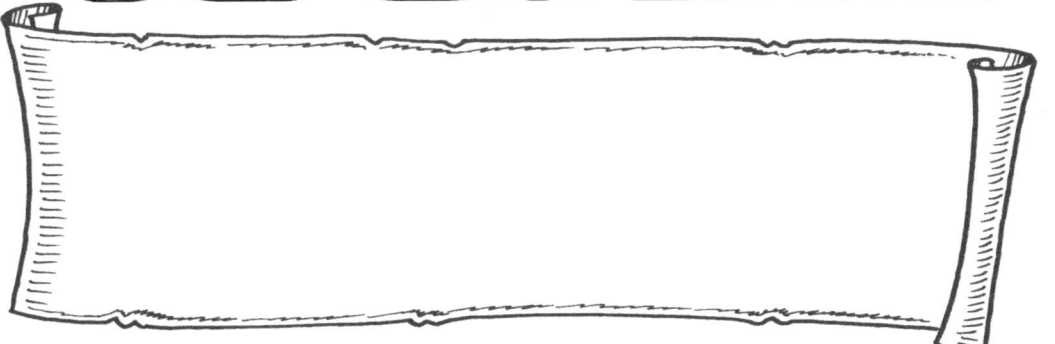

Calculating, measuring and understanding shape

BLOCK D

Unit 2 2 weeks

Calculating, measuring and understanding shape

Speaking and listening objective
- Follow an explanation or set of instructions, noting and interpreting the language associated with position, direction and movement.

Introduction
In this ten-lesson unit, children follow instructions, such as those in Lesson 7 where they give and follow instructions for movement. They solve word problems, using diagrams and number equations to help them. They reinforce their knowledge and use of addition and subtraction, multiplication and division calculation strategies and develop methods of recording their work. They link finding fractions of quantities to division. They find reflections of shapes. They use a set square to find and draw right angles.

Using and applying mathematics
- Represent the information in a puzzle or problem using numbers, images or diagrams; use these to find a solution and present it in context, where appropriate using £.p notation or units of measure.

Lesson	Strand	Starter	Main teaching activities
1. Review	Calculate	Derive and recall multiplication facts for the 2-, 3-, 4-, 5-, 6- and 10-times tables and the corresponding division facts; recognise multiples of 2, 5 or 10 up to 1000.	**Add or subtract mentally combinations of one-digit and two-digit numbers.**
2. Teach and practise	Calculate	Use knowledge of number operations and corresponding inverses, including doubling and halving, to estimate and check calculations.	As for Lesson 1
3. Teach and apply	Calculate	As for Lesson 2	Develop and use written methods to record, support or explain addition and subtraction of two-digit and three-digit numbers.
4. Teach and practise	Calculate	Derive and recall multiplication facts for the 2-, 3-, 4-, 5-, 6- and 10-times tables and the corresponding division facts.	Use practical and informal written methods to multiply and divide two-digit numbers (eg 13×3, $50 \div 4$); round remainders up or down, depending on the context.
5. Teach, practise and evaluate	Calculate Measure	As for Lesson 4	• Find unit fractions of numbers and quantities (eg $^1/_2$, $^1/_3$, $^1/_4$ and $^1/_6$ of 12 litres). • Know the relationships between kilometres and metres, metres and centimetres, kilograms and grams, litres and millilitres; choose and use appropriate units to estimate, measure and record measurements.
6. Teach and practise	Shape	Use knowledge of number operations and corresponding inverses, including doubling and halving, to estimate and check calculations.	**Draw and complete shapes with reflective symmetry and draw the reflection of a shape in a mirror line along one side.**
7. Teach and apply	Shape	As for Lesson 6	Read and record the vocabulary of position, direction and movement, using the four compass directions to describe movement about a grid.
8. Teach and practise	Shape	Derive and recall multiplication facts for the 2-, 3-, 4-, 5-, 6- and 10-times tables and the corresponding division facts; recognise multiples of 2, 5 or 10 up to 1000.	Use a set-square to draw right angles and to identify right angles in 2D shapes; compare angles with a right angle; recognise that a straight line is equivalent to two right angles.
9. Teach and apply	Use/apply	**Add or subtract mentally combinations of one- and two-digit numbers.**	Represent the information in a puzzle or problem using numbers, images or diagrams; use these to find a solution and present it in context, where appropriate using £.p notation or units of measure.
10. Teach, practise and evaluate	Use/apply	As for Lesson 9	As for Lesson 9

SCHOLASTIC

Lessons 1-5

Preparation
A3 photocopies of 'Hundred square' and 'Fractions of quantities'.

You will need
Photocopiable pages
'Hop it' (page 150), 'Splitting tens and units' (page 151), 'Record it!' (page 152), 'Multiplication and division' (page 153) and 'Fractions of quantities' (page 154) for each child.
CD resources
Support and extension versions of 'Splitting tens and units', 'Record it!' and 'Multiplication and division'; 'Hundred square' for each child (see General resources).
Equipment
Counting stick.

Learning objectives

Starter
● Derive and recall multiplication facts for the 2-, 3-, 4-, 5-, 6- and 10-times tables and the corresponding division facts; recognise multiples of 2, 5 or 10 up to 1000.
● Use knowledge of number operations and corresponding inverses, including doubling and halving, to estimate and check calculations.

Main teaching activities
2006
● Add or subtract mentally combinations of one- and two-digit numbers.
● Develop and use written methods to record, support or explain addition and subtraction of two-digit and three-digit numbers.
● Use practical and informal written methods to multiply and divide two-digit numbers (eg 13 × 3, 50 ÷ 4); round remainders up or down, depending on the context.
● Find unit fractions of numbers and quantities (eg ½, ⅓, ¼ and ⅙ of 12 litres).
● Know the relationships between kilometres and metres, metres and centimetres, kilograms and grams, litres and millilitres; choose and use appropriate units to estimate, measure and record measurements.
1999
● Use mental calculation strategies - several objectives, including: use known number facts and place value to add/subtract mentally; add and subtract mentally a 'near multiple of 10'; add mentally three or four small numbers; find a difference by counting up.
● Use known number facts and place value to carry out mentally simple multiplications and divisions.
● Begin to find remainders after simple division; round up or down after division, depending on the context.
● Recognise unit fractions such as ½, ⅓, ¼, ⅕, ¹⁄₁₀ ... and use them to find fractions of shapes and numbers.
● Measure and compare using standard units (km, m, cm, kg, g, l, ml).
● Know the relationships between kilometres and metres, metres and centimetres, kilograms and grams, litres and millilitres.
● Begin to use decimal notation for metres and centimetres.
● Suggest suitable units and measuring equipment to estimate or measure length, mass or capacity.

Vocabulary
problem, solution, puzzle, pattern, methods, sign, operation, symbol, number sentence, equation, mental calculation, written calculation, informal method, jottings, diagrams, pictures, images, add, plus, sum, total, subtract, take away, minus, difference, double, halve, inverse, multiply, times, multiplied by, product, share, share equally, divide, divided by, divided into, left, left over, remainder, fraction, part, equal parts, one whole, one half, one third, one quarter, one fifth, one sixth, one tenth, measure, estimate, unit, length, distance, weight, capacity, ruler, tape measure, balance, scales, measuring cylinder/jug, angle, right angle, set square, units of measurement and abbreviations: metre (m), centimetre (cm), millimetre (mm), kilogram (kg), gram (g), litre (l), millilitre (ml)

BLOCK D

Lesson 1 (Review)

Starter

Recall: Practise counting in fives, starting from zero, using a counting stick. Point to different positions on the stick asking both whole-class and individual questions such as: *How many fives in 50?* Ask the children to only think of multiples of 5 when responding to your questions. Then invite them to close their eyes and think of a multiple less than 25, and double it. Ask: *What possible answers are there?* List the answers and ask the children to spot which possible answers are missing.

Main teaching activities

Whole class: Explain to the children that in this lesson they will be adding three or four numbers together. Provide each child with a copy of general resource sheet 'Hundred square', which they can use as an aid for addition, and remind them that they can also use an empty number line if they find this helpful. Write the addition $15 + 35 + 45 = \square$ on the board. Ask the children to calculate the answer. Ask: *How did you work this out?* Invite different methods, such as beginning with the largest number or adding the tens first. Repeat for another addition such as $31 + 26 + 37$.

Repeat for additions such as $36 + 15$. Ask the children to work mentally, where they can, or to use the 'Hundred square'. They could say: *36 add 10 is 46, add 4 is 50, add 1 is 51.* Repeat for other examples.

Individual work: Ask the children to complete the 'Hop it' activity sheet. They are asked to find six different solutions to the addition sentence $\square + \square = 80$.

Review

Ask for volunteers to draw one of their solutions for the 'Hop it' activity sheet on an empty number line on the board. Move their box and triangle numbers around, asking the class what difference it makes to the total (none). However, they may express a preference for the order they would like to add the numbers.

Differentiation

Less confident learners: Decide whether to work with this group to find different solutions. Use an empty number line to demonstrate each possible solution.

More confident learners: Challenge the children to find more solutions, say ten in total. They can write their additional solutions on the back of their sheet.

Lesson 2 (Teach and practise)

Starter

Reason: Explain that you would like the children to halve some numbers. Ask them to halve 100, 90, 80, 70, 60, 50, 40, 30, 20 and 10. Ask: *Which numbers did you find easier to halve? How did you halve 90?* For example, did they consider partitioning the division into $80 \div 2$ and $10 \div 2$ and then recombining the results?

Main teaching activities

Whole class: Explain that today you would like the children to consider in which order they would add a series of numbers, and to add by partitioning into tens and units. Write on the board: $26 + 43 = \square$ and ask the class to think about how they would calculate the answer. Now write up $26 + 43 = (20 + 6) + (40 + 3) = (20 + 40) + (6 + 3) = 60 + 9 = 69$. Model this on an empty number line.

Then write $43 + 26 = (40 + 3) + (20 + 6) = (40 + 20) + (3 + 6) = 60 + 9 = 69$ and ask: *Does it make any difference in which order we add? No. Which way round do you think was easier? Why do you think that?* Children may vary in their views, so be accepting of this. Repeat for $17 + 52$, $25 + 61$ and $34 + 25$.

Individual work: Provide copies of the activity sheet 'Splitting tens and units' and ask the children to complete them, working individually.

Review

Write on the board the numbers 24, 67 and 82. Ask the children to partition each of these. Now ask: *How would you add 24 and 67?* Invite suggestions and ask a child to record the suggestions on the board. Discuss whether

Differentiation

Less confident learners: Use the support version of the activity sheet for this group. You may wish to provide apparatus such as an A3 hundred square or number line as a calculation aid.
More confident learners: The extension version of the activity sheet challenges the children to think about the order of the two-digit numbers to be added.

it is easier to calculate 24 + 67 or 67 + 24 and why they think this. Now challenge the more confident children. Invite them to calculate 67 + 82. Discuss the size of the answer before beginning, saying: *Will the answer be more or less than 100? How do you know?* Record a suggestion for calculating on the board, such as:

$$67 + 82 = 82 + 67$$
$$= (80 + 60) + (2 + 7)$$
$$= 140 + 9$$
$$= 149$$

Repeat for 24 + 82.

Lesson 3 (Teach and apply)

Starter
Recall: Take the children on 'number walks'. This involves the children listening to your calculations and then making jottings as the number walk progresses. Only accept an answer right at the end. For example: *I start on the number 15, double it* (pause for jotting), *then to move on I add the number 20* (pause). *I halve this number and add 3* (pause). *Where do I end up?* (28) Repeat the process for other examples, such as: *I start on the number which is double 5. Then I add 30. I halve this number and subtract 4. Where do I end up?* (16)

Main teaching activities
Whole class: Explain that today the children will be using written methods to record and explain their addition and subtraction. Explain that this can be done by adding the most significant digits first. Write on the board: 58 + 34 = (50 + 30) + (8 + 4) = 80 + 12 = 92. Repeat this for another example, such as 48 + 56.

Now extend this to adding two- and three-digit numbers, such as: 360 + 58: 300 + (60 + 50) + 8 = 300 + 110 + 8 = 418.

Repeat for subtraction. Write up 87 – 50 and ask: *How can you work this out?* Children may suggest counting up from 50 to 80 in tens then adding 7 to make 37. Draw an empty number line to model this and write: 87 – 50 = 80 – 50 + 7 = 37. Repeat for another example, such as 234 – 8, and ask for suggestions for how to solve this, and what to record in order to explain how the problem was worked out.
Paired work: Ask the children to work in pairs to find solutions to the number problems on the 'Record it!' activity sheet.

Review
Review some of the examples which the children tried. Ask them to write their recording method. Ask: *Who tried a different method? Which one do you think is better? Why do you think that?*

Differentiation

Less confident learners: Decide whether to use the support version of the sheet.
More confident learners: There is an extension version of the sheet available.

Lesson 4 (Teach and practise)

Starter
Recall: Explain that you will ask some multiplication table questions. Ask, for example: *What is 6 multiplied by 4? What is 8 times 3?* and so on.

Main teaching activities
Whole class: Explain that in this lesson the children will multiply and divide two-digit numbers, using the table facts that they have been learning. Explain also that they will record their working. Say: *My table top at home is 90cm along each side. How far is it all the way around? How could you work this out? What sort of calculation do you need?* Agree that this is a multiplication problem: 90 × 4. Write this on the board. Ask: *How can we work this out?* The children should remember that if they know 9 × 4, then they can derive 90 × 4. Write the answer: 360cm. Ask: *How many metres is this?* Write 3m 60cm. Repeat for a division problem, such as: *I have 12*

▷

metres of ribbon. I want to cut this into 4 metre lengths. How many lengths of ribbon can I make? What sort of calculation is this? Agree that it is a division problem. Write on the board: 12 ÷ 4 = 3. Now repeat this for one with a remainder, such as: I need to cut a 25cm length of tape into 4cm lengths. How many can I cut? How much tape will be left? Discuss the type of calculation needed and write on the board: 25 ÷ 4 = 6 remainder 1. Ask: How long is the piece left over?

Paired work: Ask the children to work in pairs with activity sheet 'Multiplication and division'. They work independently to find the answers, write their method, then compare how they have worked out the answer.

Review

Invite children from each ability group to explain how they found their answers and to write their recording for others to see and compare. Ask questions such as: What two multiplication facts could you use to calculate 14 × 4?

Differentiation

Less confident learners: Decide whether to use the support version of the sheet that uses table facts from the 2-, 5- and 10-times tables only.
More confident learners: Decide whether to use the extension version of the sheet that includes table facts from the 6-times table.

Lesson 5 (Teach, practise and evaluate)

Starter
Recall: Repeat the Starter from Lesson 4, this time for deriving division facts. Say, for example: What is 30 divided by 5?

Main teaching activities
Whole class: Explain that in today's lesson children will find fractions of quantities. Say: Paul has a bottle of juice which holds 500ml. He pours equal $^1/_5$ amounts of the juice into some glasses until there is none left. How much is in each glass? What sort of calculation do you need to do? Agree that in order to find $^1/_5$ of 500ml the calculation needed is 500ml ÷ 5 = 100ml. Ask: What must we do now? Children may suggest repeated subtraction of 100 from 500, or know that 100 × 5 = 500.

Say: A bar of chocolate weighs 240g. Tamsin cuts it into four equal pieces. What fraction of the bar is each piece? How much does each piece weigh? Agree that each piece is ¼ of the bar and that the calculation is 240 ÷ 4.

Paired work: Provide a copy of activity sheet 'Fractions of quantities' for each child. Ask them to work in pairs to find the fractions.

Review
Using the A3 enlargement of the sheet, review the questions together. Ask: How did you find the answer? What sort of calculation did you need to use? So what fraction was this? What have you learned about fractions?

Differentiation

Less confident learners: Decide whether to have the children work as a group, as the sheet is not differentiated. Discuss each fraction and how it can be found using division.
More confident learners: Set the challenge to find $^2/_5$, ¾... of the quantities once the unit fraction quantity has been found.

◯

Lessons 6–10

Preparation
Enlarge photocopiable page 'Guess my rule' to A3.

You will need
Photocopiable pages
'Guess my rule' (page 155).
CD resources
Core, support and extension versions of 'Bugs alive', support and extension versions of 'Guess my rule'; 'Angles' (see General resources). ITP Symmetry.
Equipment
Mirrors; ten beanbags; Roamer; set squares.

Learning objectives

Starter
● Use knowledge of number operations and corresponding inverses, including doubling and halving, to estimate and check calculations.
● Derive and recall multiplication facts for the 2-, 3-, 4-, 5-, 6- and 10-times tables and the corresponding division facts; recognise multiples of 2, 5 or 10 up to 1000.
● Add or subtract mentally combinations of one-digit and two-digit numbers.

Main teaching activities
2006
● Draw and complete shapes with reflective symmetry and draw the reflection of a shape in a mirror line along one side.
● Read and record the vocabulary of position, direction and movement, using the four compass directions to describe movement about a grid.

▷

Unit 2 ▶ 2 weeks

- Use a set-square to draw right angles and to identify right angles in 2D shapes; compare angles with a right angle; recognise that a straight line is equivalent to two right angles.
- Represent the information in a puzzle or problem using numbers, images or diagrams; use these to find a solution and present it in context, where appropriate using £.p notation or units of measure.

1999
- Identify and sketch lines of symmetry in simple shapes, and recognise shapes with no lines of symmetry.
- Sketch the reflection of a simple shape in a mirror line along one edge.
- Read and begin to write the vocabulary related to position, direction and movement, eg describe and find the position of a square on a grid of squares with the rows and columns labelled.
- Recognise and use the four compass directions N, S, E, W.
- Identify right angles in 2D shapes and the environment.
- Recognise that a straight line is equivalent to two right angles.
- Compare angles with a right angle.
- Choose and use appropriate operations (including multiplication and division) to solve word problems, and appropriate ways of calculating: mental, mental with jottings, pencil and paper.
- Recognise all coins and notes. Understand and use £.p notation (for example, know that £3.06 is £3 and 6p).

Vocabulary

problem, solution, puzzle, pattern, methods, sign, operation, symbol, number sentence, equation, mental calculation, written calculation, informal method, jottings, diagrams, pictures, images, map, plan, compass point, north (N), south (S), east (E), west (W), turn, whole turn, half turn, quarter turn, right, left, up, down, ascend, descend, forwards, backwards, sideways, across, angle, right angle, set square

Lesson 6 (Teach and practise)

Starter
Reason: Ask the children to say the doubles of numbers that you say. Begin with simple ones such as double 11... 14... Then extend to double 23... 29... Ask: *How did you work out the answer?*

Main teaching activities
Whole class: Display the ITP Symmetry and click on squares to build a 2 × 3 rectangle. Ask: *Where do you think this shape will be reflected in the mirror?* Ask the children to quickly sketch the shape on squared paper, with the mirror line drawn in, then to sketch where they think the reflection will be. Display the reflection for them to check. Repeat for other shapes and for the mirror in both horizontal and vertical alignment.

Paired work: Provide more squared paper. Ask the children to draw in their mirror line, either horizontally or vertically. Then they draw a shape which touches the mirror. They swap papers with their partner and draw in the reflection. They check their drawings with a mirror.

Differentiation
Less confident learners: Decide whether to work as a group and encourage the children to use the vocabulary of shape to explain where they think the reflection will be.
More confident learners: Challenge the children to draw more complex shapes, away from the mirror line so that they need to calculate the position on the other side of the mirror for the reflection.

Review
Invite the children to draw their shapes using the ITP Symmetry. The others sketch the shape and its reflection, then they check by revealing the reflection on Symmetry. Ask questions, such as:
- *Which letters of the alphabet have line symmetry?*
- *Which letters have more than one line of symmetry?*
- *Which letter, when reflected in the mirror, makes a different letter?* (b, d)

BLOCK D

Lesson 7 (Teach and apply)

Starter

Recall: Remind the class that 19 and 21 are 'near doubles'. Ask the children for other examples of near doubles. Tell them to divide their whiteboards into two with a vertical line. Ask for a double and near double, such as 34/35, where 34 is double 17 and 35 is, for example, 17 + 18. Share the responses and test out the 'doubleness' of the left-hand number by halving. What is the hardest example they can show you?

Main teaching activities

Whole class: Before the lesson begins, mark the four points of the compass clearly on the classroom floor. Give out five beanbags, one to each of five children. The first child moves around the room and places their beanbag saying 'My beanbag is underneath the chair'. The next child has to remember this and then repeat this by touching the first child's bag and moving to place their own beanbag in their choice of place. Continue until all five bags are out. Ask the children what positional vocabulary has been used from today's list. Extend to ten beanbags.

Now point to the four compass points on the floor and ask the children to explain what these mean. Write 'North', 'South', 'East' and 'West' on the board, spread well out, to show the four points of the compass. Repeat the beanbag activity, this time asking the children to place their beanbags using compass directions, such as the first child steps 'North, 1 step' (drop bag); second child repeats and adds 'turn clockwise through a right angle, 1 step' (drop bag), and so on. Each time, the children decide in which direction the child is facing when the beanbag is dropped. Sketch the route on the board, marking the route and referring to the compass direction each time.

Group work: Using the vocabulary of compass points, direction and movement, the children work in small teams to script a short route to drop the beanbags. Each child tries out their script before drawing the route.

Differentiation

Less confident learners: Provide adult support to act as a scribe for this group.

More confident learners: Challenge these children to program Roamer to follow their route.

Review

Ask one group to walk their route. Then display two of the drawn routes. Can the children reason which is the correct drawing? Encourage them to direct a child along a beanbag route. Ask: *Which way should he/she turn next? How can you tell that? In which direction is he/she facing now?* If the more confident children have programmed Roamer, invite them to show what they have done and to explain how they programmed Roamer.

Lesson 8 (Teach and practise)

Starter

Rehearse: Use the counting stick again, labelling one end 0 and the other 30. Now count along it with the children and, for each position, say the relevant 3-times table fact. Do this several times, keeping a good pace to the chanting. Now point to a place on the stick and ask for the fact for where your finger is pointing and repeat the activity.

Main teaching activities

Whole class: Explain to the children that in this lesson they will be comparing right angles with other angles to see which is greater. Ask them to take a sheet of paper, fold it in half and then across into quarters, making sure that the creases are firm. Then ask the children to identify the right angle, where the paper has all the folds. Now ask them to compare their right angle with angles that they can see around them, such as the edge of their desk. Ask: *Is this a right angle?* Now ask the children to put two pieces of folded paper together so that the right angles touch, as if one is a reflection of the other. Suggest the children look at the straight edge that runs from one side of the two right angles to the other, explaining that a straight line can be seen as being the same as two right angles.

Differentiation
Less confident learners: Decide whether to have these children complete this activity as a group. Encourage them to use the vocabulary of angles as they answer.
More confident learners: Challenge these children to sketch some straight-line shapes and to label the angles 'L' for larger than a right angle and 'S' for smaller. They can mark the right angles with an 'R'.

Provide each child with a set square. Show them, by using a board set-square, how to draw a right angle with it, then how to check a right angle. Ask the children to use the set square to find some right angles in the classroom. Check that everyone is secure with using a set square.
Individual work: Provide each child with a copy of general resource sheet 'Angles'. Ask them to use a set square to check which angles are right angles, and which are larger/smaller than a right angle.

Review
Draw a hexagon with some right angles on the board. Ask: *How can we check which angles are right angles?* Invite a child to demonstrate using the teaching set square. Now, using the teaching ruler and the set square, ask: *How can we draw a square which measures six units along each side?*

Lesson 9 (Teach and apply)

Starter
Rehearse: Write some subtraction sentences on the board, such as 47 – 25 = 22. Ask the children to think of the three related number sentences: two for addition and another for subtraction.

Main teaching activities
Whole class: Ask the class to decide which operation was used for the following problems: *I start with the number 10 and end up with 15; I start with 25 and end up with 17; I start with 54 and end up with 27.* Discuss each question in turn, inviting the children to explain why it is addition or subtraction. Give each child a copy of the differentiated activity sheet 'Guess my rule' and ask them to work out the rule for the function machines.

Differentiation
Less confident learners: Provide the children with the support version of 'Guess my rule'.
More confident learners: Give the children the extension version of the activity sheet.

Review
Use an A3 enlargement of 'Guess my rule'. Invite all the children to help explain what the rule is for each function machine. Ask questions such as: *How did you work out whether to add, subtract, multiply or divide?* Encourage the children to explain this in their own words. Give praise to those who use mathematical vocabulary appropriately.

Lesson 10 (Teach, practise and evaluate)

Starter
Derive: Repeat the Starter for Lesson 9. This time write up, for example, 45 + 36 = ☐ or 95 – 67 = ☐ and ask the children to complete the number sentence, before deriving the other three sentences.

Main teaching activities
Whole class: Explain that the problems to be solved in this lesson centre around a class who are collecting minibeasts on a science trip. Pose this problem: *Dana has 15 slugs. Andy has 23 slugs. How many more slugs does Andy have than Dana?* On the board, write this grid formation and solve it.

Differentiation
Less confident learners: Decide whether to use the support version of the activity sheet with simpler calculations. Discuss with the children the range of calculation strategies that they could use to solve these problems.
More confident learners: There is an extension version available which extends the number range for these children.

Problem	Calculation	Final answer	Checking calculation
15 slugs, 23 slugs; How many more?	23 – 15	8 slugs more	15 + 8 = 23

By carrying out a checking calculation they can check the answer. Repeat for another problem, such as: *Seema has collected 24 woodlice. Mark has only half as many woodlice as Seema. How many woodlice does Mark have?*
Individual work: Ask the children to complete the activity sheet 'Bugs alive'.

Review
Review together some of the problems from the activity sheets. Invite feedback on what the children have learned this week.

Name _____ Date _____

Hop it

Write in the missing numbers.

Find six different solutions.

 +  =

 +  =

 +  =

 +  =

 +  =

 +  =

Name _____   Date _____

Splitting tens and units

Work out these calculations.

Show how you solved each one, step-by-step. One has been done for you.

37 + 25

        = (30 + 7) + (20 + 5)
        = (30 + 20) + (7 + 5)
        = 50 + 12 = 50 + 10 + 2
        = 62

1. 48 + 25 = ☐	**2.** 45 + 32 = ☐
3. 38 + 44 = ☐	**4.** 29 + 16 = ☐
5. 56 + 17 = ☐	**6.** 28 + 43 = ☐

Calculating, measuring and understanding shape

BLOCK D

Name _____ Date _____

Record it!

Find the answers to these number problems.

Show your workings.

Number problem	Solution	Answer
1. 56 + 35		
2. 84 − 37		
3. 346 + 40		
4. 345 − 30		
5. 642 − 7		

Name _____ Date _____

Multiplication and division

Work out the answers to these questions.

Make some jottings to help you to work out the answer.
Compare what you did with your partner.

Problem	Jottings	Answer
1. Marc buys four bags of sweets. Each bag weighs 120g. How much do the sweets weigh in total?		
2. Poppy measured a picture frame. All the sides were the same size. Altogether the frame measured 80cm. How long was each side?		
3. A small cup holds 60ml of juice. How much will three of these cups hold?		
4. Each side of a square book measures 14cm. How far is it all around the book?		
5. Five sweets weigh 100g. How much does each sweet weigh?		

Calculating, measuring and understanding shape

BLOCK D

Name _____   Date _____

Fractions of quantities

1. Aidan has 100cm of tape. Which of these quantities can he cut exactly?

Be careful! Aidan does not want any fractions of centimetres!

Write the answers, and show how long each fraction of the tape would measure.

Fraction	Quantity	Is this an exact amount?
$\frac{1}{2}$		
$\frac{1}{4}$		
$\frac{1}{5}$		
$\frac{1}{6}$		
$\frac{1}{10}$		

2. Aidan now wants to divide 240g of chocolate into different amounts.

Write the answers showing how much each fraction of the chocolate would weigh.

Fraction	Quantity	Is this an exact amount?
$\frac{1}{2}$		
$\frac{1}{4}$		
$\frac{1}{5}$		
$\frac{1}{6}$		
$\frac{1}{10}$		

Name _____   Date _____

Guess my rule

Look at the numbers in the first column.
Decide how they have been changed into the numbers in the second column.

Write underneath each function box what rule you think applies.

Write in the missing numbers.

2	4
3	6
0	0
10	

My rule is _____

44	35
	59
36	27
22	13

My rule is _____

25	21
52	48
	6
100	96

My rule is _____

27	32
41	46
75	80
58	

My rule is _____

24	8
30	10
15	5
	9

My rule is _____

36	
42	21
68	34
44	22

My rule is _____

Calculating, measuring and understanding shape

BLOCK D

Unit 3 2 weeks

Calculating, measuring and understanding shape

Speaking and listening objective

● Explain a process or present information, ensuring that items are clearly sequenced, relevant details are included and accounts ended effectively.

Introduction

In this ten-lesson unit, children should be encouraged to present information in a logical sequence, using appropriate mathematical vocabulary and be prepared to answer questions from other children. They solve problems which involve addition, subtraction, multiplication and division, and use appropriate methods to record their work. They develop their understanding that division is the inverse of multiplication and use this understanding to solve problems. They sketch shapes, and recognise right angles. They read scales for capacity, make estimates and checks in practical situations. They tell the time in five-minute intervals, and record using digital time. They also write sentences about time intervals.

Using and applying mathematics

● Solve one-step and two-step problems involving numbers, money or measures, including time, choosing and carrying out appropriate calculations.

Lesson	Strand	Starter	Main teaching activities
1. Teach and apply	Knowledge	Derive and recall multiplication facts for the 2-, 3-, 4-, 5-, 6- and 10-times tables and the corresponding division facts.	Use knowledge of number operations and corresponding inverses, including doubling and halving, to estimate and check calculations.
2. Teach and apply	Calculate	As for Lesson 1	Develop and use written methods to record, support or explain addition and subtraction of two-digit and three-digit numbers.
3. Teach and apply	Calculate	**Derive and recall all addition and subtraction facts for each number to 20.**	As for Lesson 2
4 Teach and apply.	Calculate	Read, write and order whole numbers to at least 1000 and position them on a number line; count on from and back to zero in single-digit steps or multiples of 10.	As for Lesson 2
5 .Teach, apply and evaluate	Calculate	Derive and recall multiplication facts for the 2-, 3-, 4-, 5-, 6- and 10-times tables and the corresponding division facts.	Use practical and informal written methods to multiply and divide two-digit numbers (eg 13 × 3, 50 ÷ 4); round remainders up or down, depending on the context.
6. Teach and practise	Calculate	**Derive and recall all addition and subtraction facts for each number to 20.**	Understand that division is the inverse of multiplication and vice versa; use this to derive and record related multiplication and division number sentences.
7. Teach and apply	Calculate	Read, write and order whole numbers to at least 1000 and position them on a number line; count on from and back to zero in single-digit steps or multiples of 10.	As for Lesson 6
8. Teach and apply	Shape	**Derive and recall all addition and subtraction facts for each number to 20.**	Use a set-square to draw right angles and to identify right angles in 2D shapes; compare angles with a right angle; recognise that a straight line is equivalent to two right angles.
9. Teach and apply	Measure	As for Lesson 8	**Read, to the nearest division and half-division, scales that are numbered or partially numbered; use the information to measure and draw to a suitable degree of accuracy.**
10. Teach, practise and evaluate	Measure	As for Lesson 8	Read the time on a 12-hour digital clock and to the nearest five minutes on an analogue clock; calculate time intervals and find start or end times for a given time interval.

Unit 3 ▪ 2 weeks

Lessons 1-5

Preparation
Make two sets of 0 to 20 cards, using CD page 'Numeral cards 0–20'. Use CD page 'Add or subtract 1, 10 or 100' to make cards.

You will need
Photocopiable pages
'At the bookstore' (page 164) and 'Missing numbers' (page 165) for each child.
CD resources
Support and extension versions of 'At the bookstore' and 'Missing numbers'; 'Numeral cards 0–20' and 'Add or subtract 10 or 100' cards' (see General resources).
Equipment
Pots of coins.

Learning objectives

Starter
● Derive and recall multiplication facts for the 2-, 3-, 4-, 5-, 6- and 10-times tables and the corresponding division facts.
● Derive and recall all addition and subtraction facts for each number to 20.
● Read, write and order whole numbers to at least 1000 and position them on a number line; count on from and back to zero in single-digit steps or multiples of 10.

Main teaching activities
2006
● Use knowledge of number operations and corresponding inverses, including doubling and halving, to estimate and check calculations.
● Develop and use written methods to record, support or explain addition and subtraction of two- and three-digit numbers.
● Use practical and informal written methods to multiply and divide two-digit numbers (eg 13 × 3, 50 ÷ 4); round remainders up or down, depending on the context.
1999
● Check subtraction with addition, halving with doubling and division with multiplication.
● Repeat addition or multiplication in a different order.
● Check with an equivalent calculation.
● Use informal pencil and paper methods to support, record or explain HTU ± TU, HTU ± HTU.
● Begin to use column addition and subtraction for HTU ± TU where the calculation cannot easily be done mentally.
● Use known number facts and place value to carry out mentally simple multiplications and divisions.
● Begin to find remainders after simple division; round up or down after division, depending on the context.

Vocabulary
problem, solution, puzzle, pattern, methods, sign, operation, symbol, number sentence, equation, mental calculation, written calculation, informal method, jottings, diagrams, pictures, images, add, plus, sum, total, subtract, take away, minus, difference, double, halve, inverse, multiply, times, multiplied by, product, share, share equally, divide, divided by, divided into, left, left over, remainder

Lesson 1 (Teach and apply)

Starter
Recall: Say a multiplication fact, such as 4 × 5. Ask the children to work in pairs to write the two multiplication facts and two division facts, with answers, from your starting point. Use the 2-, 3-, 4-, 5- and 10-times tables.

Main teaching activities
Whole class: Explain that today and in the next lesson the children will be solving money problems. Hold up a 20p and 50p coin and say: *What is the total? How did you work it out? So, if I have 70p in total and spend 20p how much do I have left?* Agree that if 20 + 50 = 70, then 70 - 20 = 50. Remind the children that they can use subtraction to check addition, multiplication to check division, doubling for halving, and so on. Now ask the children to use the pots of money on their tables and, working in groups, to decide what different amounts of money they can make if they choose three silver coins each time.

Give the children about five minutes to do this. Invite a response from each group and write these on the board. Ask: *How did you find your solutions? How did you check your results? Give me a check calculation.* Write the check calculation on the board.

Paired work: Ask the children to work in pairs. Set the challenge: *How many different amounts can you make with four silver coins?* Ask the children to record their work and remind them that it will be an advantage to them if they think about doing this systematically. For each amount ask them to think about a check calculation they could use. For example, if four 20p coins make 80p, a good check calculation would be dividing 80 by 4.

Review

Invite the children from the core group to feed back their results. Write these on the board, ordering them so that only one coin changes each time. Discuss the patterns of results that are revealed.

Differentiation

Less confident learners: Decide whether to ask the children to use just three copper or silver coins each time.
More confident learners: Challenge these children to work with five silver coins each time.

Lesson 2 (Teach and apply)

Starter

Recall: Repeat the Starter from Lesson 1, this time including facts from the 6-times table.

Main teaching activities

Whole class: Set a challenge. Ask: *If I buy a toy which costs 36p and use two silver coins to pay for this, what change might I get?* Now extend this to include the £1 and £2 coins and ask: *If I buy a book which costs £3.65 and use two coins to pay for this, what coins could I use? What change would I get?* Ask the children to use written recording to show how they worked out the answer. Discuss how children worked out the answer, and how they recorded their workings.

Individual work: Provide copies of 'At the bookstore'. Ask the children to find solutions to the problems and to record their working each time.

Review

Invite children to give their responses to the problems, and discuss the jottings that the children made and how these were useful. Ask: *How would you record 92 - 36? How would you calculate the answer?*

Differentiation

Less confident learners: Decide whether to use the support version of the activity sheet for these children. Provide pots of coins and notes where children would find these useful.
More confident learners: There is an extension version of the activity sheet which involves larger amounts of money.

Lesson 3 (Teach and apply)

Starter

Recall: Place two stacks of 0–20 numeral cards face down on the table. Invite a child to take the top card from each stack, Blu-Tacking the cards to the board for everyone to see. Then ask the children to make an addition and subtraction number sentence using the two numbers, where the addition total does not exceed 20. For example, for 19 and 13 they might make 13 + 6 = 19 and 19 - 13 = 6. Set the timer to ring at ten seconds, telling the children that as soon as the timer rings they must hold up their whiteboards to show their number sentences. Share some of the responses and swiftly move on to the next two cards to be picked up.

Main teaching activities

Whole class: By the end of the lesson the majority of children should understand that $\triangle + \square = \bigcirc$ or $\bigcirc - \triangle = \square$. Review with the children the language of addition and subtraction, focusing on numbers that encourage the children to bridge the hundreds.

Discuss the children's strategies for calculating, and how they managed to cross the hundreds, such as 82 + 19: *82 add 10 is 92, add 8 is 100, add 1 is 101.*

Now draw an empty number line on the board and invite a child to demonstrate 82 + 19. Reinforce that whilst 82 + 19 = 101, 19 + 82 = 101 and 82 - 19 = 63, 19 - 82 *cannot* equal 63. Now say: *I think of a number. I add 7. The answer is 15.* What is my number? (8) Then: *15 added to a number is 65. What is the number?* (50) Invite children to explain how they worked out the answers and to show this on an empty number line such as:

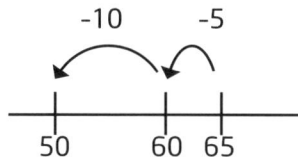

Paired work: Provide copies of the activity sheet 'Missing numbers' and ask the children to work in pairs to complete the questions. Encourage them to discuss their work with a partner and to compare methods for finding their solutions.

Review

Ask the children to substitute numbers so these statements are true:
△ - △ = 0   (both numbers must be the same)
☐ + ☐ = 102 (51)

Ask for volunteers to model one of their answers using an empty number line. (This can be done on the interactive whiteboard.)

Move on to the following question: ☐ - 12 = 101. Again, invite children to model the answer using the empty number line.

Differentiation
There are support and extension versions of the sheet available.
Less confident learners: Decide whether to provide a hundred square to assist the children in calculating.
More confident learners: If the children are confident, challenge them to use mental methods as they work.

Lesson 4 (Teach and apply)

Starter

Choose six volunteers and give each one an 'Add or subtract 1, 10 or 100' card. Ask the six children to stand in a line in any order. The first child says any number greater than 100 and the other five children then say what the number would be if they applied the rule on their card. Now the second child says a number, and so on. The class has to work out which child is adding or subtracting 1, 10 or 100.

Main teaching activities

Whole class: Review the use of an empty number line, using 36 - 15, then 176 - 43. Discuss whether there is just one way to a solution, or whether alternatives will work too. Write up △ - ☐ = 15 and, working in pairs again, ask the children to find as many solutions to this as they can in three minutes. Write some of these on the board and discuss how they worked them out. Repeat for other subtraction equations, such as △ - ☐ = 18 and 29 - △ - ☐ = 6.

Review

Invite the children to give examples of their number sentences, making up number stories for some of the sentences using the vocabulary of subtraction.

Lesson 5 (Teach, apply and evaluate)

Starter

Recall: Repeat the Starter from Lesson 2. This time begin with a division, such as 42 ÷ 6.

Main teaching activities

Whole class: Explain that in this lesson, the children will continue their work on multiplication and division. Ask: *What is 14 × 3? How can you work this out?* Write on the board: (10 × 3) + (4 × 3) = 30 + 12 = 42. Now write up 40 ÷ 3 and ask: *How can we work this out?* Ask: *What is the nearest multiplication fact for 3 that you can find?*

Unit 3 ▶ 2 weeks

▷ Write the following on the board:
$10 \times 3 = 30$
$3 \times 3 = 9$
$13 \times 3 = 30 + 9 = 39$
So, $40 \div 3 = 13$ remainder 1.

Paired work: Write some examples, such as 15×4 and $50 \div 4$. Ask the children to work in pairs, using the methods that you have just demonstrated, to find the answers.

Whole class: Review these two problems. Discuss any difficulties the children had. Now say: *There are 35 marbles to be shared between three children. How many does each child have?* Invite the children to suggest how this can be solved using multiplication: $10 \times 3 = 30$; $1 \times 3 = 3$, so $11 \times 3 = 33$. Agree that there will be a remainder of 2, so the answer is 11 marbles each.

Paired work: Set two more problems:
● *There are 50 children who want to go to the cinema. They are going in cars. Each car will take four children. How many cars are needed?* (13)
● *Three children want to go to the football match. The tickets are £16 each. How much money do they need?* (£42)

Review

Ask children to explain how they solved each problem. Invite them to display their recording. Discuss the answer to the first problem and why it is necessary to round the answer up. Invite the more confident children to read out one of their problems. Challenge the other children to solve it. Ask: *Which calculation strategies can you use?*

Differentiation

Less confident learners: Ask the children to work as a group on these problems. If necessary, simplify the problems by using just 2- and 3-times table facts.
More confident learners: Challenge the children to write a problem of their own which involves division and has a remainder.

Lessons 6–10

You will need

Photocopiable pages
'Multiplication and division problems' (page 166), 'Multiplying and dividing' (page 167) and 'Start and end times' (page 168) for each child.
CD resources
Support and extension versions of 'Multiplication and division problems' and 'Multiplying and dividing'; 'Sketching 2D shapes' for each child (see General resources). Interactive resource: 'Measuring jug'.
Equipment
For each child geostrips and fasteners, or card strips and paper fasteners; four differently-shaped containers for each group (with the capacity covered if using commercial bottles); measuring cylinder with increments in 2ml; teaching clock.

Learning objectives

Starter
● Derive and recall multiplication facts for the 2-, 3-, 4-, 5-, 6- and 10-times tables and the corresponding division facts.
● Derive and recall all addition and subtraction facts for each number to 20.

Main teaching activities
2006
● Understand that division is the inverse of multiplication and vice versa; use this to derive and record related multiplication and division number sentences.
● Use a set-square to draw right angles and to identify right angles in 2D shapes; compare angles with a right angle; recognise that a straight line is equivalent to two right angles.
● Read, to the nearest division and half-division, scales that are numbered or partially numbered; use the information to measure and draw to a suitable degree of accuracy.
● Read the time on a 12-hour digital clock and to the nearest five minutes on an analogue clock; calculate time intervals and find start or end times for a given time interval.
1999
● Recognise that division is the inverse of multiplication, and that halving is the inverse of doubling.
● Say or write a division statement corresponding to a given multiplication statement.
● Identify right angles in 2D shapes and the environment.
● Recognise that a straight line is equivalent to two right angles.
● Compare angles with a right angle.
● Read scales to the nearest division (labelled or unlabelled); record

estimates and measurements to the nearest whole or half unit (eg 'about 3.5 kg'), or in mixed units (eg '3 m and 20 cm').
- Use a ruler to draw and measure lines to the nearest half centimetre.
- Read the time to 5 minutes on an analogue clock and 12-hour digital clock; use the notation 9:40.

Vocabulary
problem, solution, puzzle, pattern, methods, sign, operation, symbol, number sentence, equation, mental calculation, written calculation, informal method, jottings, diagrams, pictures, images, multiply, times, multiplied by, product, share, share equally, divide, divided by, divided into, left, left over, remainder, measure, estimate, unit, litre (l), millilitre (ml), time, clock, watch, hours (h), minutes (min), seconds (s)

Lesson 6 (Teach and practise)

Starter
Recall: Repeat the Starter from Lesson 3. Increase the pace to encourage more rapid recall.

Main teaching activities
Whole class: Explain that you will ask some multiplication and division questions. Begin with: *I have 30 stickers. I want to put three stickers into each envelope. How many envelopes do I need?* Now ask: *What sort of problem is this? What multiplication fact will help you to find the answer?* Agree that 3 × 10 = 30 and that 30 ÷ 3 = 10; *I will need ten envelopes.*

Repeat for another problem: *There are 54 children in Year 3. Their teachers put them into six groups. How many children are there in each group?* Agree that 9 × 6 = 54, so 54 ÷ 6 = 9; there will be nine children in each group.

Individual work: Provide each child with the activity sheet 'Multiplication and division problems'. Ask them to read the problem and to find the multiplication fact that will help them to solve the problem. Tell them to record their working.

Review
Discuss the questions on the activity sheet. Ask questions such as: *I multiply 20 by 5 and divide the answer by 5. What number do I get? How do you know? How many 4-litre bottles of water do I need so that I have 28 litres in total? What sort of problem is this? How do you know? What multiplication fact would help you to find the answer?*

Differentiation

Less confident learners: There are problems that just use the 2-, 3- and 5-times tables on the support version of the sheet.
More confident learners: There are problems that also use the 8-times table on the extension version of the sheet.

Lesson 7 (Teach and apply)

Starter
Recall: Repeat the Starter from Lesson 4, this time encouraging even quicker recall.

Main teaching activities
Whole class: Write on the board 20 × 2 and ask for an answer. Now write 3 × 2 and repeat. Write up 23 × 2 and ask: *How can we work this out?* The children may suggest combining the two previous answers. Repeat for other examples, such as 31 × 3, 42 × 2, 22 × 4, 11 × 5.
Individual work: Provide copies of the activity sheet 'Multiplying and dividing' and ask the children to work individually to write the answers.

Review
Invite the children to take turns to choose one of the questions from their sheet and explain to the others how they calculated their answer.

Differentiation

Less confident learners: Give these children the support version of the activity sheet.
More confident learners: Challenge the children to complete the extension version of the activity sheet.

BLOCK D

Lesson 8 (Teach and apply)

Starter
Recall: Explain that you will say an addition sentence using numbers to 20. Ask the children to say the total. Begin with 8 + 6, 9 + 5... and extend to 13 + 8, 16 + 7, 12 + 16, 19 + 14... Keep the pace sharp, to encourage rapid recall.

Main teaching activities
Whole class: Ask the children to use their geostrips to show a right angle. Now ask them to compare their result with their neighbour. Ask: *Did you make a good estimate?* Repeat this, asking for angles less than/more than a right angle. Repeat this several times, asking the children to make a right angle again and to place this on the table. Now ask them to pair up their right angles so that these lie next to each other. Ask: *What have you made?* The children should realise that two right angles make a straight line.
Individual work: Provide set squares and rulers and copies of general resource sheet 'Sketching 2D shapes'. The children sketch the shapes asked for on the activity sheet, using a ruler and set square. Encourage them to make these sketches as accurately as they can.

Review
On the board, draw up a table with three columns headed 'All right angles', Some right angles', 'No right angles'. Ask the children to suggest 2D shapes to fit into each column. They can take turns to sketch the shapes in the correct column. Now draw two right angles, one of them with smaller arms and the right angle inverted. Ask: *What can you tell me about these? Which angle is smaller? Why do you think that?* Agree that both angles are right angles, so they are the same size, and that it is the arms of the angles which are different lengths. This does not alter the shape and size of the angle.

Differentiation
Less confident learners: Check that these children are confident with using a set square and a ruler.
More confident learners: Encourage these children to work as accurately as possible.

Lesson 9 (Teach and apply)

Starter
Recall: Repeat the Starter from Lesson 6, this time for subtraction of pairs of numbers up to 20. Begin with 9 - 4, 8 - 5..., then extend to 13 - 8, 19 - 7, 15 - 11 and so on.

Main teaching activities
Whole class: Reveal the interactive resource 'Measuring jug' and explain that in today's lesson the children will be reading scales. Set the scale to maximum 100 and increments in 2s and discuss with the children what each little line represents. Fill the container to 26 and ask the children to say how much is in the container. Fill again, this time to a point in between two of the small lines. Now ask: *How much is in the container?* Discuss how, in between two small lines represents, for example, 27, with 26 below and 28 above. Repeat for further examples.
Group work: Provide each group with four differently-shaped bottles and a measuring cylinder marked in 2ml increments. Ask the children to pour 100ml of water into the cylinder then pour this into the first container. They estimate how much the container will hold when full from where the 100ml reaches, then check by measuring. Ask them to record their results – for example, drawing pictures of the containers to help them. They repeat this for each of the containers.

Differentiation
All children can attempt this task. Check that the more confident children do not dominate their group and that the less confident children are able to contribute.

Review
Invite children to explain how they recorded their work. Ask a child from each group to explain how they went about the task. Discuss the different ways in which this was done, and which was better and why the children think that. Encourage them to report back in a sequential order. Choose one of the bottles. Ask: *How much did this hold?* Peel off the label covering the amount

that it was made to hold and ask: *Why is this different from when the bottle is full?* Discuss reasons, such as leaving space for the contents to expand in hot weather; leaving space so that when the cap is removed the contents do not spill out.

Lesson 10 (Teach, practise and evaluate)

Starter
Recall: Repeat the Starter from Lesson 6, giving a mixture of addition and subtraction equations. Keep the pace sharp.

Main teaching activities
Whole class: Explain that this lesson is about telling the time, and calculating time. Show 8.20 on the teaching clock. Ask: *What time is it? How would this time be shown on a digital clock?* Invite a child to write the time using digital clock display (08.20). Repeat for 8.25 and 8.35. For 8.35, say: *This time can be said as 25 minutes to nine. How would I show this time on a digital clock?* Invite a child to write this on the board. Repeat for other 'to the hour' times, such as 9.40, 2.55...

Now ask some time word problems such as: *My journey to school takes 20 minutes. I need to be at school by quarter past eight. What time do I need to leave home?* Ask the children to demonstrate their working using the teaching clock and to write the digital time on the board.

Paired work: Provide a copy of the activity sheet 'Start and end times' for each pair. The children take turns to choose a time from the list, then a time interval from the second list. They write a sentence using the start time, and work out the end time using the time interval. For example, if they choose 6.30 and 45 minutes, then the end time would be 7.15.

Review
Invite children to read out one of their time sentences. The other children can check to see if they agree. Invite the more confident children to read one of their 'counting back' sentences. Again, ask the other children to check that this is correct.

Ask the children to discuss in pairs what they have learned this week. Invite those children that you are targetting for assessment to give feedback.

Differentiation
Less confident learners: Use the times on the sheet and ask the children to set individual clock faces to the start time. Then they calculate the finish time. Ask them to write both times in digital format. Concentrate at this stage on the children being able to count on in five-minute intervals.
More confident learners: Challenge the children to write some sentences where they count back in time, such as: *I get to school at 8.45. My journey takes 20 minutes so I leave home at 8.25.*

Calculating, measuring and understanding shape

BLOCK D

Name _____   Date _____

At the bookstore

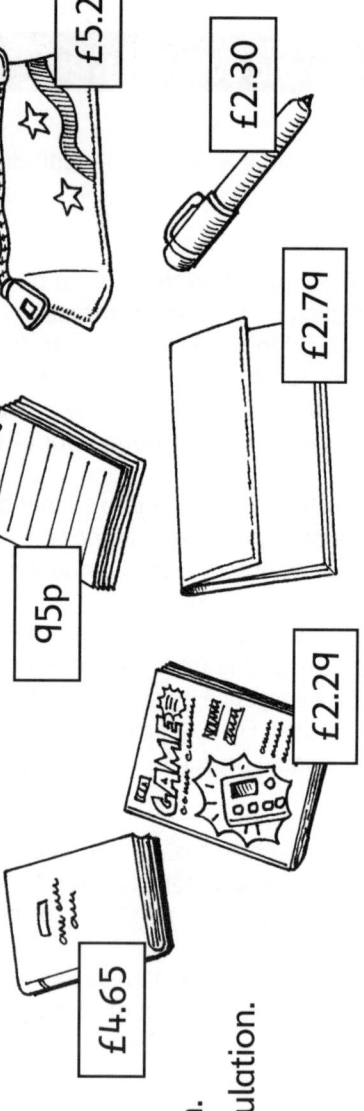

£5.25

£2.30

£2.79

95p

£2.29

£4.65

You have £10 to spend at the bookstore.

Choose two items each time.
Total the two items and record the calculation.
Find the change from £10 and record the calculation.

Repeat this four more times.

I bought	Recording	Total spent	Recording	Change

Name _____   Date _____

Missing numbers

Find the missing numbers in these number sentences.

Show your working.

1.   19 + ☐ = 25

_____

2.   52 + ☐ = 64

_____

3.   ☐ + 45 = 63

_____

4.   36 + ☐ = 93

_____

5.   42 + 38 = ☐

_____

6.   64 + ☐ = 100

_____

Now find four different solutions to this number sentence.

☐ + ☐ = 40

☐ + ☐ = 40

☐ + ☐ = 40

☐ + ☐ = 40

SCHOLASTIC PHOTOCOPIABLE

Calculating, measuring and understanding shape

BLOCK D

Name _____   Date _____

Multiplication and division problems

Read each problem.

Decide which multiplication fact will help you to find the answer.

Write this down. Now write the calculation. Write the answer.

Problem	Multiplication fact	Calculation	Answer
1. How many 10-minute cartoons can I watch in 50 minutes?			
2. I share a bag of 60 sweets between six people. How many sweets does each person get?			
3. A book is 5cm deep. How many copies of the book are needed to make a pile that is 70cm high?			
4. There are 64 cakes. Each cake box holds six cakes. How many cake boxes are needed?			

Name _____   Date _____

Multiplying and dividing

Write the answers to these questions.

1. 6 × 10 = ☐

2. 5 × 100 = ☐

3. 6 × ☐ = 600

4. 7 × ☐ = 70

5. 700 ÷ 100 = ☐

6. 400 ÷ 10 = ☐

7. What is one tenth of 90? ☐

8. What is one hundredth of 300? ☐

9. What is double 45? ☐

10. ☐ × 2 = 70

11. 90 ÷ 2 = ☐

12. ☐ ÷ 2 = 40

13. 60 × 2 = ☐

14. 20 × ☐ = 100

15. 33 × 3 = ☐

16. 13 × ☐ = 26

17. What is 11 multiplied by 5? ☐

18. What is 24 multiplied by 2? ☐

19. What is 12 multiplied by to make 24? ☐

20. What is 100 divided by to make 10? ☐

Name _____   Date _____

Start and end times

Work with a partner.

Take turns to choose a start time from the clocks below. Now choose a time interval from the table below. Work out the end time, using the start time and the time interval. Write a sentence which uses these times. Use the table to record your work.

Start times

Time intervals

Start time	Time interval	End time	Sentence
	30 minutes		
	15 minutes		
	20 minutes		
	45 minutes		
	50 minutes		
	40 minutes		

Calculating, measuring and understanding shape

BLOCK D

Block E

Securing number facts, relationships and calculating

Key aspects of learning
- Enquiry
- Problem solving
- Reasoning
- Creative thinking
- Social skills
- Communication
- Motivation

Expected prior learning
Check that children can already:
- solve one-step word problems involving all four operations
- choose and use suitable equipment when following a given line of enquiry
- select, organise and present information in lists, tables and simple diagrams
- partition two-digit numbers and recognise the importance of place value
- recognise simple fractions and find halves and quarters of sets of objects and small numbers
- recall addition and subtraction facts for all numbers to 10 and multiples of 10
- understand inverse operations and use the inverse relationships of addition and subtraction to generate number facts
- understand multiplication and division and derive and recall multiplication and division facts for 2, 5 and 10.

Objectives overview
The text in this diagram identifies the focus of mathematics learning within the block.

Following lines of enquiry and solving problems

Deriving and consolidating knowledge of number facts for all four operations

Solving problems by identifying patterns and relationships in numbers

Block E: Securing number facts, relationships and calculating

Interpreting and using proper fractions

Finding unit fractions of quantities

Developing practical and written methods for adding, subtracting, multiplying and dividing two-digit numbers

Interpreting remainders in context

BLOCK E

Securing number facts, relationships and calculating

Lesson	Strands	Starter	Main teaching activities
1. Teach and practise	Knowledge	**Derive and recall all addition and subtraction facts for each number to 20, sums and differences of multiples of 10 and number pairs that total 100.**	**Derive and recall all addition and subtraction facts for each number to 20, sums and differences of multiples of 10 and number pairs that total 100.**
2. Teach and apply	Knowledge	As for Lesson 1	As for Lesson 1
3. Teach and apply	Knowledge	Derive and recall multiplication facts for the 2-, 3-, 4-, 5-, 6- and 10-times tables and the corresponding division facts.	As for Lesson 1
4. Teach and practise	Knowledge	As for Lesson 3	Derive and recall multiplication facts for the 2-, 3-, 4-, 5-, 6- and 10-times tables and the corresponding division facts; recognise multiples of 2, 5 or 10 up to 1000.
5. Teach, practise and evaluate	Knowledge	As for Lesson 3	As for Lesson 4
6. Teach and apply	Calculate	As for Lesson 3	Use practical and informal written methods to multiply and divide two-digit numbers (eg 13×3, $50 \div 4$); round remainders up or down, depending on the context.
7. Teach and practise	Calculate	As for Lesson 3	As for Lesson 6
8. Teach and practise	Calculate	As for Lesson 3	As for Lesson 6
9. Teach and apply	Calculate	As for Lesson 3	As for Lesson 6
10. Teach, apply and evaluate	Use/apply	As for Lesson 3	Identify patterns and relationships involving numbers or shapes, and use these to solve problems.
11. Teach and apply	Calculate	**Derive and recall all addition and subtraction facts for each number to 20, sums and differences of multiples of 10 and number pairs that total 100.**	Find unit fractions of numbers and quantities (eg $\frac{1}{2}$, $\frac{1}{3}$, $\frac{1}{4}$ and $\frac{1}{6}$ of 12 litres).
12. Teach and practise	Calculate	Derive and recall multiplication facts for the 2-, 3-, 4-, 5-, 6- and 10-times tables and the corresponding division facts.	As for Lesson 11
13. Teach and apply	Use/apply	**Derive and recall all addition and subtraction facts for each number to 20.**	Identify patterns and relationships involving numbers or shapes, and use these to solve problems.
14. Teach and apply	Use/apply	As for Lesson 13	As for Lesson 13
15. Teach, apply and evaluate	Use/apply	As for Lesson 13	As for Lesson 13

Securing number facts, relationships and calculating

BLOCK E

Unit 1 ⬜ 3 weeks

Speaking and listening objective

- Sustain conversation, explain or give reasons for their views or choices.

Introduction

In this 15-lesson unit, children develop their ability to make decisions when solving problems, and to use tables and charts to make clear the data they have collected. Lessons 10 and 13-15 are devoted to using and applying mathematics in problem-solving situations. However, the using and applying aspect of mathematics is included in all work in this unit. Children are encouraged throughout the unit to explain their thinking and to give their view and choices. When working with a partner or in small groups, encourage them to discuss their work and to sustain their conversation so that they develop their abilities to discuss in more detail.

Using and applying mathematics

- Identify patterns and relationships involving numbers or shapes, and use these to solve problems.

Lessons 1-5

Preparation

Copy CD page 'Blank hundred square' onto an OHT for the teacher's/LSA's reference and also copy onto card.

You will need

Photocopiable pages
'Make the total' (page 182), 'Looking at multiples of ten' (page 183) and 'Find the numbers' (page 184) for each child.

CD resources
Support and extension versions of 'Make the total' and 'Find the numbers'; 'Blank hundred square' and '2-, 4-, 5- and 10-times tables' for each child (see General resources).

Equipment
Multilink; strings of 100 beads; an empty number line (ENL); OHP calculator; calculators.

Learning objectives

Starter

- Derive and recall all addition and subtraction facts for each number to 20, sums and differences of multiples of 10 and number pairs that total 100.
- Derive and recall multiplication facts for the 2-, 3-, 4-, 5-, 6- and 10-times tables and the corresponding division facts.

Main teaching activities

2006
- Derive and recall all addition and subtraction facts for each number to 20, sums and differences of multiples of 10 and number pairs that total 100.
- Derive and recall multiplication facts for the 2-, 3-, 4-, 5-, 6- and 10-times tables and the corresponding division facts.

1999
- Know by heart: all addition and subtraction facts for each number to 20; all pairs of multiples of 100 with a total of 1000 (eg 300 + 700); all pairs of multiples of 5 with a total of 100 (eg 35 + 65).
- Derive quickly all number pairs that total 100 (eg 62 + 38, 75 + 25, 40 + 60).
- Know by heart multiplication facts for the 2-, 5- and 10-times tables; begin to know the 3- and 4-times tables. Derive quickly the corresponding division facts.
- Recognise two-digit and three-digit multiples of 2, 5 or 10, and three-digit multiples of 50 and 100.
- Begin to know multiplication facts for the 6-times tables.

Vocabulary

sign, equals (=), operation, symbol, number operation, number sentence, equation, mental calculation, written calculation, informal method, jottings, number line, count on, count back, add, plus, sum, total, subtract, take away, minus, difference, double, halve, inverse, multiply, times, multiplied by, product, share, share equally, divide, divided by, divided into

Lesson 1 (Teach and practise)

Starter

Rehearse: Explain that you will say a number between 0 and 20. Ask the children to say the number that adds to your number to make 20. Invite the children to explain how they derived their answer, and praise those who 'know' the answer. Say, for example: *12, 16, 9, 14...*

Main teaching activities

Whole class: Explain that in this and the next lesson the children will continue to develop their knowledge of addition and subtraction facts to 20. Write on the board: 7, 11, 15, and ask: *What would the next number be?* (19) Ask for an explanation of how children worked this out. Agree that the difference between each pair of numbers is 4, so that the next number is 4 more than 15. Repeat this for other examples, such as: 2, 8, 14; 4, 9, 14; 19, 16, 13…

Paired work: Ask the children to work in pairs. They both write a number sequence where the difference between each pair of numbers is the same. Remind the children that the numbers must stay below 20. They swap papers and their partner works out the sequence rule and the next number in the pattern. Ask the children to find at least five different patterns, with a range of differences.

Review

Ask pairs of children to write one of their sequences on the board, but with the last number missing. The other children work out the difference and then what the next number is. Repeat this for several different patterns, and each time invite children to explain how they worked out the answer: what facts they used, and what other facts they could have used instead. Ask some of the more confident children to write up their patterns which extend the sequences to up to 30 and challenge everyone to solve the problem.

Differentiation

Less confident learners: Decide whether to limit the sequences to differences of 2 and 5.
More confident learners: Challenge the children, when they have completed five different patterns, to write some patterns which extend up to 30.

Lesson 2 (Teach and apply)

Starter

Recall: Repeat the Starter for Lesson 1. Keep the pace sharp.

Main teaching activities

Whole class: Write on the board 5 ☐ 11 = 16 and ask: *What is the missing symbol? How can you tell this is an addition?* Repeat this for 17 ☐ 14 = 3. Now write on the board 7 ☐ 6 ☐ 4 = 9 and invite the children to work out what the missing signs are. Give the children about a minute to complete this. Ask for suggestions and write in the signs: 7 + 6 - 4 = 9. Repeat for other examples such as 14 ☐ 11 ☐ 7 ☐ 2 = 12. (14 - 11 + 7 + 2 = 12.) Each time, ask the children to explain how they worked out the answer, including the number facts that they used.

Individual work: Provide each child with a copy of the activity sheet 'Make the total'. Ask the children to use mental methods as far as possible to find combinations of numbers from 1 to 20 to solve the problems, but reassure them that if they do need to make jottings then that is fine.

Review

Invite children to write one of their number sentences on the board. Ask: *What number facts did you use to work this out? Would anyone have worked it out using different number facts?* Challenge everyone at the end of the lesson by providing one of the more confident problems, with a total of more than 20, for everyone to try.

Differentiation

Less confident learners: There is a support version of the activity sheet with numbers to 10 for making totals.
More confident learners: There is an extension version of the activity sheet which contains some totals beyond 20.

Lesson 3 (Teach and apply)

Starter

Rehearse: Say together the multiplication tables for 2, 5 and 10. Then say those for 3, 4 and 6. Keep a good pace for this. Now explain that you will ask a multiplication fact. Ask the children to say the answer together. Again, keep the pace sharp.

Main teaching activities

Whole class: Say: *We are going to use what we know about addition and subtraction to 10 and to 20 to help us to add and subtract multiples of 10* to make 100. Write on the board 60 + 40 and ask: *How can we use what we already know to find the answer?* Agree that if 6 + 4 = 10 then 60 + 40 = 100. Repeat for other addition of multiples of 10 to make 100. Now ask: *What is 80 subtract 50?* Agree that if 8 – 5 = 3 then 80 – 50 = 30. Repeat for other differences between pairs of multiples of 10.

Paired work: Provide each child with the activity sheet 'Looking at multiples of ten'. Ask the children to work in pairs and to discuss their solutions. The sheet is not differentiated because all answers can be found using complements for 10.

Review

Ask questions such as: *What do I add to ___ to make one hundred? What is the difference between 40 and 60?* And of the more confident children: *How many different solutions did you find to the final question?* Write up the solutions, inviting everyone to contribute.

Lesson 4

Starter

Rehearse: Ask the children to sit in a circle. Taking turns, one child chooses a multiplication fact from the 2-, 5- or 10-times tables (such as 2 × 10 = 20). The next child then says a related fact and a completely different fact from the 2-, 5- or 10-times tables – for example, 10 × 2 = 20 for the related fact, followed by 5 × 3 = 15 as an unrelated fact. The third child might then say 15 ÷ 3 = 5 for the related fact and 7 × 5 = 35 for the unrelated fact.

When the children understand the activity, split the class into three separate groups to continue the activity. This will give each child more opportunities to speak and help to keep the pace sharp.

Main teaching activities

Whole class: Explain to the children that this lesson is about making arrays and repeated addition to represent multiplication facts. Ask them to arrange some of the card tiles from general resource sheet 'Blank hundred square' onto the OHT of the 'Blank hundred square' to show some multiplication facts. For example, if you asked a child to come and show 2 multiplied by 5 and 5 multiplied by 2, they could show it in two ways:

5 × 2 =

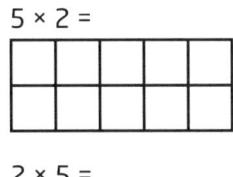

2 × 5 =

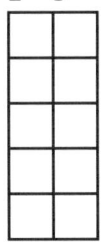

Invite the children to check the calculation by totalling. For example, for 2 × 5, this is 2 + 2 + 2 + 2 + 2 = 10, and 5 × 2, it is 5 + 5 = 10. Also try 3 × 5, 5 × 3; 2 × 7, 7 × 2; 3 × 8, 8 × 3. They derive the related division facts from the known multiplication facts, such as 3 × 5 = 15, 5 × 3 = 15, 15 ÷ 3 = 5 and 15 ÷ 5 = 3.

Paired work: Provide general resource sheet '2-, 4-, 5- and 10-times tables' and ask the children to complete the missing table facts. They should show the fact using the empty hundred grid and cards, then write the answer on the sheet. If they do not 'know' the answer, then suggest that they use repeated addition to work it out.

Differentiation

Less confident learners: Decide whether to limit the table facts to those for the 2- and 5-times tables.
More confident learners: Challenge the children to find all the facts for the 3-times table, modelling these in the same way.

Review

Ask the children to draw arrays on their individual whiteboards using dots for 3 × 6 and ask: *What other multiplication fact uses these numbers? Yes, 6 × 3. Now try 4 × 2 in the same way.* Then invite the children to write the calculation for this story: *A farmer sells three boxes of half a dozen eggs. How many eggs does he sell? How many eggs does he sell if he doubles his sales?* Repeat for other multiplication stories.

Lesson 5 (Teach, practise and evaluate)

Starter

Rehearse: Show the children the following triangle of facts:

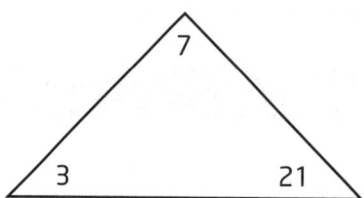

Working in groups of four, ask the children to choose any multiplication fact they know. The children then work round their foursome: child one chooses the starting multiplication fact, child two says the related multiplication fact, child three suggests a division fact and child four the related division fact. Challenge the groups to perform their calculations for the class by saying them rapidly in sequence. Ask each group to prepare for performance three different multiplication facts and their related division facts.

Main teaching activities

Whole class: Explain that today's lesson continues the work begun in the previous lesson. Write on the board 5 × 6 and ask: *How can we work this out?* The children may suggest making arrays of using repeated addition. Invite a child to draw some dots on the board to represent 5 × 6 as an array. Now, using the OHP and an OHP calculator set to perform repeated addition (usually, number then ++= will set this, but check the manufacturer's instructions as some calculators operate differently), input 5, then press =. This should give 10. Repeat this for a different multiplication, such as 8 × 6. Ask the children to keep count of how many eights are added until six of them are totalled.
Paired work: Provide pairs with a calculator between them. Ask them to try these for themselves: 4 × 6, 9 × 6, 5 × 4 and 8 × 3. Then ask the children to feed back the answers.

Now write on the board: 24 ÷ 3 = ☐ and ask: *How can we work this out?* The children may suggest counting in threes to find how many are needed to reach 24. Do this together, then show how 24 can be placed in three rows using dots on the board. Ask: *How many dots are there in each row?* Repeat this for another example, such as 18 ÷ 6 = ☐.
Individual work: Provide each child with a copy of the activity sheet 'Find the numbers' and ask them to complete the sheet individually.

Differentiation

Less confident learners: Give the children the support version of the activity sheet that uses only multiples of 3. Assist this group by relating all their questions to concrete materials, eg Multilink or bead chains.
More confident learners: Give these children the extension version of the activity sheet with multiples of 6. Ask them to write out the 6-times table by doubling the 3-times table. Show the group jumps of 6 on an empty number line. ▶

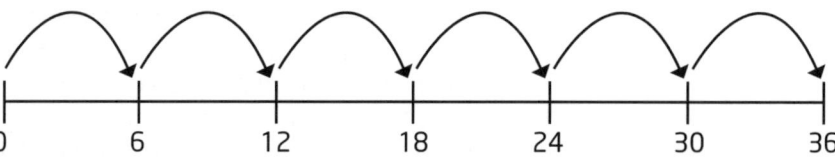

Review

Ask questions such as: *Ten times what equals 80? What times five equals 30?* Now ask: *What multiplication sentences could give the answer 60?* Invite the children to write their responses on the board, such as 12 × 5,

6 × 10 and 30 × 2, and so on. Using the OHP and the calculator set to repeated addition, check the children's suggestions so that they can all follow these multiplications.

Invite the children to give feedback on what they have learned in this series of lessons.

Lessons 6-10

Preparation
Enlarge CD page 'Word problems (2)' to A3.

You will need
Photocopiable pages
'Word problems (2)' (page 185) and 'Money multiplication' (page 186) for each child.
CD resources
Support and extension versions of 'Word problems (2)' and 'Money multiplication'.

Learning objectives

Starter
● Derive and recall multiplication facts for the 2-, 3-, 4-, 5-, 6- and 10-times tables and the corresponding division facts.

Main teaching activities
2006
● Use practical and informal written methods to multiply and divide two-digit numbers (eg 13 × 3, 50 ÷ 4); round remainders up or down, depending on the context.
● Identify patterns and relationships involving numbers or shapes, and use these to solve problems.
1999
● Use known number facts and place value to carry out mentally simple multiplications and divisions.
● Begin to find remainders after simple division; round up or down after division, depending on the context.
● Solve mathematical problems or puzzles, recognise simple patterns and relationships, generalise and predict. Suggest extensions by asking 'What if...?'
● Describe and extend number sequences.
● Investigate a general statement about familiar numbers or shapes by finding examples that satisfy it.

Vocabulary
double, halve, inverse, multiply, times, multiplied by, product, share, share equally, divide, divided by, divided into

Lesson 6 (Teach and apply)

Starter
Rehearse: Explain that you will ask for multiplication and division facts from the 2-, 5- and 10-times tables. Say, for example: *Find four facts that use the numbers 12, 2 and 6.* (2 × 6 = 12; 6 × 2 = 12; 12 ÷ 2 = 6; 12 ÷ 6 = 2). The children write their four facts on their whiteboards and, when you say *Show me,* they hold up their boards for you to check.

Main teaching activities
Whole class: Explain that in today's lesson children will find the solutions to word problems using the 2-, 5- and 10-times tables. Write on the board the following: 'If I have three 5p coins, how much money do I have?' Ask: *How did you solve that?* Check that the children have understood that this problem can be solved using the multiplication 3 × 5. Now ask: *If I have 40p in 10p coins, how many coins do I have?* Check that the children understand that this can be solved using the division 40 ÷ 10. Repeat this for other questions, such as: *I buy five lollies at 9p each. How much do I spend?; I spend 70p on ten pencils. How much does each pencil cost?*
Individual work: Provide each child with a copy of the activity sheet 'Word problems (2)'. Ask the children to work individually to solve these problems using mental methods to find the table facts.

Differentiation
Less confident learners: Give these children the support version of the activity sheet.
More confident learners: Give these children the extension version of the activity sheet.

Review
Using an A3 enlargement of 'Word problems (2)', invite children to explain the table facts that they used to solve each of the problems. Encourage them to explain why they chose that particular fact and how the multiplication fact relates to the division fact, as appropriate.

Lesson 7 (Teach and practise)

Starter
Recall: Repeat the Starter from Lesson 6, this time for table facts from the 3-times table.

Main teaching activities
Whole class: Explain that in this lesson the children will be using informal methods to record multiplication. Begin with an example, such as 13 × 5. Explain that this can be seen as 10 × 5 add 3 × 5. Use an empty number line on the board and draw this diagram:

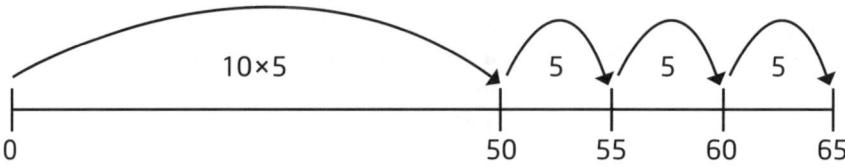

Underneath the diagram write: 13 × 5 = 10 × 5 add 3 × 5 = 50 + 15 = 65. Now provide further examples for the children to try for themselves: 14 × 3; 16 × 2; 18 × 4. Give the children about five minutes to work through the examples for themselves then review these together, using empty number lines on the board and writing out the number sentence as shown above.
Paired work: Ask the children to work in pairs. Write the two-digit numbers 12, 15 and 17 on the board, and the single-digit numbers 2, 3, 5 and 10. Encourage the children to work together, using an empty number line to help them to model multiplication facts and to write the multiplication sentences.

Review
Review some of the paired work examples. Invite children to draw their empty number line diagrams on the board, write the multiplication sentences, and to explain which number facts they chose to use. Ask, for example: *Did everyone do this in this way? Which number facts did you use?* If there is sufficient time, invite some of the more confident children to show the challenge that they tried and to explain how they solved the problem.

Differentiation
Less confident learners: Decide whether to have these children work as a group and to try simpler examples, using just the 2-, 5- and 10-times tables, such as 12 × 5, 14 × 5, and so on.
More confident learners: Challenge these children to try more complex multiplications such as 23 × 5.

Lesson 8 (Teach and practise)

Starter
Recall: Repeat the Starter from Lesson 6, this time for the 4-times table facts.

Main teaching activities
Group work: Review the work from the previous lesson. Write on the board 15 × 4. Ask the children to suggest how this can be solved using an empty number line. Write the number sentence 15 × 4 = (10 × 4) + (5 × 4) = 40 + 20 = 60. Repeat this for further examples, such as 14 × 3, 16 × 5, and so on.
Individual work: Write on the board 11, 13, 14, 15 and 16, and 3 and 4. Ask the children to multiply each teen number by 3, then by 4, and to record each multiplication using an empty number line and writing the multiplication sentence.

Unit 1 ⬛ 3 weeks

Differentiation

Less confident learners: Work with this group to solve 11 × 3, 13 × 3 and 14 × 3.
More confident learners: Provide some more challenging examples such as 22 × 4.

Review

Review the children's work, as in the previous lesson. Invite the more confident to explain how they worked without the empty number line and to demonstrate the solution to their challenge.

Lesson 9 (Teach and apply)

Starter

Recall: Repeat the Starter from Lesson 6, this time for 6-times table facts.

Main teaching activities

Whole class: Explain that in today's lesson children will be solving problems involving multiplication. Reveal the first word problem on the activity sheet 'Money multiplication'. Ask the children to suggest how they could solve it. Ask them to use either an empty number line and write the multiplication sentence, or if they feel confident to work mentally, just to write the multiplication sentence. When the children have solved the problem, invite suggestions for how to solve it, the number facts used and the solution.
Individual work: Provide each child with a copy of activity sheet 'Money multiplication'. Ask the children to work on their own to solve the problems. Remind them that there is an empty number line for each problem which they can use, and also to write out their multiplication sentences.

Differentiation

Less confident learners: There is a support version of the sheet that uses 2-, 3-, 5- and 10-times tables facts.
More confident learners: The extension version of the sheet has more complex multiplications of two-digit numbers by a single digit.

Review

Invite children to explain how they solved each problem. Ask: *How did you find the answer? Did you need the empty number line? What number facts did you use?*

Lesson 10 (Teach, apply and evaluate)

Starter

Recall: Repeat the Starter for Lesson 6, this time for all table facts for the 2-, 3-, 4-, 5-, 6- and 10- times tables.

Main teaching activities

Whole class: Explain that in this lesson the children will investigate the digits that multiples of 2 and 3 end in. Begin with the multiples of 10 and ask: *What is the last digit each time? Is it always a zero? How do you know?* Repeat this for multiples of 5, agreeing that multiples of 5 always end in 5 or 0. Demonstrate how to record using a digit wheel for multiples of 2.

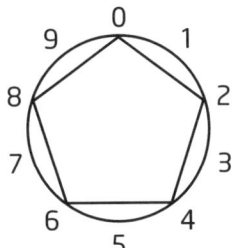

Paired work: Ask the children to work together to produce a digit wheel for multiples of 2, then to do this for multiples of 3. Ask them to record their results in a table: the multiple; the last digits; and the shape they form on the digit wheel. Explain that they will continue this work next week and to leave room to add in the results for the multiples of 4, 5, 6 and 10.

Differentiation

Less confident learners: The children may find it beneficial to mark the multiples onto a number line before they begin to make the digit wheel.
More confident learners: Challenge the children to identify multiples of 2 and of 3 between 120 and 130.

Review

Review the children's work. Ask for results and produce a class digit wheel for each of the multiples of 2 and of 3. Ask: *How many multiples of 2 are there between 50 and 60? 85 and 95? 124 and 137? How did you work this out?* Invite feedback on what the children have learned about multiplication and division.

Lessons 11-15

You will need
Photocopiable pages
'Spot the pattern (2)' (page 187) for each child.
CD resources
Support and extension versions of 'Spot the pattern (2)'; 'Fractions of shapes' for each child (see General resources).
Equipment
Counting stick; counters; interlocking cubes.

Learning objectives

Starter
● Derive and recall all addition and subtraction facts for each number to 20.
● Derive and recall multiplication facts for the 2-, 3-, 4-, 5-, 6- and 10-times tables and the corresponding division facts.

Main teaching activities
2006
● Find unit fractions of numbers and quantities (eg $\frac{1}{2}$, $\frac{1}{3}$, $\frac{1}{4}$ and $\frac{1}{6}$ of 12 litres).
● Identify patterns and relationships involving numbers or shapes, and use these to solve problems.
1999
● Recognise unit fractions such as $\frac{1}{2}$, $\frac{1}{3}$, $\frac{1}{4}$, $\frac{1}{5}$, $\frac{1}{10}$..., and use them to find fractions of shapes and numbers.
● Solve mathematical problems or puzzles, recognise simple patterns and relationships, generalise and predict. Suggest extensions by asking 'What if...?'
● Describe and extend number sequences.
● Investigate a general statement about familiar numbers or shapes by finding examples that satisfy it.

Vocabulary
problem, solution, calculate, calculation, inverse, answer, method, explain, predict, estimate, reason, pattern, relationship, compare, order, information, test, list, table, diagram, fraction, part, equal parts, one whole, parts of a whole, number of parts, one half, one third, one quarter, one fifth, one sixth, one tenth, two thirds, three quarters, three fifths, unit fraction

Lesson 11 (Teach and apply)

Starter
Recall: Repeat the Starter for Lesson 1, choosing different examples and a range of addition and subtraction vocabulary.

Main teaching activities
Whole class: Explain that in today's lesson the children will continue their work on counting patterns. Begin by writing on the board: 'When you count in fives the units form a pattern'. Ask: *Is this true? How do you know it is true? What pattern could the units form?* Agree that, if starting on zero, the pattern of the units is 0, 5, 0, 5 and so on. Ask: *What would the pattern be if the count started on 1... 2... 3... 4?*
Paired work: Ask the children to continue their work from the previous lesson, this time exploring the multiples of 4 and 6. They complete digit wheels, fill in their tables and add in the data for multiples of 5 and 10.

Review
Review the results for multiples. Now invite the children to give a general statement about multiples of 2 (for example, the last digit is always even), 3, 4, 5, 6 and 10. Write these on the board. Now say: *If I count in 6s starting on zero, every number is even. Is this true? How do you know that?*

Differentiation
Less confident learners: These children may find it beneficial to mark the multiples onto a number line before they begin to make the digit wheel.
More confident learners: Challenge the children to identify multiples of 4 and 6 between 120 and 130.

SCHOLASTIC

Lesson 12 (Teach and practise)

Starter

Recall: Repeat the Starter for Lesson 6, this time keeping the pace sharp to encourage rapid recall of facts.

Main teaching activities

Whole class: Explain that in this lesson the children will find simple fractions of shapes. Provide each child with a sheet of A4 paper and ask them to find a way to fold it in half. Ask: *What can you say about each half?* Agree that the two pieces are each half and are the same shape and size. Now ask the children to fold the paper into quarters and again agree that all four pieces are the same size and shape. Discuss how two of the quarters are equivalent to a half, and that four quarters are equivalent to two halves or a whole. Finally ask the children to fold the paper into eighths and agree that each piece is the same size and shape and discuss the equivalents. On the board write: $\frac{1}{2} = \frac{1}{4} + \frac{1}{4}$; $\frac{1}{4} = \frac{1}{8} + \frac{1}{8}$.

Individual work: Provide each child with a copy of general resource sheet 'Fractions of shapes'. They shade in the appropriate fractions on each shape.

Review

Discuss the work together. Ask questions such as: *How many quarters… eighths… are equivalent to a half… a whole?* Discuss the second part of the activity sheet. Ask the children to name, as a fraction, the part that is shaded.

Differentiation

Less confident learners: Decide whether to work with these children as a group and discuss the fractions, using fraction vocabulary.

More confident learners: Challenge the children to find unit fractions of regular shapes with 9, 10, 11 and 12 sides.

Lesson 13 (Teach and apply)

Starter

Recall: Repeat the Starter from Lesson 6, keeping the pace sharp.

Main teaching activities

Whole class: Explain that in today's lesson the children will find fractions of groups of objects. Ask the children to count out 40 counters. Say: *How can you find half?* Ask them to work in pairs to find half by sharing the counters into two piles. Ask: *How many counters in each pile? So what fraction of 40 is 20?* Now ask the children to find half of one of the piles. Write on the board: $\frac{1}{2}$ of 40 = 20. $\frac{1}{2}$ of 20 = 10. Ask: *What fraction is 10 of 40?* Agree that it is a quarter. Now ask the children to share one of the ten piles into two and ask: *What fraction is 5 of 40?* Agree that it is an eighth and write on the board: $\frac{1}{8}$ of 40 is 5.

Discuss how the number at the bottom of the fraction refers to 'sharing', that is, that $\frac{1}{8}$ of 40 is the same as dividing 40 by 8. Draw an empty number line on the board. Label one end 0 and the other end 1. Ask the children to say where $\frac{1}{2}$ fits, then $\frac{1}{4}$ and $\frac{1}{8}$.

Paired work: Ask the children to find half, quarter and one eighth of 36 counters and to record on paper their results. Then ask them to repeat this for 48 counters.

Review

Discuss the work with the children. Check that they understand the relationship between $\frac{1}{2}$, $\frac{1}{4}$ and $\frac{1}{8}$. Invite children to give their answers to the problems that they were set. Ask: *Which is heavier, $\frac{1}{2}$ of 18kg or $\frac{1}{4}$ of 32kg? How would you work out $\frac{1}{8}$ of 32?* Agree that the children could find $\frac{1}{2}$ of 32, $\frac{1}{2}$ of 16 then $\frac{1}{2}$ of 8.

Differentiation

Less confident learners: Decide whether to ask the children to find just half and a quarter of 24 and 32.

More confident learners: Challenge the children to repeat the activity for 64.

Securing number facts, relationships and calculating

BLOCK E

Securing number facts, relationships and calculating

BLOCK E

Lesson 14 (Teach and apply)

Starter

Rehearse: Explain that you will say an addition or subtraction fact and ask the children to write the answer on their whiteboards. They hold up their boards when you say *Show me*. Use a variety of vocabulary for this, such as: *8 add 7, 9 plus 4, 17 subtract 11; What is 5 less than 12? What is 8 more than 6? What is the difference between ___ and ___? How many more should I add to ___ to make ___?* and so on. Keep the pace sharp to encourage rapid recall. Check who responds accurately and who will need further help with recall.

Main teaching activities

Whole class: Practise counting sequences, which cross the hundreds boundaries, with the children by chanting, pointing to the numbers on a counting stick as you do so, such as 29, 39, 49... 99, 109, 119, 129. Lead the children both in sequence but also by hopping your finger around the stick. If you hold the stick in one hand with a thumb at the centre point of the stick this will give the children a visual clue of where numbers come on the stick. Try using these numbers:

- Jumping in tens from 9, 28 and 32.
- Jumping in tens from 120, 222 and 314.
- Jumping in hundreds from 30, 100, 58 and 247.

Include chanting backwards with the counting sequences.

Now ask: *How can we tell if a number is odd or even?* If the children are unsure, make a tower of ten cubes and ask: *Is this odd or even?* Invite a child to break the tower into two and to note that the two smaller towers are the same height. Repeat for an odd number of cubes. Explain that even numbers will halve exactly; odd numbers will always have one left over. Invite the children to list all the single-digit even numbers and the odd numbers. These can be written on the board as two ordered lists. Then ask: *Is 12 even or odd? What about 17? 39? 124?* Elicit from the children that if the units digit is even then it is an even number, and if it is odd, then it is an odd number.

Group work: Ask the children to work in pairs. They take turns to say a three-digit start number less than 900, then count on in tens, stopping after saying ten numbers and writing down the numbers that they say. They decide whether their numbers are odd or even. Ask the pairs to generate at least five even number patterns and five odd number patterns.

Review

Invite children from each group to give one of their counting patterns. The other children can join in the chant, forwards and back again. Ask: *Is this an odd or an even pattern? How can you tell?* Ask the children to count in tens from, say, 178. Ask questions such as: *Is this an odd or even pattern? How can you tell? But the starting number tens digit is odd and so is the hundreds digit. Doesn't that make a difference? Can you explain why not?*

Differentiation

Less confident learners: Decide whether the children should start their counting patterns with a two-digit number between 70 and 99 so that they cross the first hundreds boundary in their counting.

More confident learners: Challenge the children to find counting patterns which cross the thousands boundary.

Lesson 15 (Teach, apply and evaluate)

Starter

Recall: Repeat the Starter for Lesson 1, choosing different examples, and using a variety of addition and subtraction vocabulary.

Main teaching activities

Whole class: Ask: *What is half of 24?* Write on the board: ½ of 24 = 12. *What is a quarter of 24?* Write up ¼ of 24 = 6. *What is an eighth of 24?* Write up ⅛ of 24 = 3. Ask: *What do you notice?* Agree that the answers are halves: 3 is half of 6; 6 is half of 12 and 12 is half of 24.

Now ask: *What is half of 48? What is a quarter of 48? What is an eighth of 48?* Again, consider the pattern that this gives of 24; 12; 6. Invite the children to explain the pattern.

Now write up this sequence:

74   69   ☐   59   54   49   ☐

Ask: *How can we find the missing numbers in this count?* Agree that the children can count back in ones to check the difference between each two numbers. Repeat this for another sequence such as:

71   67   ☐   59   55   51   ☐

Paired work: Provide copies of the activity sheet 'Spot the pattern (2)'. Ask the children to discuss with their partner the patterns that they see before they write their answers.

Differentiation

Less confident learners: Decide whether to use the support version of the activity sheet which uses smaller numbers.
More confident learners: Decide whether to use the extension version of the activity sheet which contains more complex number patterns.

Review

Discuss the children's answers from their activity sheets. Invite children to explain their reasoning. Ask questions such as, for the counting patterns: *How did you work out what the pattern was?* For the fraction questions, ask: *Why are the answers half of each other? What do you spot about the fractions? Yes, these follow the same pattern.*

Invite the children to give feedback about what they have learned about fractions, and about solving problems.

Securing number facts, relationships and calculating

BLOCK E

Name _____   Date _____

Make the total

Choose four of these numbers each time.

1	2	3	4	5	6	7	8	9	10
11	12	13	14	15	16	17	18	19	20

Decide whether to add, subtract, or use both operations to make the target total. **Write a correct number sentence for each total.**

1.	= 10
2.	= 15
3.	= 0
4.	= 17
5.	= 8
6.	= 11
7.	= 12
8.	= 9
9.	= 16
10.	= 3

Securing number facts, relationships and calculating

BLOCK E

Name _____   Date _____

Looking at multiples of ten

Work with a partner. Use this number grid for each task.

1. Take turns to choose one number from the grid.
Your partner chooses another number from the grid.
Your two numbers must total 100.

50	30	70	90	10
40	80	20	60	50

Write your number sentences here.

_____

_____

2. Take turns to choose two numbers from the grid.

Find the difference between the two numbers. _____

Write your number sentence here.

_____

Do this nine more times.

_____

_____

_____

_____

_____

_____

_____

3. Choose groups of three numbers from the grid that total 100.
Write an addition sentence for each group.

[   ] + [   ] + [   ] = 100   [   ] + [   ] + [   ] = 100

[   ] + [   ] + [   ] = 100   [   ] + [   ] + [   ] = 100

Find three more ways to achieve a total of 100, using three numbers

Securing number facts, relationships and calculating

BLOCK E

Name _____   Date _____

Find the numbers

1. Circle the multiples of 6.

    3   18   12   14   25   24

2. Fill in the missing numbers.

    ☐ x 3 = 18   6 x ☐ = 30   24 ÷ ☐ = 3 21 ÷ 7 = ☐

    5 x ☐ = 25   ☐ x 4 = 4   45 ÷ 5 = ☐   6 x ☐ = 36

3. Write the calculation needed to solve this problem.
Vicky bought 3 tubes of chocolate buttons. Each tube cost 25p.
How much did she spend? ☐

My calculation

Name _____ Date _____

Word problems (2)

Answer the following problems. Draw pictures to help.

1. How many stamps would you have if you bought 2 books with each book having 10 stamps?

2. Maddy has 5 stamps. How many stamps has Delyth if she has twice as many as Maddy?

3. Mei Mei walks 4km, which is twice as far as Paul. How far does Paul walk?

4. Joolz makes 8 cakes. Mark eats half of them. How many cakes are left?

■SCHOLASTIC PHOTOCOPIABLE

Securing number facts, relationships and calculating

BLOCK E

Name _____   Date _____

Money multiplication

Read each problem carefully.

You can use an empty number line to help you.

Write out the multiplication sentence. Write the answer.

---

1. Ananti buys 14 buttons.

Each button costs 5p.
How much does Ananti spend?

---

2. Sameer sees 13 pencils in the shop.

Each pencil costs 6p.

Sameer buys all the pencils.
How much change will he have from £1.00?

---

3. Sarah has 18 pens.

She decides to sell these at a car boot sale.

She asks 4p for each pen.
How much money will she collect if she sells all the pens?

---

4. Carl has 15 marbles.

Each marble cost him 6p.
How much did he spend on marbles?

Securing number facts, relationships and calculating

BLOCK E

PHOTOCOPIABLE  SCHOLASTIC

Name _____   Date _____

Spot the pattern (2)

Work with a partner. Together, look at each number sequence.

Agree on what pattern you can see. Write the missing numbers.

1. 23   27   ☐   35   39   ☐ ☐

2. 94   90   ☐ ☐   78   74   ☐

3. 93   83   ☐   63   ☐ ☐ ☐

4. 46   52   58   ☐ ☐ ☐ ☐

Now find the answers to these questions.

Write down what you notice about the answers.

5. Find $\frac{1}{2}$ of 40. ☐   **What do you notice?** _____

Find $\frac{1}{4}$ of 40. ☐   _____

Find $\frac{1}{8}$ of 40 . ☐   _____

6. Find $\frac{1}{3}$ of 60. ☐   **What do you notice?** _____

Find $\frac{1}{6}$ of 60. ☐   _____

Find $\frac{1}{12}$ of 60. ☐   _____

7. When you count in fours, starting on 2, every number is even. Is this true? _____

Write an explanation of how you know.

_____

_____

_____

_____

Securing number facts, relationships and calculating

BLOCK E

Securing number facts, relationships and calculating

Lesson	Strands	Starter	Main teaching activities
1. Teach and apply	Counting	Derive and recall multiplication facts for the 2-, 3-, 4-, 5-, 6- and 10-times tables.	Read and write proper fractions (eg $^3/_7$, $^9/_{10}$), interpreting the denominator as the parts of a whole and the numerator as the number of parts; identify and estimate fractions of shapes; use diagrams to compare fractions and establish equivalents.
2. Teach and apply	Counting	As for Lesson 1	As for Lesson 1
3. Teach and practise	Knowledge	As for Lesson 1	Derive and recall multiplication facts for the 2-, 3-, 4-, 5-, 6- and 10-times tables and the corresponding division facts; recognise multiples of 2, 5 or 10 up to 1000.
4. Teach and apply	Knowledge	As for Lesson 1	As for Lesson 3
5. Teach, practise and evaluate	Knowledge	As for Lesson 1	As for Lesson 3
6. Teach and practise	Calculate	As for Lesson 1	Multiply one-digit and two-digit numbers by 10 or 100, and describe the effect.
7. Teach and practise	Calculate	As for Lesson 1	Use practical and informal written methods to multiply and divide two-digit numbers (eg 13 × 3, 50 ÷ 4); round remainders up or down, depending on the context.
8. Teach and practise	Calculate	As for Lesson 1	As for Lesson 7
9. Teach and practise	Calculate	As for Lesson 1	Understand that division is the inverse of multiplication and vice versa; use this to derive and record related multiplication and division number sentences.
10. Teach, apply and evaluate	Calculate	As for Lesson 1	As for Lesson 9
11. Teach and practise	Calculate	Read and write proper fractions (eg $^3/_7$, $^9/_{10}$) interpreting the denominator as the parts of a whole and the numerator as the number of parts; identify and estimate fractions of shapes; use diagrams to compare fractions and establish equivalents.	Find unit fractions of numbers and quantities (eg $^1/_2$, $^1/_3$, $^1/_4$ and $^1/_6$ of 12 litres).
12. Teach and apply	Calculate	As for Lesson 11	As for Lesson 11
13. Teach and apply	Use/apply	Multiply one-digit and two-digit numbers by 10 or 100, and describe the effect.	Solve one-step and two-step problems involving numbers, money or measures, including time, choosing and carrying out appropriate calculations.
14. Teach and apply	Use/apply	Use knowledge of number operations and corresponding inverses, including doubling and halving, to estimate and check calculations.	As for Lesson 13
15. Teach, apply and evaluate	Use/apply	As for Lesson 14	As for Lesson 13

Unit 2 ◻ 3 weeks

Speaking and listening objective
● Develop and use specific vocabulary in different contexts.

Introduction
In this 15-lesson unit, children develop and use mathematical vocabulary for solving problems, multiplication and division, and for fractions. They solve word problems as well as writing their own for given equations. They develop their practical and written methods for division, including division involving remainders, and consolidate recall for table facts, including those for the 6-times table. They multiply one- and two-digit numbers by 10 or 100 and observe the effect. They begin to recognise that the same fraction can be expressed in different ways (equivalence) and that fractions can be ordered by their size.

Using and applying mathematics
● Solve one-step and two-step problems involving numbers, money or measures, including time, choosing and carrying out appropriate calculations.

Lessons 1-5

Preparation
Make an OHT of squared paper.

You will need
Photocopiable pages
'Fractions' (page 200) and 'Wheels' (page 201) for each child.
CD resources
Support and extension versions of 'Fractions' and 'Wheels'; 'Shading fractions' for each child (see General resources).
Equipment
OHT calculator; 12 interlocking cubes.

Learning objectives

Starter
● Derive and recall multiplication facts for the 2-, 3-, 4-, 5-, 6- and 10-times tables.
● Read and write proper fractions (eg $3/7$, $9/10$), interpreting the denominator as the parts of a whole and the numerator as the number of parts.

Main teaching activities
2006
● Read and write proper fractions (eg $3/7$, $9/10$), interpreting the denominator as the parts of a whole and the numerator as the number of parts; identify and estimate fractions of shapes; use diagrams to compare fractions and establish equivalents.
● Derive and recall multiplication facts for the 2-, 3-, 4-, 5-, 6- and 10-times tables and the corresponding division facts; recognise multiples of 2, 5 or 10 up to 1000.
1999
● Recognise unit fractions such as $½$, $⅓$, $¼$, $⅕$, $1/10$ ... and use them to find fractions of shapes and numbers.
● Begin to recognise simple fractions that are several parts of a whole, such as $¾$, $⅔$ or $3/10$.
● Compare familiar fractions, eg know that on the number line one half lies between one quarter and three quarters.
● Begin to recognise simple equivalent fractions, eg five tenths and one half, five fifths and one whole.
● Estimate a simple fraction.
● Know by heart: all addition and subtraction facts for each number to 20; all pairs of multiples of 100 with a total of 1000 (eg 300 + 700); all pairs of multiples of 5 with a total of 100 (eg 35 + 65).

Vocabulary
problem, solution, calculate, calculation, inverse, answer, method, explain, predict, estimate, reason, pattern, relationship, compare, order, information, test, list, table, diagram, double, halve, inverse, multiply, times, multiplied by, product, share, share equally, divide, divided by, divided into, left, left over, remainder, round up, round down, fraction, part, equal parts, one whole, parts of a whole, number of parts, one half, one third, one quarter, one fifth, one sixth, one tenth, two thirds, three quarters, three fifths, unit fraction

BLOCK E

Lesson 1 (Teach and apply)

Starter

Reason: Use an OHT calculator to repeatedly add threes (3++=) up to 30. Ask the children if they can spot any patterns, such as alternate odd/even in the units. Continue adding threes up to 90, each time writing the result on the board so the children can begin to see the 3, 6, 9, 2, 5, 8, 1, 4, 7 and 0 pattern repeating in the units. Each time, encourage the class to predict what will come next, using the pattern that they have already spotted.

Main teaching activities

Whole class: Invite a child to count out 12 interlocking cubes and agree that 12 cubes make a whole stick of cubes. Ask: *How many would half of these be?* Write on the board $1/2 + 1/2 = 1$. Demonstrate this by breaking the stick into two halves, then combining to make a whole again. Repeat for $1/4$, asking the children to say how many that would be. Now ask: *So how many is $1/4$?* Agree that $3 + 9 = 12$ (number of cubes) so that $1/4 + 3/4 = 1$. Repeat this for ten cubes, using tenths, such as $5/10 + 5/10 = 1$; $6/10 + 4/10 = 1$, and so on. Now draw a 5 × 2 rectangle on OHT squared paper, and shade in three squares. Ask: *How many squares are there altogether in this rectangle?* (10) *How many are shaded?* (3) *So $3/10$ are shaded.* Write the fraction on the board and explain that the bottom number (denominator) shows how many parts the whole is divided into, and the numerator (top number) gives the 'fraction' or the part of the whole. Repeat this for another rectangle, such as 4 × 3.

Individual work: Provide each child with a copy of general resource sheet 'Shading fractions'. The sheet asks them to draw rectangles of a given size, to shade in part of them, then to write the fractions that are not shaded.

Differentiation

Less confident learners: Decide whether to carry out the task as a group. Help the children to use the vocabulary of fractions appropriately.

More confident learners: Challenge the children to draw a 6 × 4 rectangle and to decide which fractions they could shade.

Review

Discuss the fractions that were shaded and what fractions were not shaded. Write some of these on the board as addition sentences to show that the pairs of fractions add to make 1. Draw a rectangle on the board (no squares this time) and shade in, say, approximately $1/3$. Ask: *What fraction do you estimate is shaded? How did you decide that? So how much is not shaded?*

Lesson 2 (Teach and apply)

Starter

Reason: Repeat the Starter for Lesson 1, this time looking at the patterns that occur in the units if you count from zero in 4s: 0, 4, 8, 2, 6, 0, 4...

Main teaching activities

Whole class: Write 1 on the board and ask the children to suggest as many equivalent fractions as they can think of. Write these on the board, such as $2/2$, $3/3$, $4/4$... Now say: *Tell me two fractions that will total 1.* Write the suggestions on the board, such as $1/4 + 3/4$. Challenge the more confident children to give more examples, such as $15/20 + 5/20$.

Now explain that you are going to ask some word problems about fractions. Say, for example: *There are ten apples in the box. If $3/10$ are sold, how many apples are left?* Ask the children to explain how they worked out the answer. Repeat for another word problem, such as: *$4/5$ of the pattern is red and the rest is white. What fraction is white?* ($1/5$) *If the pattern has ten sections altogether, how many sections are white?* (2)

Individual work: Provide the children with copies of the activity sheet 'Fractions'. Ask them to complete the sheet, which covers equivalent fractions, and fractions totalling 1.

Review

Ask: *How many eighths make a whole? What other fraction is the same as $2/8$?* ($1/4$); *$4/8$?* ($1/2$); *$6/8$?* ($3/4$); *What is $2/8$ add $6/8$?* Write this as a fraction sentence on the board: $2/8 + 6/8 = \square$. Now ask: *What other fractions are*

Unit 2 ▢ 3 weeks

Differentiation

Less confident learners: The support version of the sheet covers just halves, quarters and eighths.
More confident learners: The extension version of the sheet includes twelfths and twentieths.

worth the same as $^2/_8$ and $^6/_8$? So $^1/_4 + ^3/_4$ is worth the same as $^2/_8 + ^6/_8$. Using the challenge set to the more confident children, review with them the fractions that they found and write these on the board with their equivalents, such as $^6/_{12}$, $^1/_2$, $^3/_6$, and so on.

Lesson 3 (Teach and practise)

Starter
Recall: Repeat the Starter from Lesson 1, this time for counting in 6s from zero. Again discuss the unit's pattern: 0, 6, 2, 8, 4, 0, 6...

Main teaching activities
Whole class: Explain that in today's lesson the children will use their table facts to solve a problem. Begin by writing on the board: *There are 32 legs. How many horses is that?* Ask: *How did you work that out? Which table fact did you use?* Now say: *There are 24 legs. These could be horses' legs, or chickens' legs, or a mixture of both. How many animals do you think there are?* Give the children about five minutes, working in pairs, to suggest some solutions.

Discuss possible solutions and how the children worked this out. For example, there could be 6 horses (6 × 4) or 12 chickens (12 × 2) or a mixture of both animals such as 5 horses (5 × 4 = 20) and 4 chickens (2 × 2 = 4). There are other solutions. Discuss the table facts that the children used and how these helped them to find a solution.

Paired work: Provide each child with a copy of the activity sheet 'Wheels'. This contains a problem about how many vehicles there could be for a given number of wheels. Remind the children to use their table facts to solve the problem.

Review
Review the core sheet together. Discuss the solutions and the table facts used. Ask, for example: *Which table fact did you use? Did you use this for multiplication or division? Why? How did you decide how many of each vehicle to try?* Remind the children that with problems like this there can be more than one solution. Now ask the more confident children to report back on both parts of the problem on the more complex version of the sheet. Discuss their solutions, the table facts they needed, and the range of solutions that they found.

Differentiation

Less confident learners: There is a simpler version of 'Wheels' which uses only the 2- and 4-times tables.
More confident learners: The extension version of the sheet involves the 2-, 3-, 4- and 6-times tables.

Lesson 4 (Teach and apply)

Starter
Recall: Ask the children to count in 3s, then 5s, again looking at the pattern of the units. 3s: 0, 3, 6, 9, 2, 5, 8, 1, 4, 7, 0, 3... And 5s: 0, 5, 0, 5...

Main teaching activities
Whole class: Explain that in today's lesson children will be solving more problems using multiplication and division facts. Ask: *What is 8 times 3? So how can I use this to find 8 times 6?* Discuss how the first fact can be doubled to derive another fact. Write on the board: 24 ÷ ◯ = ◯. Ask: *How could we complete this division fact?* Write the different ways that the children suggest: 24 ÷ 6 = 4; 24 ÷ 4 = 6; 24 ÷ 8 = 3; 24 ÷ 3 = 8; 24 ÷ 2 = 12; 24 ÷ 12 = 2. Discuss how the children found the answers, such as if you know that 6 × 4 = 24, then you can derive 24 ÷ 6 = 4 and 24 ÷ 4 = 6.

Paired work: Write on the board: ◯ × ◯ = 36 and 36 ÷ ◯ = ◯. Ask the children to work in pairs to find solutions that fit both of these equations.

Review
Write on the board the answers that the children give, starting with the multiplication equation. Put the division answers alongside the multiplication fact. Discuss how, from knowing one fact, the others can be derived.

Differentiation

Less confident learners: Suggest that they try the multiplication first and that the answers to this will help them to find the division answers.
More confident learners: Challenge the children to extend their responses to, for example, 18 × 2 and 12 × 3, and so on.

Lesson 5 (Teach, practise and evaluate)

Starter
Recall: Write on the board 30 ÷ ◯ = ☐, and ask the children to suggest some solutions. Write up their responses. Each time, ask for the relevant multiplication fact as well as the division fact. Repeat this for 20 ÷ ◯ = ☐; 40 ÷ ◯ = ☐.

Main teaching activities
Whole class: Explain that in this lesson the children will explore ways of recognising multiples of 2, 5 and 10. Ask the children to count in twos starting from zero. Do this slowly and for each number they write just the unit digit: 0, 2, 4, 6, 8, 0, 2, 4… Ask: *What is special about these numbers?* Agree that these are even numbers, and that any multiple of 2 will have an even unit digit. Write these numbers on the board: 50, 79, 62, 245, and ask: *Which are multiples of 2? Which are not? How can you tell?* Now repeat this for counting in fives and agree that all multiples of 5 will have a 0 or a 5 as their unit digit. Say: *Tell me a three-digit number that is a multiple of 5.* Encourage the children to think of at least ten examples and agree that each must end with 5 or 0. Repeat this for counting in tens and that a multiple of 10 always has 0 as its unit digit.

Paired work: Arrange the children into pairs and ask them to find five three-digit numbers between 200 and 250 which are multiples of 2, 5 and 10. Ask them to write a sentence to explain their thinking.

Review
Invite children to explain their results and to read out their sentence. Ask the more confident children to say which three-digit number they found that is a multiple of 2, 3, 4, 5 and 10 (240). Point out that this is also a multiple of 6: 6 × 40 = 240. Now say: *If I know that 4 × 5 is 20, what is 4 × 50?* Repeat for other examples, such as 6 × 5, 9 × 2 and so on. Ask: *What have you learned about fractions, and multiplication and division?*

Differentiation
Less confident learners: Decide whether to limit the number range to 0 to 50.
More confident learners: Decide whether to challenge these children to find a three-digit number that is not only a multiple of 2, 5 and 10 but also a multiple of 3 and 4, in the range 200 to 250. (240).

Lessons 6-10

You will need
Photocopiable pages
'Multiply by 10 and 100' (page 202), 'Division and remainders' (page 203) and 'Arrays' (page 204) for each child.
CD resources
Support and extension versions of 'Multiply by 10 and 100', 'Division and remainders' and 'Arrays'. ITP 'Remainders after division'.

Learning objectives

Starter
● Derive and recall multiplication facts for the 2-, 3-, 4-, 5-, 6- and 10-times tables.

Main teaching activities
2006
● Multiply one-digit and two-digit numbers by 10 or 100, and describe the effect.
● Use practical and informal written methods to multiply and divide two-digit numbers (eg 13 × 3, 50 ÷ 4); round remainders up or down, depending on the context.
● Understand that division is the inverse of multiplication and vice versa and use this to derive and record related multiplication and division number sentences.
1999
● Multiply mentally by 10/100 by shifting the digits one/two places to the left.
● Use known number facts and place value to carry out mentally simple multiplications and divisions.
● Begin to find remainders after simple division; round up or down after division, depending on the context.
● Recognise that division is the inverse of multiplication, and that halving is the inverse of doubling.

● Say or write a division statement corresponding to a given multiplication statement.

Vocabulary
problem, solution, calculate, calculation, inverse, answer, method, explain, predict, estimate, reason, pattern, relationship, compare, order, information, test, list, table, diagram, double, halve, inverse, multiply, times, multiplied by, product, share, share equally, divide, divided by, divided into, left, left over, remainder, round up, round down

Lesson 6 (Teach and practise)

Starter
Recall: Explain that you will say a multiple. Ask the children to give you two multiplication and two division statements that contain this number. For example, if you say '45' then they would say $9 \times 5 = 45$; $5 \times 9 = 45$; $45 \div 5 = 9$; $45 \div 9 = 5$. Keep the pace sharp to encourage rapid recall of the multiplication facts.

Main teaching activities
Whole class: Explain that in today's lesson the children will multiply one- and two-digit numbers by 10 or 100. Begin by writing on the board 16. Ask the children to multiply this by 10 and write up the answer (160). Ask: *What is the value of the 1... 6... 0 in your answer?* Ask: *What would change 24 into 240? How do you know that? What is the value of the 2... 4... 0... in the answer?* Now write 4 and ask the children to multiply this by 10 (40); now multiply 40 by 10 (400). Ask: *What is the value of each digit in 400?* Discuss how what they have done is the same as multiplying 4 by 100. Repeat for multiplying 6 by 100.
Paired work: Provide each child with a copy of the activity sheet 'Multiply by 10 and 100'. The children choose one of the numbers from the top grid, then find the answer reached when multiplying by 10 or 100 in the second grid. They explain to their partner what they have done, then record this as a multiplication equation.

Review
Write on the board '56', and ask: *How can I change this into 560? What operation do I need?* Now write '6', and ask: *How can I change this into 600? What operation do I need?* Invite the children to explain what happens to each digit as they multiply by 10 or 100.

Differentiation
Less confident learners: The support version of the sheet (called 'Multiply by 10') concentrates on multiplying by 10.
More confident learners: The extension version of the sheet includes two-digit numbers multiplied by 100.

Lesson 7 (Teach and practise)

Starter
Recall: Repeat the Starter from Lesson 6, choosing different multiples.

Main teaching activities
Whole class: Explain that in this and the next lesson, the children will consider practical and written methods for multiplication and division. Begin by demonstrating with the ITP 'Remainders after division'. Show 9 rows of three counters, plus one more counter. Say: *This shows 28 divided by 3. Can you see what the answer will be?* Discuss which table facts will help the children to find the solution, eg $9 \times 3 = 27$. Discuss the solution, and reveal this by pressing the 'equals' button. Now put these numbers into a word problem: *Three children count how many marbles they have altogether. The total is 28. If they share these equally how many will they have each?* Discuss how this can be calculated. Ask: *What sort of calculation is it? Which word tells you that?* Repeat for another division which has a remainder, such as 36 divided by 5 and set this onto the ITP screen. Invite the children to say which multiplication fact will help them to solve this ($7 \times 5 = 35$) and to suggest their own word problem for this division.

Paired work: Provide squared paper. Write the following division questions on the board: 25 ÷ 4; 37 ÷ 4; 52 ÷ 6; 38 ÷ 5; 45 ÷ 6. Ask the children to draw a rectangle, and to draw rows/columns of spots to represent the counters, for each division. Explain that they must show the remainder as a column which does not have sufficient spots in it to complete it. They write the division equation underneath, write the multiplication fact they need as well, and write the answer. Challenge the children to write a word problem for each division equation.

Review

Review the questions on the board using the ITP 'Remainders after division'. Discuss for each one the multiplication fact needed to help to solve it, and the remainder. Ask children from each ability group to read out their word problems. Ask: *How do you know that this is a division question? And what is the answer?*

Lesson 8 (Teach and practise)

Starter

Recall: Repeat the Starter for Lesson 7, again choosing different multiples.

Main teaching activities

Whole class: Remind the children of what they did in the previous lesson by showing the ITP 'Remainders after division' again and using a division equation, such as 46 ÷ 5.

Individual work: Provide each child with a copy of the activity sheet 'Division and remainders' and ask them to work individually with this. Provide squared paper if the children find this helpful.

Review

Invite children from each ability group to explain how they worked out their answers. Ask: *When you divide a number that ends in 3 by 10, what will the remainder be? Why is this?*

Lesson 9 (Teach and practise)

Starter

Recall: Explain that you will ask multiplication questions from the 6-times table. Say, for example: *What is 5 times 6? What is 8 multiplied by 6?* Keep the pace sharp to encourage rapid recall.

Main teaching activities

Whole class: Ask the children to double numbers that you say, such as double 15, 18, 7… Write these as multiplication sentences on the board: 15 × 2 = ☐, with their answers. Now ask: *What is half of 30? So 30 divided by 2 is 15.* Write alongside the multiplication sentences the relevant division sentences, in this case 30 ÷ 2 = 15.

  Now write up 5 × 3 and ask the children to work out the answer. Write up 15 ÷ 3 and ask for the answer. Discuss how, if you know a multiplication fact, you can work out the related division. Write: 5 × 3 = 15; 3 × 5 = 15; 15 ÷ 3 = 5; 15 ÷ 5 = 3. Repeat this for other facts, such as 7 × 3, 9 × 6….

Paired work: Ask the children to work in pairs. They take turns to write a multiplication fact for which they know the answer. They write two multiplication facts and two division facts, such as: 8 × 3 = 24; 3 × 8 = 24; 24 ÷ 3 = 8; 24 ÷ 8 = 3. Ask the children to complete ten different sets of facts.

Review

Invite children to give examples of their multiplication and division facts. Discuss how each fact can be seen to be part of a family of multiplication and division facts, and how useful this is; children can find division facts from

Unit 2 3 weeks

multiplication facts that they know. Ask questions such as: *What is double 30? So what is half of 60? What is 4 multiplied by 5? So what is 40 divided by 10?* Check from their responses that children understand the inverse nature of multiplication and division, and of doubling and halving.

Lesson 10 (Teach, apply and evaluate)

Starter
Recall: Repeat the Starter from Lesson 9, this time extending the questions to include all the multiplication tables that the children have learned: 2-, 3-, 4-, 5-, 6- and 10-times tables. Keep the pace sharp to encourage rapid recall.

Main teaching activities
Whole class: Draw an array on the board for 5 × 4 and say: *This diagram shows two multiplication facts. Count how many squares across; count how many squares down; count all the squares. What multiplication facts does this array show?* Agree that it is 5 × 4 and 4 × 5. Repeat this for another pair of facts such as 5 × 2 and 2 × 5. Now ask: *What division facts are linked to this array?* Repeat this for another array, such as 6 × 3. Discuss how, if you know a multiplication fact then you can derive another multiplication fact and two division facts.
Individual work: Provide copies of the activity sheet 'Arrays'. Ask the children to write the four facts associated with each array.

Review
Review together some of the arrays from each sheet. Discuss how the children found the solutions. Ask the more confident children to display some of their different arrays. Challenge all the children to calculate the facts for these. Ask questions such as: *If I use a calculator to find the answer to 32 ÷ 4, the answer is 8. What operation do I need to put into the calculator to turn the 8 back into 32? Tell your partner what you now know about division and remainders, and multiplying by 10 and by 100.*

Differentiation
Less confident learners: There is a support version of the sheet that concentrates on multiplication tables 2, 5 and 10. Encourage the children to use the vocabulary of multiplication and division to explain how they found each fact.
More confident learners: After they have completed the extension version of the activity sheet, challenge the children to draw some different arrays and to write the corresponding facts.

Lessons 11-15

Preparation
Make OHTs of CD pages 'Fraction number lines', 'Fraction cards' (cut out the fraction cards) and 'Inside the Post Office'.

You will need
Photocopiable pages
'Post Office problems' (page 205) for each child.
CD resources
Core, support and extension versions of 'Easter egg parade', support and extension versions of 'Post office problems'; 'Fraction cards' and 'Fraction number lines' for each child, 'Inside the Post Office' (see General resources).

Learning objectives

Starter
● Multiply one- and two-digit numbers by 10 or 100, and describe the effect.
● Use knowledge of number operations and corresponding inverses, including doubling and halving, to estimate and check calculations.
● Read and write proper fractions (eg $3/7$, $9/10$), interpreting the denominator as the parts of a whole and the numerator as the number of parts; identify and estimate fractions of shapes; use diagrams to compare fractions and establish equivalents.

Main teaching activities
2006
● Find unit fractions of numbers and quantities (eg $1/2$, $1/3$, $1/4$ and $1/6$ of 12 litres).
● Solve one-step and two-step problems involving numbers, money or measures, including time, choosing and carrying out appropriate calculations.
1999
● Recognise unit fractions such as $1/2$, $1/3$, $1/4$, $1/5$, $1/10$... and use them to find fractions of shapes and numbers.
● Solve word problems involving numbers in 'real life', money and measures, using one or more steps, including finding totals and giving change, and working out which coins to pay. Explain how the problem was solved.

Securing number facts, relationships and calculating

BLOCK E

Vocabulary

problem, solution, calculate, calculation, inverse, answer, method, explain, predict, estimate, reason, pattern, relationship, compare, order, information, test, list, table, diagram, fraction, part, equal parts, one whole, parts of a whole, number of parts, one half, one third, one quarter, one fifth, one sixth, one tenth, two thirds, three quarters, three fifths, unit fraction

Lesson 11 (Teach and practise)

Starter

Reason: Explain that you will say a fraction. Ask the children to think of some fractions that are equivalent to the ones that you say. Say, for example: ½, ¼...

Main teaching activities

Whole class: Explain that in this and the next lesson, the children will be comparing unit fractions. Provide each child with some squared paper and some scissors and ask them to cut three strips of squares, each strip to have ten squares. Now ask them to colour in half of one strip, a fifth of another and a tenth of the third. Ask the children to put the strips in front of them, with one strip under another. Ask: *Are all the strips the same size? Find the strip with five coloured squares. What fraction are the five coloured squares of the whole strip?* Agree that the fraction is $^5/_{10}$ or ½ and write both of these on the board. Ask: *What fraction are the two squares of the whole strip?* Agree that this is $^2/_{10}$ or $^1/_5$ and again write the fractions on the board. For the third strip ask: *What fraction is one square of the whole?* Write $^1/_{10}$ on the board. Now ask: *Which is the larger fraction? Which is the smaller one? Order your strips with the coloured parts in order from smallest to largest.* Discuss how the strips are all the same length, but the coloured fractions of the strips can be ordered from smallest to largest. Agree that $^1/_{10}$ is smaller than $^1/_5$, which is smaller than ½.

Paired work: Provide more squared paper. Ask the children to cut four strips of 12 squares. They colour $^1/_2$, $^1/_3$, $^1/_4$ and $^1/_6$ of the squares, then order their strips. Ask them to write a sentence about their results.

Review

Discuss the children's results. Invite children from each group to read out their sentence. Ask questions such as: *Which is the largest of these fractions? Don't move your strips of paper, but if you ordered them from largest to smallest, which would be larger than $^1/_4$ but smaller than $^1/_2$? How do you know that?*

Differentiation

Less confident learners: Decide whether to have these children work as a group and encourage them to use fraction vocabulary to describe what they find.
More confident learners: Ask the children to write some equivalent fractions for each of their unit fractions.

Lesson 12 (Teach and apply)

Starter

Reason: Repeat the Starter from Lesson 11, this time saying $^3/_4$, $^2/_{10}$...

Main teaching activities

Whole class: Explain that in this lesson the children will be placing fractions on a number line. Show the OHT 'Fraction number lines' and write on one number line 0 at the beginning and 1 at the end. Point to the mid-point of the line and ask: *What fraction is this?* Agree that it is $^1/_2$ and place that fraction card in place. Place the other fraction cards from general resource sheet 'Fraction cards' around the edge of the OHT so that the children can see what these are. Ask: *What other cards could go here?* Praise those who suggest $^2/_4$ and $^5/_{10}$ and ask for explanations of why these are correct. Place the fifth cards and the tenth cards.

Mark a second number line from 3 to 4 and ask: *What number is half way between 3 and 4?* Write in $3^1/_2$. Point to other positions on the line and ask the children to say which fractions would go there.

Draw a line on the board and ask the children to help you to put in all the fractions of halves and quarters from 0 to 10. Do this systematically: 0, $^1/_4$, $^1/_2$, $^3/_4$, 1, 1$^1/_4$, 1$^1/_2$... 10. When the line is complete, read it forwards and backwards several times until the children are confident. Cover the line over with some large sheets of paper and ask questions such as: *What number is half way between 5 and 6? What number is between 4$^1/_2$ and 5? Tell me any number between 8 and 9.* Write down the children's responses, then uncover the line so that they can check that the answers are true.

Paired work: Provide each pair with a copy of general resource sheet 'Fraction cards'. Ask the children to cut out the cards and to place them, shuffled, in a pile. They take turns to take a card and place the cards in front of them. The object is to work together to make a fraction line for halves, quarters, fifths and tenths, placing the fractions in order.

Review

Using the OHT 'Fraction number lines', invite a child to write in the fractions for halves on the first line. Agree that the start is 0, $^1/_2$ is at the mid-point, and 1 is at the far end. Repeat this for tenths and fifths. Now discuss quarters. Explain that there are only four quarters in a whole, so that the children will need to look at the mid-point between 0 and $^1/_2$ for $^1/_4$ and the mid-point between $^1/_2$ and 1 for $^3/_4$.

Differentiation

Less confident learners: Decide whether to have these children work as a group so that they work together to decide where the cards should go. Encourage them to read each card and say where it belongs in the line.

More confident learners: Challenge the children to make their own fraction line, using a copy of general resource sheet 'Fraction number lines'. They can decide which set of fractions they would like to use.

Lesson 13 (Teach and apply)

Starter

Recall: Explain that you will ask a multiplication by 10 or 100 question. Say, for example: *What is 12 multiplied by 10? What is 36 multiplied by 10? How can I change 5 into 500?*

Main teaching activities

Whole class: Talk briefly about why people use post offices (to collect pensions, send parcels, pick up passport forms, pay car tax and so on). Share the general resource sheet 'Inside the Post Office' with the class, covering the word problem at the end of the sheet. The sheet shows that stamps are 30p and that a 500g parcel would be 70p to send. Ask:

● *How much would three stamps cost?*
● *How much would it cost to send two parcels, each weighing 500 grams?* Explain how you worked it out.

Make jottings on a whiteboard to accompany the children's explanations, for example: Three stamps would be 30p + 30p + 30p = 90p. One child might have jotted 60p and then 90p, as if keeping a running addition record. Point out that the child is using repeated addition. An alternative might be thinking 3 × 30p = 90p.

Move on to explain repeated subtraction for the following problem: *Mia buys two 30p stamps using a pound coin. What change should she receive?* (Tell the children to think of £1 as 100p when using the empty number line.) Her change should be 100p − 30p − 30p = 40p. Show the class how to use an empty number line (ENL) to show their thinking.

Alternatively, the children might say they worked the answer out by multiplying 30p × 2 to equal 60p, and then subtracting 60p from one pound. This could be expressed as working out the difference between 60p and 100p or as 100p, jump backwards 60p to reach 40p. Both responses are acceptable.

Refer again to the general resource sheet 'Inside the Post Office' and ask the children:

● *What information on the picture have we not used so far?* (The date is visible.)
● *What units are the problems likely to be in?* (Pounds and pence, grams and kilograms, and so on.)
● *Looking at the picture, what do you anticipate the problems might be about?* (Money.)

Differentiation

Less confident learners: This group can work on the support version of the activity sheet in pairs to solve simpler problems. They calculate a total, then choose which coin/s to pay with from a selection.

More confident learners: This group can work on two-step operations on the extension version of 'Post Office problems', which has challenging mathematical expressions such as 'three times the amount'. Provide calculators for the final part of the sheet, where children invent their own problems.

● *What operations do you think you might be using, and why?*
Uncover the word problem on the OHT 'Inside the Post Office'. The problem is: *Melinda went to the Post Office to buy a set of six special edition stamps. The stamps were all the same price – 50p each. How much did she spend? How much change did she get from £5?* Invite the children to explain in their own words what is to be calculated, and how. They may suggest multiplication (6 × 50p) or repeated addition, perhaps using an empty number line. Encourage them to use their table facts and to derive division ones where necessary.

Individual work: Ask the children to complete the word problems on the activity sheet 'Post Office problems'.

Review

Invite children from each ability group to explain how they solved one of their problems. Ask: *Did anyone have a different way of calculating this? Which do you think is better? Why do you think that?* Challenge the children to make up a word problem using the division 42 ÷ 6. Ask: *How do you know that this problem will involve division?*

Lesson 14 (Teach and apply)

Starter

Recall: Explain that you will say a number and that you want the children to say its double. Choose numbers that are multiples of 5, from 5 to 50, such as 15, 10, 25, 40, 35... Give sufficient thinking time for the majority of the children to derive the answer.

Main teaching activities

Whole class: Explain that this and the next lessons are about solving problems. Tell the class that you will read a story about a disastrous dinner party. Ask the children to jot down their answers, using mental or pencil and paper methods as necessary, each time you pause. Here is the story:

There are six visitors coming to tea. How many pieces of cutlery will you need if they and you each have a knife, spoon and fork? (7 × 3 = 21)

You only have five table settings-worth of cutlery, so you decide to have a Chinese meal instead, for which you will need seven pairs of chopsticks. How many chopsticks will be on the table? (14)

Sadly, the dog decides to chew two chopsticks, so how many do you have left? (12)

You think to yourself, 'I wish we'd eaten out!'

You find some plastic picnic spoons. You discover that you have twice as many spoons as there will be people at the party – but don't forget yourself! So how many spoons are there? (14)

Review the children's answers to each part of the story and ask individuals to explain how they worked out their answers.

Individual work: Provide copies of the activity sheet 'Easter egg parade'. Ask the children to work individually to calculate their answers.

Review

Explain that you are going to tell another story. Ask the children to keep a note of their answers, and make jotting as necessary. Say:

I decided to take my friends on a picnic. There were four of us altogether. Each of us would eat four sandwiches. How many sandwiches would I need to make? (16)

We all like cakes. I made six chocolate cakes and four times that number of strawberry cakes. How many cakes did I make altogether?
(6 + (6 × 4) = 30)

Another friend gave me two more cakes. How many cakes are there now? (32)

But only a quarter of the cakes were eaten. How many were eaten? (8)

Review the children's answers, and encourage them to explain how

Differentiation

Less confident learners: There is a support version of the activity sheet available for this group which uses halving and doubling.

More confident learners: There is an extension version of the sheet available for this group which includes finding quarters.

they worked each one out. Ask them to check each answer, for example by doubling or halving, as appropriate.

Lesson 15 (Teach, apply and evaluate)

Starter
Recall: Repeat the Starter from Lesson 14, this time increasing the pace to encourage rapid recall.

Main teaching activities
Whole class: Ask word problems such as: *I have 60 apples. I put a quarter of the apples into a bowl. How many apples are in the bowl?* Discuss how the children worked out the answer, such as halving and halving again. Discuss also how the answer can be checked by doubling and doubling again.

Repeat this for another example, such as: *There are 48 chickens to go to market. Only a quarter of them will fit into each crate. How many chickens is that?*

Paired work: On the board write some number sentences such as $80 \div 4$, $100 \div 4$, 25×4, $400 \div 4$ and so on. Challenge the children to work in pairs to invent their own word problem for each number sentence, find the answer, then check it by halving for doubling, or doubling for halving.

Review
Invite the children to read out their number sentences, say their answers and explain how they checked them. Ask questions such as: *How did you work that out? Did anyone try a different method? Which do you think was the more effective method? Why do you think that?*

Ask the children that you are targetting for assessment to say what they have learned from this series of lessons.

Differentiation
Less confident learners: Offer these children simpler number sentences.
More confident learners: For these children, add in some more complex number sentences, such as $160 \div 4$.

Securing number facts, relationships and calculating

BLOCK E

Name _____ Date _____

Fractions

Write the fraction for the shaded part.

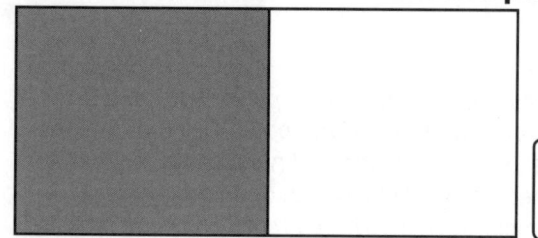 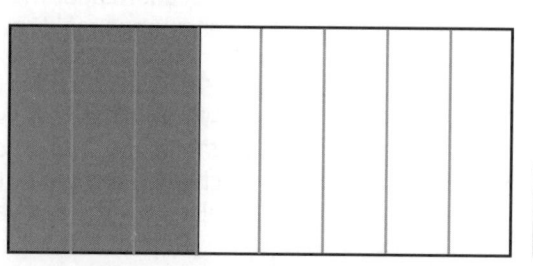

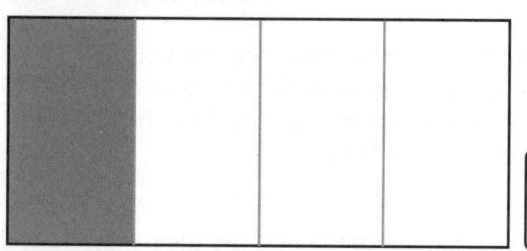 

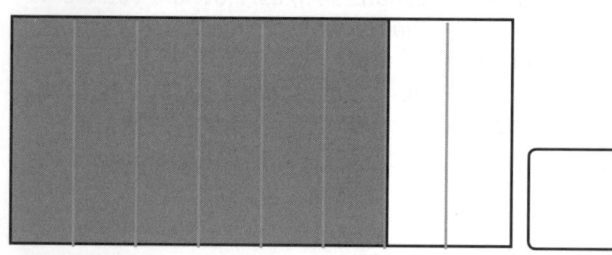 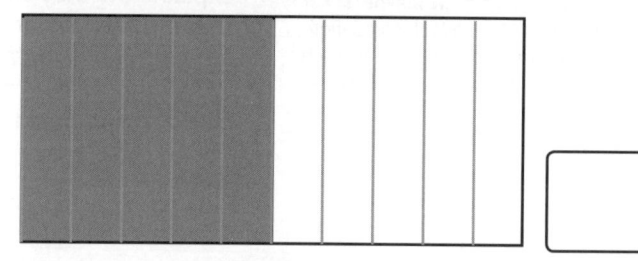

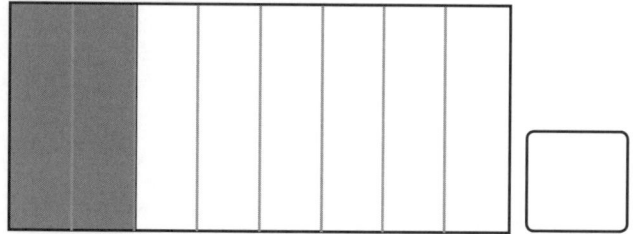 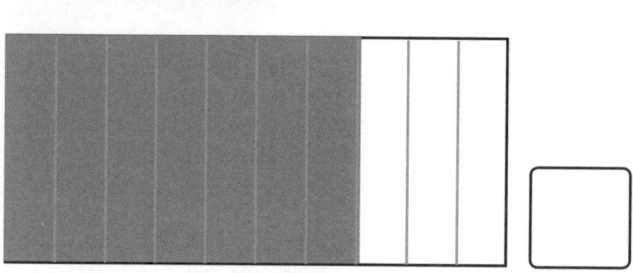

Write in the fraction that makes 1 whole.

$\frac{1}{2}$ + ⬜ = 1

$\frac{3}{4}$ + ⬜ = 1

$\frac{3}{8}$ + ⬜ = 1

$\frac{7}{10}$ + ⬜ = 1

Securing number facts, relationships and calculating

BLOCK E

Name _____   Date _____

Wheels

Sam counts how many wheels she can see in the staff car park.

She counts 36 wheels.

Some of the vehicles are cars.

Some of the vehicles are bicycles.

Some of the vehicles are cars with just three wheels.

How many of each type of vehicle do you think there are?

Use this space to find a solution to the problem.

Show your working out.

Discuss this with your partner.

Securing number facts, relationships and calculating

BLOCK E

Name _____   Date _____

Multiply by 10 and 100

Work with a partner.

Take turns to choose a number from grid **A**.

From grid **B**, find the total you get when you multiply your number by 10 or 100.

A

5	2	9	37	6	18	27	33	19	23
17	54	92	1	99	4	46	8	35	7

B

270	100	800	460	500	700	230	540	600	990
180	190	900	350	330	920	400	200	170	370

Write a multiplication sentence for each of your chosen numbers.

Securing number facts, relationships and calculating

BLOCK E

Name _____   Date _____

Division and remainders

Write the answer to each division.

Show any working out that you do.

You can use squared paper if that will help you.

Division	Working out	Answer
1. 24 ÷ 5		
2. 38 ÷ 6		
3. 39 ÷ 4		
4. 25 ÷ 3		
5. 95 ÷ 10		

Securing number facts, relationships and calculating

BLOCK E

Name _____ Date _____

Arrays

Write the two multiplication facts for each of these arrays.

Now write the two linked division facts for each array. The first has been done for you.

Array	Answers							
1×4 ●●●●	1	$\times$	4	$= 4$	4	$\div$	1	$= 4$
	4	$\times$	1	$= 4$	4	$\div$	4	$= 1$
1. 6×3	☐ × ☐ = ☐				☐ ÷ ☐ = ☐			
	☐ × ☐ = ☐				☐ ÷ ☐ = ☐			
2. 9×2	☐ × ☐ = ☐				☐ ÷ ☐ = ☐			
	☐ × ☐ = ☐				☐ ÷ ☐ = ☐			
3. 8×4	☐ × ☐ = ☐				☐ ÷ ☐ = ☐			
	☐ × ☐ = ☐				☐ ÷ ☐ = ☐			
4. 7×5	☐ × ☐ = ☐				☐ ÷ ☐ = ☐			
	☐ × ☐ = ☐				☐ ÷ ☐ = ☐			

Now draw these arrays onto the squared paper.

Write all four facts for each array.

5. 3×4	☐ × ☐ = ☐ ☐ ÷ ☐ = ☐	
	☐ × ☐ = ☐ ☐ ÷ ☐ = ☐	
6. 10×2	☐ × ☐ = ☐ ☐ ÷ ☐ = ☐	
	☐ × ☐ = ☐ ☐ ÷ ☐ = ☐	

Name _____   Date _____

Post Office problems

The prices that you need are in the picture.

1. Cal spent 90p on stamps. How many stamps did he buy? [ ]

2. Eleanor spent twice as much as Cal on stamps. How much did she spend? [ ]

How many stamps did she buy? [ ]

3. How much would it cost to send one 500g parcel and two letters? [ ]

4. It costs 70p to send a 500g parcel. How much will it cost to send a 2kg parcel? [ ]
How much change would you get from £3.00? [ ]

5. How much does a parcel weigh if it cost £3.50 to post? [ ]

6. What is the difference in cost between a stamped letter and a 500g parcel? [ ]

Now use the data in the picture to write your own problem here, and work out the answer. You may want to make some jottings on some spare paper to remind you how you worked this out.

_____

_____

Securing number facts, relationships and calculating

BLOCK E

Unit 3 ▢ 3 weeks

Securing number facts, relationships and calculating

Lesson	Strands	Starter	Main teaching activities
1. Teach and practise	Counting	Read, write and order whole numbers to at least 1000 and position them on a number line; count on from and back to zero in single-digit steps or multiples of 10.	**Partition three-digit numbers into multiples of 100, 10 and 1 in different ways.**
2. Teach and apply	Use/apply	Derive and recall multiplication facts for the 2-, 3-, 4-, 5-, 6- and 10-times tables.	Identify patterns and relationships involving numbers or shapes, and use these to solve problems.
3. Teach and apply	Use/apply	As for Lesson 2	As for Lesson 2
4. Teach and apply	Use/apply	As for Lesson 2	As for Lesson 2
5. Teach, apply and evaluate	Counting Use/apply	As for Lesson 2	• **Partition three-digit numbers into multiples of 100, 10 and 1 in different ways.** • Identify patterns and relationships involving numbers or shapes, and use these to solve problems.
6. Teach and practise	Counting	Read and write proper fractions (eg $3/7$, $9/10$), interpreting the denominator as the parts of a whole and the numerator as the number of parts; identify and estimate fractions of shapes; use diagrams to compare fractions and establish equivalents.	Read and write proper fractions (eg $3/7$, $9/10$) interpreting the denominator as the parts of a whole and the numerator as the number of parts; identify and estimate fractions of shapes; use diagrams to compare fractions and establish equivalents.
7. Teach and practise	Counting	As for Lesson 6	As for Lesson 6
8. Teach and practise	Knowledge	Derive and recall multiplication facts for the 2-, 3-, 4-, 5-, 6- and 10-times tables and the corresponding division facts.	Derive and recall multiplication facts for the 2-, 3-, 4-, 5-, 6- and 10-times tables and the corresponding division facts.
9. Teach and practise	Knowledge	As for Lesson 8	As for Lesson 8
10. Teach, practise and evaluate	Calculate	As for Lesson 8	Find unit fractions of numbers and quantities (eg $\frac{1}{2}$, $\frac{1}{3}$, $\frac{1}{4}$ and $\frac{1}{6}$ of 12 litres).
11. Teach and practise	Calculate	Round two- or three-digit numbers to the nearest 10 or 100 and give estimates for their sums and differences.	Develop and use written methods to record, support or explain addition and subtraction of two- and three-digit numbers.
12. Teach and practise	Calculate	Round two- or three-digit numbers to the nearest 10 or 100 and give estimates for their sums and differences.	As for Lesson 11
13. Teach and practise	Calculate	Derive and recall multiplication facts for the 2-, 3-, 4-, 5-, 6- and 10-times tables and the corresponding division facts.	Use practical and informal written methods to multiply and divide two-digit numbers (eg 13 × 3, 50 ÷ 4); round remainders up or down, depending on the context.
14. Teach and apply	Calculate	As for Lesson 13	As for Lesson 13
15. Teach, apply and evaluate	Use/apply	As for Lesson 13	Solve one-step and two-step problems involving numbers, money or measures, including time, choosing and carrying out appropriate calculations.

Unit 3 ◗ 3 weeks

Speaking and listening objective
- Sustain conversation, explaining or giving reasons for their views or choices.

Introduction
In this 15-lesson unit, the children are involved in making decisions about how to calculate, which methods to use and record. They solve one- and two-step problems and discuss the choices they made, giving reasons for this. They develop their skills in partitioning numbers, identify patterns and relationships to help them to calculate. They further develop their skills in addition, subtraction, multiplication and division, and use both informal and formal written methods. They find fractions of shapes and quantities and link this to division. By now they should have rapid recall of all multiplication facts in the 2-, 3-, 4-, 5-, 6- and 10-times tables and derive the related division facts swiftly.

Using and applying mathematics
- Solve one-step and two-step problems involving numbers, money or measures, including time, choosing and carrying out appropriate calculations.
- Follow a line of enquiry by deciding what information is important; make and use lists, tables and graphs to organise and interpret the information.

Lessons 1-5

Preparation
Prepare sets of 0-9 digit cards, using CD page 'Numeral cards 0-20'; make an OHT of CD page 'Hairyonymus'.

You will need
Photocopiable pages
'Ordering numbers' (page 218) for each child.
CD resources
Support and extension versions of 'Ordering numbers'; 'Numeral cards 0-20' and 'Hairyonymus' for the teacher's/LSA's and children's reference (see General resources).
Equipment
Beanbag.

Learning objectives

Starter
- Read, write and order whole numbers to at least 1000 and position them on a number line; count on from and back to zero in single-digit steps or multiples of 10.
- Derive and recall multiplication facts for the 2-, 3-, 4-, 5-, 6- and 10-times tables.

Main teaching activities
2006
- Partition three-digit numbers into multiples of 100, 10 and 1 in different ways.
- Identify patterns and relationships involving numbers or shapes, and use these to solve problems.
1999
- Know what each digit represents, and partition three-digit numbers into a multiple of 100, a multiple of ten and ones (HTU).
- Solve mathematical problems or puzzles, recognise simple patterns and relationships, generalise and predict. Suggest extensions by asking 'What if...?'
- Describe and extend number sequences.
- Investigate a general statement about familiar numbers or shapes by finding examples that satisfy it.

Vocabulary
problem, solution, calculate, calculation, inverse, answer, method, explain, predict, estimate, reason, pattern, relationship, compare, order, information, test, list, table, diagram, place value, partition, ones, tens, hundreds, one-digit number, two-digit number, three-digit number

Lesson 1 (Teach and practise)

Starter
Recall: Ask the class to stand in a circle to play a game, as follows. Give a beanbag to a child to hold and ask him to say a two-digit number. He then passes the beanbag to his left. The next person has to add 10 to the number, pass on the beanbag, and so on, until someone says 'Inverse reverse'. This means the rule changes to subtract 10 and the direction of the beanbag also changes. Tell the children that they may each say 'Inverse reverse' only once

during the game. It may take a few tries before the children can pick up the speed! You may like to double up children if you have a large class by asking one child to stand behind a partner and to whisper the answer for the person in front to call out.

Main teaching activities

Whole class: Explain to the children that by the end of the lesson they should feel more confident in placing three-digit numbers in order quickly. Draw this simple grid on the board and ask the children to quickly draw it on their whiteboards.

Hundreds	Tens	Units

Explain that you will show the children a number card with a single digit on it and they must decide where to write that number – that is, as a hundreds, tens or units digit. The aim of the game is to make the largest number they can, but once they have written the digit into a place it cannot be altered. Play the game two or three times, before asking questions such as: *Did you always make the largest number possible? What is the largest number we could make with these three digits? What is the smallest number that we could make?*

Now write two numbers on the board with a space between them, such as: 245 ☐ 368. Ask the children to give you as many facts as they can about the two numbers, such as: *Which is the larger number? Which is the smaller number? Think of some numbers that are larger than the smaller number.* Write the responses on the board, then repeat this for three-digit numbers that are smaller than the larger number. Again, write the children's responses on the board. Compare their answers, asking: *What is the hundreds digit? Is it a 2 or a 3? Why is that important? What about the tens digit? Can that be any number? Why do you think that? What about the units digit – can that be any number in this example?* Discuss how the hundreds digit must be a 2 or a 3; and that the tens digit can be any number between 4 and 9 if the hundreds digit is a 2, or between 0 and 6 if the hundreds digit is a 3. Ask the children to explain what the units digit can or cannot be.

Now draw an empty number line and place the two numbers on it: 245 ☐ 368. Repeat this for another example, such as 678 ☐ 804.

Paired work: Ask the children to complete the activity sheet 'Ordering numbers'. This gives the children two numbers, and they must find a third, from a list given, which will fit between the two given numbers. Point out that some answers will fit more than one question.

Review

Ask a child to write a three-digit number on the board. Now invite another child to write a second three-digit number that is larger than the first number. Challenge the class to suggest numbers that will fit between so that the three numbers are in order. Ask: *How can you tell that that number will fit?* Repeat this for another pair of numbers. Challenge the more confident children by including four-digit numbers.

Differentiation

Less confident learners: The support version of the sheet gives examples using only two-digit numbers.

More confident learners: The extension version of the sheet asks the children to write in two numbers, in order, to fit between each pair of numbers. There is no list of numbers given. The children must work these out for themselves.

Lesson 2 (Teach and apply)

Starter

Recall: Say together the facts for the 3-times table: *0 multiplied by/times 3 is 0; 1 multiplied by/times 3 is 3,* and so on. Then ask the children questions about the 3 times-table, such as: *What is 8 multiplied by 3? What is 9 multiplied by 3?*

Keep the pace sharp and encourage the children to begin to 'know' these facts by praising those with good recall.

Main teaching activities

Whole class: Explain that today, and during the following two lessons, the children will be solving number-based puzzles, using patterns that they find to help them. Check that they understand the terminology of 'sum' and 'product' by asking them to think of a pair of numbers that have a sum of 19 and a product of 90. (10 and 9.) Discuss the strategies that the children used to find the solution. Explain that it is useful to make jottings when finding solutions to puzzles and problems, because it helps you to remember what you have tried, what worked, and what did not.

Work through the following examples with the children:
Find a pair of numbers with: a sum of 10 and a product of 25 (5, 5); *a sum of 16 and a product of 60* (10, 6); *a sum of 12 and a product of 32* (8, 4).

Using the same products, change the examples so they now read:
Find a pair of numbers with: a difference of 0 and a product of 25 (5 and 5); *a difference of 4 and a product of 60* (10 and 6); *a difference of 4 and a product of 32* (8 and 4).

Ask the children to consider whether the following are possible: *a pair of numbers with: a sum of 1 and a product of 5* (No); *a sum of 0 and a product of 9* (No); *a difference of 0 and a product of 9* (Yes: 3, 3).

In each instance, ask the children for a clear example to show whether it is possible or not.

Paired work: Ask pairs of children to try an example you write on the board: *If the sum of a pair of numbers is 7, how many different products can you find?* (1 × 6, 2 × 5 and 3 × 4.) Now ask them to think of another example and find how many products they can find for that.

Review

Review the children's findings for the sum of 7, for example. Ask: *What pattern did you spot?* Check that the children understood that they could use the multiples of 1 and 6, 2 and 5, and so on, and that if ordered it is easier to spot if any possible products are missing.

Differentiation

Less confident learners: Decide whether to work as a group. Encourage the children to discuss how they can work out some solutions and how they would record these. Then continue with the first investigation by extending it to: *If a sum of a pair of numbers is 10, how many different products can you find?* (1 × 9, 2 × 8, 3 × 7, 4 × 6, 5 × 5.) Discuss any patterns that the children can see.

More confident learners: Challenge the children to try several different sums, using small numbers.

Lesson 3 (Teach and apply)

Starter

Rehearse: Label the ends of a counting stick 0 and 40 and count along it in fours several times, then point to different positions on the stick and ask the children to name the number. Now repeat the counting along the stick, this time saying the 4-times table facts aloud. Then point to different positions on the stick and ask the children to say the 4-times table multiplication fact that belongs at that point.

Main teaching activities

Whole class: Write a puzzle on the board: *Using 2, 4 and 5, and the signs +, × and =, how many different answers can you make?* Invite the children to suggest how to begin the puzzle. Remind them that they may use the 2, 4 and 5 as many times as they need. Give the children about five minutes to try this, working in pairs. Then invite the children to feed back their results to the whole class. Discuss the importance of being systematic when approaching a problem. Remind the class that by recording everything that they try, even if it does not give the answer that they need, they will have a record of what has been tried, what worked, and what did not, so that they can spot patterns in their record.

Paired work: Show an OHT of general resource sheet 'Hairyonymus'. Ask the children to try this puzzle, working systematically in pairs.

Review

Discuss the day's learning. Write up the activity sheet findings in order as number sentences. For example: 2 + 2 + 2 + 2 + 2 + 5 = 15; 5 + 5 + 5 = 15; 5 + 10 = 15. Ask: *Is there any other combination that we could try? What other combinations could we have for the Hairyonymus babies? Why*

Differentiation

Less confident learners: Decide whether to work as a group to solve the problem.

More confident learners: Challenge the children to write their own problem for other children in the group to solve.

is this the only combination? (We need to make a 5 or 10 in order to add to the teenager's or adult's hair.) Discuss how the children went about finding solutions and how they recorded these. Praise those who worked systematically.

Lesson 4 (Teach and apply)

Starter
Repeat the Starter for Lesson 3, this time concentrating on using the counting stick to generate facts for the 6-times table.

Main teaching activities
Whole class: Draw a triangle with six circles:

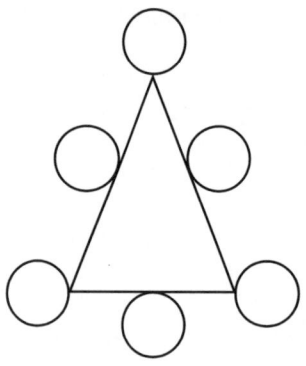 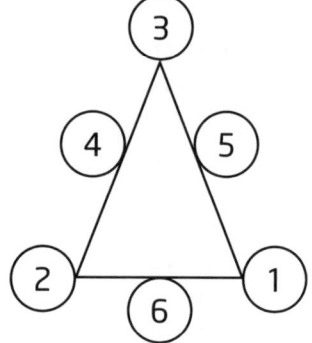

Ask the children to decide how to put the numbers 1 to 6 into the circles so that each side of the triangle totals 9. One solution is shown.
Paired work: Ask the children to try the triangle totals again, this time making totals of 10, then 11.

Review
Discuss what the children did, and how they recorded their work.

Differentiation
Less confident learners:
Provide numeral cards 1–6 for the children to place and move as necessary until they have found the solution.
More confident learners:
Challenge the children to find more than one solution for each puzzle.

Lesson 5 (Teach, apply and evaluate)

Starter
Recall: Repeat the Starter for Lesson 2, this time for the 3-, 4- and 6-times table facts. Keep the pace sharp.

Main teaching activities
Whole class: Explain that in this lesson, the children will use what they know about partitioning numbers to explore number patterns. Write on the board: 64 = 60 + 4. Say: *This can be partitioned into 50 + 14.* Write this on the board. Ask: *What would the next partition in the pattern be?* Agree that this would be 40 + 24. Ask the children to say how the pattern would continue. Write up their responses: 30 + 34, 20 + 44, 10 + 54, 0 + 64.

Now write up 742 = 700 + 42, then 742 = 600 + ☐ and ask the children to work out what comes next. Together continue the pattern.
Paired work: Provide two sets of 0–9 cards for each pair. The children take turns to take three cards from the shuffled pack and make the largest three-digit number they can from their cards. So, if they chose 1, 6 and 2, their largest number would be 621. Then they both write the partitions as a pattern: 621 = 600 + 21; 621 = 500 + 121, and so on.

Review
Invite a child to give one of their three-digit numbers. Ask the other children to begin the partition pattern. Write their responses on the board, and continue the pattern.

Now ask questions such as: *I have £1. How many 10p coins is that worth? How many 10p coins is £2 worth? How did you use the answer to the first*

Differentiation
Less confident learners: Decide whether to ask the children to choose just two cards each time and to write the TU partition: 62 = 60 + 2; 62 = 50 + 12, and so on.
More confident learners: Decide whether to challenge the children to make all the three-digit numbers possible from a set

Unit 3 ◻ 3 weeks

of three cards. They then write the partition patterns for each of these numbers.

question to help you to work out the answer to the second one? So, how many 10p coins are in £3, £4... £10?

Invite the children to say what strategies they have found helpful in solving problems.

Lessons 6–10

Preparation
Copy the CD page '1cm squared paper' onto an OHT.

You will need
Photocopiable pages
'Divide and multiply' (page 219) for each child.
CD resources
Support and extension versions of 'Divide and multiply'; '1cm squared paper' (see General resources).

Learning objectives

Starter
● Read and write proper fractions (eg $3/7$, $9/10$), interpreting the denominator as the parts of a whole and the numerator as the number of parts; identify and estimate fractions of shapes; use diagrams to compare fractions and establish equivalents.
● Derive and recall multiplication facts for the 2-, 3-, 4-, 5-, 6- and 10-times tables and the corresponding division facts.

Main teaching activities
2006
● Read and write proper fractions (eg $3/7$, $9/10$), interpreting the denominator as the parts of a whole and the numerator as the number of parts; identify and estimate fractions of shapes; use diagrams to compare fractions and establish equivalents.
● Derive and recall multiplication facts for the 2-, 3-, 4-, 5-, 6- and 10-times tables and the corresponding division facts; recognise multiples of 2, 5 or 10 up to 1000.
● Find unit fractions of numbers and quantities (eg $1/2$, $1/3$, $1/4$ and $1/6$ of 12 litres).
1999
● Recognise unit fractions such as $1/2$, $1/3$, $1/4$, $1/5$, $1/10$... and use them to find fractions of shapes and numbers.
● Begin to recognise simple fractions that are several parts of a whole, such as $3/4$, $2/3$ or $3/10$.
● Compare familiar fractions, eg know that on the number line, one half lies between one quarter and three quarters.
● Begin to recognise simple equivalent fractions, eg five tenths and one half, five fifths and one whole.
● Estimate a simple fraction.
● Know by heart multiplication facts for the 2-, 5- and 10-times tables; begin to know the 3- and 4-times tables. Derive quickly the corresponding division facts.
● Recognise two-digit and three-digit multiples of 2, 5 or 10, and three-digit multiples of 50 and 100.
● Begin to know multiplication facts for the 6-times table.

Vocabulary
problem, solution, calculate, calculation, inverse, answer, method, explain, predict, estimate, reason, pattern, relationship, compare, order, information, test, list, table, diagram, fraction, part, equal parts, one whole, parts of a whole, number of parts, one half, one third, one quarter, one fifth, one sixth, one tenth, two thirds, three quarters, three fifths, unit fraction, multiply, times, multiplied by, product, share, share equally, divide, divided by, divided into, left, left over, remainder, round up, round down

Securing number facts, relationships and calculating

BLOCK E

 **SCHOLASTIC**

Lesson 6 (Teach and practise)

Starter
Recall: Draw an empty number line on the board. Label one end 3 and the other 4. Invite a child to write where they think 3½ lies. Repeat for other fractions such as: 3¼, 3¾, 3¹/₅, 3²/₅... and then tenths.

Main teaching activities
Whole class: Reveal the '1cm squared paper' OHT. Draw a rectangle of 3 × 2 and ask: *How can I shade in one half?* Shade in the first suggestion, then ask: *Is there another way to do this?* Repeat. Now draw a 3 × 1 rectangle and shade in half of one of the squares. Ask: *Have I shaded a third? How can you tell that I have not? What fraction have I shaded?* Draw a 4 × 3 rectangle and invite suggestions for shading ⁵/₆. Discuss how, with 12 squares, two of these make ¹/₆, so 10 will make ⁵/₆. Agree that the denominator, or bottom number, gives how many parts make a whole, and the top number, or numerator, gives the fraction of the whole.
Paired work: Provide each child with some squared paper. Ask them to draw a rectangle 4 × 3. They ask them to find different ways of shading in ¾.

Review
Discuss the different ways in which children shaded. Discuss also that each of these represents the same fraction. Ask questions such as: *If you shade in ¾ of a 4 × 3 rectangle, how many squares did you shade each time? So what fraction was left unshaded? How many squares is that?*

Differentiation
Less confident learners: Decide whether to ask the children initially to shade ¼, then ½, then ¾. Discuss what the denominator and numerator mean.
More confident learners: Challenge the children to draw a 6 × 4 rectangle and to find different ways to shade in ³/₈.

Lesson 7 (Teach and practise)

Starter
Recall: Repeat the Starter from Lesson 6, this time focusing on quarters and eighths.

Main teaching activities
Whole class: Make a fraction wall together on the board for halves, fifths and tenths. Discuss which fractions are equivalent and how the children know that.
Paired work: Now ask the children to work in pairs and make a fraction wall for halves, quarters and eighths. Decide whether to work with the less confident children. Challenge the more confident children to say which fraction family will be next (sixteenths) and to extend their fraction wall to include sixteenths.

Review
Discuss the children's work. Say: *Find a fraction equivalent to one half. Now find a fraction equivalent to three quarters...,* and so on.

Lesson 8 (Teach and practise)

Starter
Recall: Explain that you will write a multiplication or division calculation on the board. Ask the children to give the answer as a word problem sentence. For example, if you write 5 × 4 they might say: *I save 5p for 4 weeks. Now I have 20p.* Restrict this to the 2-, 5- and 10-times tables for this lesson.

Main teaching activities
Whole class: Explain that in this and the next lesson the children will investigate multiplication and division facts. Write up on the board 24 ÷ 3 and ask: *What multiplication fact can you use to solve this?* Agree that 8 × 3 = 24 would be appropriate. Write some more division facts such as 35 ÷ 5, 48 ÷ 6... and ask the children to decide which multiplication fact would help them to answer the question.

Differentiation
Less confident learners: The support version of the sheet uses facts from the 2-, 3-, 4-, 5- and 10-times tables.
More confident learners: The extension version of the sheet includes facts from the 8-times table.

■SCHOLASTIC

Individual work: Provide copies of the activity sheet 'Divide and multiply' for each child. The sheet includes some division and multiplication problems to solve.

Review

Discuss the table facts used for the core sheet. Ask the children to circle any answers that they were unsure of. Suggest that they learn these multiplication facts. Now ask: *If I cannot remember a 4-times table fact, how could I work it out?* Children may suggest doubling 2-times table facts to find the answer. Ask: *And if I cannot remember a 6-times table fact, how could I find the answer?* Agree that the 3-times table fact could be doubled to give the answer.

Lesson 9 (Teach and practise)

Starter

Recall: Repeat the Starter from Lesson 8, this time including the 3-, 4-, and 6-times tables.

Main teaching activities

Whole class: Ask the children to find some division calculations which give the answer of 5. Write their suggestions on the board and for each one, ask the children to say what multiplication fact they used to find the answer. Ask the children to work in pairs to find five division calculations which give the answer 7 (for example, 70 ÷ 10; 35 ÷ 5; 28 ÷ 4; 42 ÷ 6).

Review

Discuss which calculations the children found. Now set a new challenge for everyone: find division calculations that give the answer 6.

Differentiation

Less confident learners: Decide whether to work as a group with the children to carry out this work.
More confident learners: Challenge the children to find more calculations.

Lesson 10 (Teach, practise and evaluate)

Starter

Recall: Repeat the Starter from Lesson 9. Keep the pace really sharp to encourage rapid recall.

Main teaching activities

Whole class: Explain that in this lesson the children will use their knowledge of division facts to solve fraction problems. Say: *I have 30 sweets. I eat $\frac{1}{5}$ of them. How many have I eaten?* Agree that the way to solve this is to find $\frac{1}{5}$ of 30, or 30 ÷ 5. Now say: *There are 20 cakes. These are shared equally between four plates. What fraction of the cakes is on each plate?* Discuss the answer, $\frac{1}{4}$. Ask: *How did you find the answer?* Agree that dividing by 4 is equivalent to finding one quarter.
Paired work: Write the fractions $\frac{1}{2}$, $\frac{1}{3}$, $\frac{1}{4}$, $\frac{1}{5}$, $\frac{1}{6}$ and $\frac{1}{10}$ on the board. Now ask the children: *Is it possible to find $\frac{1}{2}$, $\frac{1}{3}$, $\frac{1}{4}$, $\frac{1}{5}$, $\frac{1}{6}$ and $\frac{1}{10}$ of 40?* Ask the children to record their work, and to show how they worked out their answers.

Differentiation

Less confident learners: Decide whether to reduce the number to 24 and use just $\frac{1}{2}$, $\frac{1}{3}$ and $\frac{1}{4}$.
More confident learners: Challenge the children to find a number which allows all of these fractions to be made exactly (60).

Review

Invite children to explain how they solved the problem. Discuss how they worked out each fraction and what recording they used. Invite the more confident children to explain how they solved their challenge (60 is the first number which can be divided exactly by 2, 3, 4, 5, 6 and 10). Ask: *Would you rather have $\frac{1}{3}$ of 15 sweets or $\frac{1}{4}$ of 20 sweets? Why?*

Invite children who you are targeting for assessment to say what they have learned about multiplication, division and fractions during this week.

Lessons 11-15

You will need

Photocopiable pages
'Column addition for HTU' (page 220) and 'Solving problems' (page 221) for each child.

CD resources
Core, support and extension version of 'Two-digit by one-digit multiplication', support and extension versions of 'Column addition for HTU', 'Two-digit by one-digit multiplication' and 'Solving problems'.

Learning objectives

Starter

● Round two-digit or three-digit numbers to the nearest 10 or 100 and give estimates for their sums and differences.
● Derive and recall multiplication facts for the 2-, 3-, 4-, 5-, 6- and 10-times tables and the corresponding division facts.

Main teaching activities

2006
● Develop and use written methods to record, support or explain addition and subtraction of two- and three-digit numbers.
● Use practical and informal written methods to multiply and divide two-digit numbers (eg 13 × 3, 50 ÷ 4); round remainders up or down, depending on the context.
● Solve one-step and two-step problems involving numbers, money or measures, including time, choosing and carrying out appropriate calculations.

1999
● Use informal pencil and paper methods to support, record or explain HTU ± TU, HTU ± HTU.
● Begin to use column addition and subtraction for HTU ± TU where the calculation cannot easily be done mentally.
● Use known number facts and place value to carry out mentally simple multiplications and divisions.
● Begin to find remainders after simple division; round up or down after division, depending on the context.
● Solve word problems involving numbers in 'real life', money and measures, using one or more steps, including finding totals and giving change, and working out which coins to pay. Explain how the problem was solved.

Vocabulary

problem, solution, calculate, calculation, inverse, answer, method, explain, predict, estimate, reason, pattern, relationship, compare, order, information, test, list, table, diagram, sign, equals (=), operation, symbol, number sentence, equation, mental calculation, written calculation, informal method, jottings, number line, count on, count back, add, plus, sum, total, subtract, take away, minus, difference, double, halve, inverse, multiply, times, multiplied by, product, share, share equally, divide, divided by, divided into, left, left over, remainder, round up, round down

Lesson 11 (Teach and practise)

Starter

Rehearse: Ask: *What are the rules for rounding up or down to the nearest 100?* Check that the children are clear that if the tens digit is a 1, 2, 3 or 4, that the number rounds down to the nearest 100, and if the tens digit is a 5, 6, 7, 8 or 9, it rounds up. Ask the children to say the rounded number when you hold up your hand, allowing no more than five seconds of thinking time. Say: *Tell me the rounded number for: 523, 665, 809 and 651.*

Main teaching activities

Whole class: Explain that in this lesson the children will learn about column addition for adding two-digit numbers to three-digit numbers, and for three-digit numbers to three-digit numbers. Write on the board '256 + 67 =' and ask the children to suggest how to solve this, working horizontally. For example: 256 + 67 = 200 + 50 + 60 + 6 + 7 = 200 + 110 + 13 = 323. Now write the same addition in columns (see example):

```
  2 5 6
+   6 7
─────────
  2 0 0
  1 1 0
    1 3
─────────
  3 2 3
```

This example has been worked adding the most significant digits first. If your school policy is to start with the least significant digits, then please use that method. Repeat this for another example, such as 497 + 63. Then provide an example of adding HTU to HTU, such as 264 + 377: 264 + 377 = (200 + 300) + (60 + 70) + (4 + 7) = 500 + 130 + 11 = 641. Repeat this using column addition, reminding the children that the columns must line up for place value.

Individual work: Ask the children to complete the additions on the activity sheet 'Column addition for HTU'. It would be helpful to leave an example on the board to act as a reminder to the children of how to set out the examples.

Review
Play 'Spot the missing number' with the class. The children will need to explain how they decide upon the missing digit. Use 127 + 78. Ask: *As the units answer is 5, what possibilities could there be for the empty units box?* (Multiples of 5.) *What explanation is there for having 200 in the answer?* The children may now like to work in pairs to invent their own example to try with the whole class.

```
  1 2 7
+   7 8
─────────
  1 0 0
  □ □
    1 5
─────────
  2 0 5
```

Differentiation

Less confident learners: There is a support version of the activity sheet called 'Column addition for TU'.
More confident learners: The extension version of the sheet 'Column addition for HTU' includes totals beyond 999.

Lesson 12 (Teach and practise)

Starter
Rehearse: Repeat the Starter from Lesson 11. This time increase the pace.

Main teaching activities
Whole class: Explain to the class that in today's lesson they will be learning how to do column subtraction. Write on the board 82 - 56 and ask the children to try this for themselves in horizontal form. Now write: 82 - 56 = (82 - 50) - 6 = 32 - 6 = 26.

Show the children the simplified column method of recording this:

$$
\begin{array}{rcccl}
82 & = & 80 + 2 & = & 70 + 12 \\
-56 & = & 50 + 6 & = & \underline{50 + 6} \\
& & & & 20 + 6 = 26
\end{array}
$$

Discuss how 80 + 2 is the same as 70 + 12, and that this makes it much easier to subtract 50 + 6.

Repeat this for another example, such as 57 - 28, then ask the children to work in pairs to solve one for themselves, such as 64 - 37 (27).

Paired work: Write on the board the following subtractions: 94 - 37, 86 - 59, 67 - 28, 65 - 28 and 82 - 35. Ask the children to work in pairs to find the solutions using column subtraction. Remind them how important it is to line up the digits correctly for place value. Provide squared paper for the children to record their work.

Differentiation

Less confident learners: Decide whether to ask the children to continue to work horizontally to find the solutions.
More confident learners: If the children are confident with this method, suggest that they work individually so that you can check their level of confidence.

Review

Ask the children to complete the following subtraction by their preferred method: 85 - 38 = ▢. This will enable you to check which method for subtraction the children prefer. At this stage, some children may still prefer to work horizontally.

Lesson 13 (Teach and practise)

Starter

Recall: Explain to the children that you will say a multiple of 5 and that you would like them to calculate its double. Say smaller multiples of 5, such as 5, 10, 15... up to about 50. Ask questions such as: *How did you work that out? If it is a double of a multiple of 5, what will its unit digit be?* (0) *How did you work that out?*

Main teaching activities

Whole class: Ask the children to share 15 between 2 mentally. Ask: *Does 15 share between 2 equally? No, you have one left over, or remainder 1.* Write on the board: 15 ÷ 2 = 7 remainder 1. Now ask the children to divide 15 by 3, 4 and 5. Write the results on the board in the same way. Discuss how 15 appears in both the 3- and 5-times tables: 3 × 5 = 15 and 5 × 3 = 15. Explain that when dividing, children will find that where there is a multiplication fact for the numbers, there will be no remainder. When there is no multiplication fact, they should look for the nearest fact which is less, and then count up to find the remainder. For example, for 18 ÷ 4, the nearest lower fact is 4 × 4 = 16, so 18 ÷ 4 = 4 remainder 2. Extend this for division calculations such as 38 ÷ 3; 54 ÷ 5, and so on.

Ask the children now to work mentally to complete some divisions, some of which have remainders, and some of which do not, such as: 32 ÷ 3, 46 ÷ 5, 47 ÷ 5 and 37 ÷ 3. Remind them that they should search for the closest multiplication fact that they know and use this as their starting fact. Remind them also to record their work.
Paired work: Ask the children to work in pairs, using the multiplication tables for 2, 3, 4, 5, 6 and 10, to divide into the numbers 16, 19, 25 and 34, which can be written on the board. Encourage the children to write their answers as division sentences and, where there is a remainder, to write this too.

Differentiation

Less confident learners: Decide whether to work with these children as a group. Concentrate on multiplication table facts with which the children are confident, such as 2, 5 and 10. Encourage this group to say each division as a sentence, using the vocabulary of division.
More confident learners: Challenge this group to try to divide the numbers on the board by 8. They will need to think about doubles.

Review

Choose one of the numbers on the board. Ask the children to take turns to write up one of their division facts, such as 16 ÷ 2 = 8 or 16 ÷ 3 = 5 remainder 1. Discuss how they worked out their answers. Repeat this for the other numbers on the board so that the children can mark their own work. Now ask: *What would 75 divided by 10 be? How did you work out that 75 divided by 10 is 7 remainder 5?* Repeat this for another division and check who has understood, and who will need more practice, from the answers that you receive.

Lesson 14 (Teach and apply)

Starter

Recall: Repeat the Starter from Lesson 13, this time asking for halves of multiples of 5.

Main teaching activities

Whole class: Explain that in this lesson the children will use partitioning to multiply two-digit numbers by one-digit numbers. On the board draw an empty number line and write 14 × 3. Explain that this can be worked out in two steps: (10 × 3) + (4 × 3).

▷

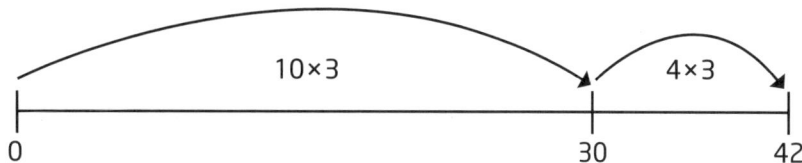

Repeat for another example, such as (17 × 4) = (10 × 4) + (7 × 4).
Paired work: Ask the children to work in pairs to use this method for 19 × 5.
Whole class: Now demonstrate the grid method. Explain to the children that this can be used to help them to multiply. Refer back to the original example of 14 × 3.

×	10	4
3	30	12

So 14 × 3 is the same as 10 × 3 + 4 × 3 = 30 + 12 = 42.
Paired work: Ask the children to complete a multiplication using the grid method: 16 × 4. Check that all children have understood the method.
Individual work: Provide each child with a copy of 'Two-digit by one-digit multiplication'. Ask them to work independently to find answers using both methods of recording their multiplication. Then they compare what they have done.

Review
Choose some examples from the core sheet and invite children to demonstrate how they found the answers. Discuss the two methods. Ask: *Peter saves 20p each week. How much will he have saved after six weeks? If he saves 18p each week, how much would he save in six weeks? How did you work that out?*

Differentiation
Less confident learners: Decide whether to use the support version of the sheet that concentrates on multiplication by 2, 3 and 4.
More confident learners: The extension version of the sheet includes multiplication by 8.

Lesson 15 (Teach, apply and evaluate)

Starter
Recall: Repeat the Starters from Lesson 13 and 14, so that children need to think about both halves and doubles. Keep the pace sharp.

Main teaching activities
Whole class: Explain that in this lesson the children will solve word problems using addition, subtraction, multiplication and division. Say: *We have 33 Lego wheels. How many four-wheeled cars can we make? How did you work that out? Are any wheels left over? How many?* Now say: *There are 14 boys and 16 girls in Class 3. The teacher wants to put the children into teams of 6. How many teams can she make?* Discuss how the children solved the problem. Ask: *Did you need to make any jottings? What sort of jottings did you make?* Discuss how children can use a number line, or write a number equation whilst doing some of the work mentally.
Individual work: Provide copies of the activity sheet 'Solving problems' which contains both one- and two-step problems for the children to solve. There is space on the sheet for the children to show their working for each problem.

Differentiation
Less confident learners: The support version of 'Solving problems' uses smaller numbers.
More confident learners: The extension version of the activity sheet has more complex problems.

Review
Discuss the problems from the core sheet. Invite children to explain how they solved the problems and any difficulties they had. Now write on the board 48 ÷ 6 and ask the children to write their own word problem for this equation. They can read out their problems for others to consider.

Ask the children to discuss with their partner which of the methods of solving more complex addition, subtraction, multiplication and division equations they feel confident with, and which they need to practise further.

Name _____   Date _____

Ordering numbers

Look at the pairs of numbers. Then read the list of numbers.

Choose a number from the list to fit between each pair of numbers.

Use each number only once.

899   375   555   502   146   101   700   292   624   209

1. 123 ▢ 156

2. 312 ▢ 398

3. 192 ▢ 392

4. 601 ▢ 715

5. 888 ▢ 999

6. 107 ▢ 654

7. 94 ▢ 108

8. 465 ▢ 503

9. 578 ▢ 776

10. 231 ▢ 642

Now write the numbers in order, so that the smallest number is first.

Name _____   Date _____

Divide and multiply

**Write the multiplication facts that would help
you to solve these division equations.**

Then write the answers to the division equations.

Division	Multiplication fact	Answer
1. 21 ÷ 3		
2. 40 ÷ 5		
3. 16 ÷ 4		
4. 36 ÷ 6		
5. 45 ÷ 5		
6. 90 ÷ 10		
7. 18 ÷ 2		
8. 18 ÷ 3		
9. 36 ÷ 4		
10. 48 ÷ 6		

Now find the multiplication facts to help you to answer these word problems.

Write the answers.

11. Marcus has 54p. How many 6p chews can he buy? _____

12. Jasmine wants to share her 40 stickers between four friends and herself.
How many do they have each? _____

13. Sam has 25 sweets. She wants to share them between her four friends.
To make sure there are none left over, how many more sweets will she need to
share them exactly?

_____

_____

_____

_____

Securing number facts, relationships and calculating

BLOCK E

Name _____ Date _____

Column addition for HTU

Use these six numbers to make as many different adding calculations as you can.

Set the numbers out under each other in columns.

124	143	255	217	329	434

H	T	U

H	T	U

H	T	U

H	T	U

H	T	U

Securing number facts, relationships and calculating

BLOCK E

Name _____ Date _____

Solving problems

Read each problem carefully.

Show your working and write the answer.

Problem	Jottings	Answer
1. There are 37 cakes. Each cake box takes 4 cakes. How many boxes are needed to fit all the cakes in?		
2. There are 15 blue stickers, 14 red stickers and 12 yellow stickers. The children take any 3 stickers each time. How many children can have 3 stickers each?		
3. There are 4 children who buy 3 lollies each. There are 28 children in the class. How many more lollies are needed so that everybody can have one?		
4. James has 36 marbles. He gives $\frac{1}{4}$ of his marbles to John. Peter has 30 marbles and gives John $\frac{1}{5}$. How many marbles does John have now?		

Securing number facts, relationships and calculating

BLOCK E

Pupil name _____   Class name _____

Comments

Year 3 End-of-year objectives	✓	Comments
Partition three-digit numbers into multiples of 100, 10 and 1 in different ways.		
Derive and recall all addition and subtraction facts for each number to 20, sums and differences of multiples of 10 and number pairs that total 100.		
Add or subtract mentally combinations of one-digit and two-digit numbers.		
Draw and complete shapes with reflective symmetry; draw the reflection of a shape in a mirror line along one side.		
Read, to the nearest division and half-division, scales that are numbered or partially numbered; use the information to measure and draw to a suitable degree of accuracy.		
Use Venn diagrams or Carroll diagrams to sort data and objects using more than one criterion.		

Teacher name _____   Class name _____

	Partition three-digit numbers into multiples of 100, 10 and 1 in different ways.	Derive and recall all addition and subtraction facts for each number to 20, sums and differences of multiples of 10 and number pairs that total 100.	Add or subtract mentally combinations of one-digit and two-digit numbers.	Draw and complete shapes with reflective symmetry; draw the reflection of a shape in a mirror line along one side.	Read, to the nearest division and half-division, scales that are numbered or partially numbered; use the information to measure and draw to a suitable degree of accuracy.	Use Venn diagrams or Carroll diagrams to sort data and objects using more than one criterion.

Year 3 End-of-year objectives

Mainly level 3

Recording sheet

CLASS